GIANMARIO PIGA

English Translation
Mother M. Xavier McMonagle O.S.B.

# The Path
# of Mother Adèle Garnier

(1838-1924)

*Foundress of the Congregation
of Adorers of the Sacred Heart of
Jesus of Montmartre, OSB*

**A.S.H. – O.S.B.**
admin@tyburnconvent.org.uk
Telephone: +44 207 723 7262

madonna.della.eucaristia@gmail.com
Telephone: +39 06 633 765

English translation from the Italian: Mother M. Xavier McMonagle O.S.B.

© Adorers of the Sacred Heart of Jesus of Montnartre Congregation Trust 2012
First Published in 2012
Second Impression October 2012
Printed in Italy by the Vatican Press

Published by Adores of the Sacred Heart of Jesus of Montmartre Congregation Trust, Tyburn Convent, 8 Hyde Park Place, London, W2 2LJ, England

ISBN 978-1-909474-00-0

*For my parents*
*Pietro and Piuccia*

# CONTENTS

## THE LIFE OF MOTHER ADÈLE GARNIER

### Chapter I: The Road toward Montmartre

### Chapter II: The road to Tyburn

## Chapter III: From Daughter to Mother

# APPENDIX

# PREFACE

Notwithstanding the diffusion of secularism and the pressure of the mentality of relativism, the man of our day is not in fact, indifferent to the experience of the supernatural. On the contrary, almost anxious on account of his nostalgia for the invisible, he manifests a clear interest in transcendent truth.

The marvellous work of grace continues to touch and invade the life of persons, who perceiving are able to grasp the Mystery, and dedicate themselves to growing in the compelling wonder of the Eternal even to the attaining of a painful mystical union with God.

Such was the spiritual experience of Mother Adèle Garnier, narrated by Don Gianmario Piga, through his study of the manuscript letters of this french nun. The author of this volume, editing the transcription and translation of around 1,500 letters, in language close to human feelings, describes the eruption of the divine presence which gave to the Foundress of the Adorers of the Sacred Heart an itinerary to sanctity that joins together eucharistic faith and adoration of the Sacred Heart.

It needs faith to accept and appreciate the Eucharist. Mother Adèle had understood how to discover and to draw close to Jesus, present under the signs of bread and wine and that there was no other way than that of faith: a faith not born as resignation from incapacity and confession of weakness in the face of the darkness of the mystery, but born from power from on high. She lived a sublime eucharistic experience. Always whenever she found herself before the Blessed Sacrament she perceived in her soul something extraordinary, that gave her no longer power to think, to ask, or to do anything whatsoever.

The Eucharist was like her own true magnet and daily she felt for it an insatiable hunger. Dazzled by its splendour, she perceived it as an interior fire, a light like a flame, which opened her mind to spiritual realities.

Adèle Garnier knew well that the Eucharist is a "permanent" sacrament, in the sense that the presence of Christ, always salvific "perdures" also after the eucharistic celebration. To this permanent presence, therefore, she loved to respond with prolonged and fervent adoration where the Heart of Christ manifested Himself as source and mode of prayer. So why not now build a Church at Montmartre in honour of the Sacred Heart where there would be perpetual exposition of the Blessed Sacrament?

In the Sacrament of the Altar, in fact, as in a mirror the devout Adèle reread the entire earthly life of the Son of God in the light of His crucified Heart. In her contemplation she was consoled by the events in the life of Christ where His human heart pulsated with love. This most ardent love manifested itself as compassion for the crowds (cf. Mk 8:2), as reproach to Jerusalem (cf. Mt 23:37) as holy indignation towards the traders in the Temple, (cf. Mt 21:13). Above all in the hour of His Passion, Jesus gave proof of love and fear in the face of pain and impending death; love and intense affliction over the traitor's kiss; love and compassion for the women of Jerusalem. Upon the Cross, then, Jesus felt his heart become like an impetuous torrent, superabounding with the most varied sentiments – of intense love, of anguish, of mercy, of burning desire and of serene calm.

Finally, in the very moment of death his transfixed Heart remains forever the vivid image of that spontaneous charity, which God himself was constrained to give his Only Begotten Son for the redemption of mankind, and with which Christ himself loved us all with such overwhelming love, offering himself as victim of bloody immolation on Calvary.

Therefore Mother Adèle speaks of the adoration of the Sacred Heart, having recourse to the use of attributes that harmonise feelings, sentiments, and affectivity. From this point her language thrusts forward towards the paradoxical overturning of its nature and function, by which "to tell you" becomes "to understand you". She translates the language of lovers into the language of mystical love. Separation and desire, the search for each other and the meeting with each other, the self renunciation and the mutual gift of self, are presented as movements of the soul enveloped by God.

So, in this way, that "pati divina" becomes manifest which stimulates growth in the awareness of the Eternal. The light of language cannot take away completely the darkness (cf. 2 Cor 12:1-4). Its task is that of helping us to pass from one darkness to another more precious where the divine presence imposes itself more strongly, till finally we reach the ultimate darkness – so very, very close to the definitive Light – where solitude and union are thus conjoined so as practically to coincide (Psalm 139:11, 12).[1] And how profoundly it was granted her to comprehend *who* she adores in the mystery of faith, the opened side of the

---

[1] *Were I to say: 'Surely darkness will hide me' then the night would become as light around me. Even darkness obscures nothing before Thee; the night shines as the day, the darkness is as the light.*

15

Redeemer, in conscious manner and in the form of blessedness and also in a form painfully purifying like gold in the
crucible.

In the letters of the Foundress, the Heart of Christ is the
centre of the Christian revelation, and of the sacramental
life.

Therefore it is not from the symbolism of the heart that
we ascend to the Heart of Christ. No, it is the gift of his
Heart that is proposed to us that we are called to perceive as
the sacrament of his person in the Holy Eucharist. And it is
the Lord who communicates himself to us by means of his
Heart and his own Heart becomes

– the fount of our relationship with Him and of our
prayer,

– the object of our confidence in Him

– the reference point of our spiritual life.

In the most precious ark of the Heart of Jesus is found
the fulness of the Charism of Mother Adèle, the gift of the
Spirit, who inspires heroic fortitude in teaching and testifying the truth of the *mysterium fidei* even to the shedding of
blood.

The Foundress, considering herself as a host in the Sacrifice of the Mass, invited her daughters to offer themselves as
victims to be immolated for the salvation of all. She told
them to take the body with its senses, the soul with its
thoughts, the will with its desires, the heart with its affections, and deliver up their entire existence to Him Who gave
Himself up for us right to the end.

To you who have in your hands this volume, a spiritual
path is offered, which sets out to educate your heart and not

only your mind and your hands, teaching you to dedicate your love in the school of the eucharistic Jesus. This can become the stimulus for ever present evangelisation, as in the Heart of Christ the heart of man learns
 – to know the true and only meaning of life and his destiny,
 – to comprehend the value of an authentically christian life,
 – to safeguard himself from certain perversions of the heart,
 – to unite filial love of God with love of his neighbour.

For this message, dear to the tradition and magisterium of the Church I thank dearest Don Gianmario, apostle of the Sacred Heart and lover of the EUCHARIST.

✠ VINCENZO PELVI
*Archbishop*[2]

---

[2] Ordinario Militare per l'Italia.

# INTRODUCTION

This work is the fruit of years of study on the spirituality of Mother Mary of Saint Peter (born Adèle Garnier),[i] the french nun foundress of the Adorers of the Sacred Heart of Jesus of Montmartre, of the Order of Saint Benedict.

A dozen years ago, I had the opportunity to spend a period of study in London, as a guest of a cloistered benedictine monastery. In 2004 I returned to that monastery and I was asked to collaborate with the transcription of a huge heritage of correspondence in french and english, of about 1,500 letters written by the Foundress, Mother Marie Adèle Garnier.[1]

In the course of this painstaking and delicate work of transcription, made even more difficult by a handwriting which was not always easy to decipher, I was able to come to know and appreciate the valuable spiritual wealth of these writings. On account of the sublime degree of their spiritual clarity, these letters can be considered to be an

---

[i] Adèle Garnier was christened *Marie Adèle*, but was familiarly called Adèle – probably because she had a sister named Marie.

[1] These letters are catalogued and preserved in the Archives of the Congregation of the Benedictine Sisters of Tyburn – London, under the following classification:

H-15B-001..., H-15C-001..., H-15D-001..., H-15E-001..., H-15F-001..., H-15G-001..., H-15H-001... The classification indicates respectively:

H: History of the Congregation

15: The sections relating to the writings of Mother Marie Adele Garnier, A,B,C,D, E, F, G, H; the different volumes corresponding to the different sections. Finally, the successively numbered sequence, 001-020... refer to the progressive number of letters gathered together in chronological order.

authentic personal spiritual testament. The gradual study of the content expressed in these letters led me progressively to accompany the work of transcription with a method for cataloguing the material, which I divided into general topics that became the precise subject matter of analysis and in-depth study contained in this work.

In particular, the aspect I appreciated most was linked to the spirituality of Adèle Garnier, which I found powerfully attractive. This was because her spirituality returns, in the first place, to seek again, a path of absolute evangelical perfection, which prompted her first steps to set out from the christian ideal of abandonment in order to attain an ambitious and, in some respects, painful mystical union with God. In her search for God, Adèle Garnier adheres to the experience of the salvific reality of Christ, dedicating herself to him with a living faith, thanks to the daily encounter with the Eucharistic Jesus. However, her journey, recounted symbolically by means of the Eucharistic sacrament, spreads out abroad in many other directions. Interiorly helped and supported by the Holy Spirit, externally dynamic and active thanks to the stimulus and comfort of her religious sisters, Adèle Garnier has succeeded in offering a personal and social testimony of authentic life and christian hope.

For this reason, the present work is based principally upon the study and analysis of her letters. The choice to proceed with this type of research was prompted not solely because Adèle Garnier's corpus of letters remains largely unpublished,[2]

---

[2] The scant publications on the Mother are in English and French and refer to the years after her death, and above all on the occasion of the Beatification of Dom Columba Marmion, her spiritual father. These works are mainly biographies of Adéle Garnier.

a factor that motivates the originality of this thesis, but also because of the remarkable spiritual authority of her writings.

The work has been divided into four chapters. The first two chapters present the biography of Adèle Garnier, a figure still little known, because "the Mother", just two years after the foundation of her Community in Paris, was forced to leave France on account of the government's hostile laws, which did not safeguard contemplative religious Congregations, and to live the rest of her life remaining permanently within the walls of Tyburn Convent, London. It was this existence, therefore, that led "the Mother" to feel that she was always on the road of great sacrifice and suffering, first following *"the road toward Montmartre"* (First Chapter), land of French martyrs, and then *"the road toward Tyburn"* (Chapter Two), the place of the English martyrs.

The Third and the Fourth Chapters concentrate mainly on the spirituality of the Mother. In the third Chapter, Adèle completes a progressive stage along the path of faith. In fact, as Daughter she welcomes the teaching and counsels of her spiritual fathers, who accompany her towards her specific christian vocation, allow her to be guided by the Holy Spirit and by the intercession of our heavenly Mother. She then passes along the path of suffering, offering herself to God as a Victim, strengthened through a daily martyrdom that unites her to the sacrifice of greater authentic witnesses of the faith. She then, as Mother, would lead her daughters in the charism of the "Work" that she herself first followed and lived.

The Fourth Chapter places the emphasis upon Adèle Garnier's interior journey and her constant commitment to the fulfilment of the divine will and above all on her spirituality of eucharistic adoration of the Sacred Heart of Jesus. In this latter, she was responding to the divine voice that invited her to dwell in adoration in the future Basilica of Montmartre: "It is there that I will you to be as victim". This is her charism: the Sacred Heart of Jesus adored and revered in the Eucharist. Finally, her ascetical experience is highlighted by the spiritual images animating her and by her total surrender in intimate union with God. Hers was a life given totally to God, and her final aspiration would be the desire for holiness.

Reviewing all these stages of the Garnier spirituality I deliberately tried to summarise the most suitable citations from the different letters analysed, intent on giving a voice to the Mother: a voice strong, contemporary, profound, but rising up to God, yet which also knows how to resound today in our hearts, to help each reader strengthen his faith journey. Certainly, it would have been possible to incorporate the mysticism of the Mother within the wider context of mystical theology. But that would have led to other voices, albeit authoritative, which could have suppressed the voice of those who, for so long a time, have remained in the silence of Tyburn.

We hope that these pages may lead the reader to discover the profound and effective testimony of Adèle Garnier who has met with God, contemplating the Sacred Heart and offering her whole being in Him, and finding in the Eucharist the source and summit of the fullness of Christian life.

# The life
# of Mother Adèle Garnier

# CHAPTER I

# THE ROAD TOWARD MONTMARTRE

## 1.1. The First Steps toward Faith

Marie Adèle Garnier was born on 15 August, 1838, feast of the Assumption of Mary, Grancey-le-Château near Dijon, the fifth child of Nicholas Garnier, an architect and constructor and of Denise née Caiset, a very devout woman. Her parents had six children: the first died as a child, while the others Louise, Josephine, Marie, Adèle and Thomas[1] lived longer. Adèle was baptized on September 12, 1838, feast of the Holy Name of Mary,[2] and three years later the family moved to Is-sur-Tille, a small town in the Côte D'Or. At the age of six years Adèle lost her mother,[3] who before dying requested that the children would study at Villeneuve-sur-Yonne with the Célestine Religious. It was here that Adèle was prepared for first Communion, which she made in the Church of Notre-Dame, May 19, 1850. The whole family then moved to Dijon where all the children attended one of the best schools of the city.[4] After a time their education was given in the home, thanks to the guidance of a tutor, while

[1] Thomas was commonly called Victor.

[2] Cf. Raoul Plus, S.J. – *Adéle Garnier, Mère Marie de Saint Pierre*, Fondatrice des Religiouses Adoratrices du S.C. de Montmartre O.S.B., Edition Spes, Paris, 1934, pp. 13-14.

[3] Cf. Emile Bouvy, Mere Marie de Saint Pierre, fondatrice et premiére Supérieure Général des Soeurs Adoratrices du Sacré-Couer de Montmartre (1838-1924) Edg Dllesarde, Enghien 1933, p. 8.

[4] This school was the Pension Baillot, an Institute well renowned at that time.

Victor went to university and became an engineer. The father devoted himself totally to his profession and to the education of his children assisted in the latter by Josephine and Adèle who both showed talent for technical design.

At the age of sixteen Adèle was engaged to a young man. The engagement lasted a few years, but with the passing of time as she matured Adèle grew doubtful about this marriage prospect, mainly due to religious differences, as apparently the young man had no interest in religious matters, but rather despised them. One day, in fact, as Dom Bede Camm relates in "Sacrifice of Praise",[5] Adèle heard her fiancé express doubts about his faith. When she heard these words, she decided to put an end to their engagement and nothing could change her mind, not even the young man's threat of suicide.

In the course of time Adèle began to feel drawn to a more perfect life, even if not necessarily toward the ideal of religious life. So she wrote in her letter:

"I began to despise the vanities of the world, to grieve over, perhaps rather to be ashamed of my faults and defects, and I think that by God's grace I now began to correct them. My soul was constantly dwelling upon God and was filled with the longing to please him. Little by little the desire for a life more laborious, occupied, and at the same time more dependent on others, took hold of me and I felt thus alone could I please God. I asked my spiritual father if he would permit me to become a governess in a family. He gave his consent, and circumstances soon permitted me to find what I desired in an excellent family, in the west of France".[6]

---

[5] Cf. Dom Bede Camm, *"A Sacrifice of Praise"*, *Marie Adele Garnier and the Founding of Tyburn Convent*, St Michael's Press, 2006, pp. 10-11.

[6] *Ibidem*, p. 11.

In 1861, she went to Nantes[7] to visit her sister who was a governess. There, despite the fact that she was somewhat reticent, at the suggestion of the Jesuit Père Edouard Marquet, she began to work as a governess in the family De Crochard.[8] The priest took care of her soul, and he counselled her to be faithful to daily communion. It was in this period that she began to feel her soul purified in order to ascend to God: a strong devotion to the Sacred Heart of Jesus matured within her, along with the call to the consecrated life.

Some time later, Père Pierre Donniou became her new spiritual father, who guided her for ten years.[9] He recognized immediately the authenticity of her vocation though initially he did not encourage her because he considered her health too frail for the religious life. However, later he allowed her to make a trial of religious life, and in 1864 Adèle entered as a postulant in the novitiate of the Ladies of

---

[7] Cf. H-15D-001, Abbé Courtois: "I have told you dear Father, that Our Lord provided me, at 23 years of age, with an occasion to make a journey to the west of where my sister was a governess. I had a vague presentiment that I would stay there and become a governess. But my shyness prevented me from considering this seriously. Nevertheless I went there. At Nantes, Father Marquet, who is very determined to better my soul, immediately ordered me to receive Communion daily. After only eight days of this life, an extraordinary change took place in my way of thinking. A family that did not appeal to me asked me to be their governess. […]. But Father Marquet spoke with authority and I obeyed. He advised me to always receive Communion daily. In spite of all the goodness shown me and the confidence (alas! so little justified) which they had in me, it proved to be extreme isolation on account of this place, and this secluded life in the country, etc.!"

[8] Cf. Emile Bouvy, *op. cit.*, p. 10.

[9] Cf. H-15D-001, Abbé Courtois: "The Lord, left him to me for ten years, during that time he was a holy, enlightened and kindly guide for my soul".

Sacrè Coeur at Conflans, Chaienton-le-Pont (Val-de-Marne).[10] This experience lasted barely two months and the young Adèle, just 26 years of age had to leave the convent on account of serious ill health. The following year her condition deteriorated and the certainty that God would never abandon her was her only consolation.

Once the critical period had passed, she spent a little time with the family De Crochard at Poitiers and then worked as a governess with Madame St. Cyr. Once more, a sudden deterioration in her state of health forced her to return to her family in Dijon to regain her health. Remaining at home, she became stronger and for the first time began to receive mystical experiences. In the church sometimes she felt suddenly elevated to God by a supernatural power that filled her with an immense bliss. This state of grace lasted a few moments, but was very frequent. The young Adèle, fearing it was an illusion, could not speak of it in confession, until eventually the same confessor perceiving her embarrassment encouraged her in these experiences, confirming that they were a grace and a sign that God was calling her to perfection.

In these years Adèle spent part of her time engrossed in reading works of the saints. In particular when she understood from reading a work of Saint Theresa that some of the graces described were similar to those she was experiencing, out of humility she saw this as a temptation to pride and was smitten with shame to think that she dared to compare herself to a saint:

[10] Cf. Jacques Benoist, *Le Sacré Coeur des femmes, de 1870 à 1960*, Editions de l'Atelier, 2000, p. 1396; See also Emile Bouvy, *op. cit.*, p. 10 e H-15D-001, Abbé Courtois.

"I would have preferred to be buffeted, trampled, humiliated. But unhappily I carefully concealed these things which would have helped my confessor to guide me on the right way".[11]

## 1.2. "The Meeting" with Montmartre

A few years later, in 1868, Adèle was beginning to improve in health and resumed her activity as governess near Laval, with the family of Madame de Crozé.[12] This experience of eight years marked a turning point in her spiritual life. The countryside in which she lived was very far from the only church in the area. In view of the need she had to receive daily Communion, the family in which she worked and their spiritual father, the Jesuit Père Pierre Donniou,[13] succeeded in obtaining from the bishop permission to reserve the Blessed Sacrament in the chapel of the castle where they lived.[14] This arrangement greatly favoured the physical and spiritual health of Adèle. Her first significant spiritual experience was an apparition which took place in 1869. Adèle saw Jesus surrounded by light that indicated his Sacred Heart. This image struck her so profoundly that, once she had founded her Congregation, the habit of the new community had a medal worn on the breast in memory of this apparition.[15]

However, an event occurred in the winter 1872 that became a turning point in the life of Adèle, giving even a

---

[11] Dom Bede Camm, *op. cit.*, p. 13.
[12] Cf. Emile Bouvy, *op. cit.*, p. 11.
[13] Cf. *Ibidem.*
[14] Cf. H-15D-001, Abbé Courtois.
[15] Cf. Dom Bede Camm, *op. cit.*, p. 15.

precise address for her vocation. Following this she entered a period that she calls "great interior trials".[16] Adèle, in the drawing-room heard an article read aloud from the UNIVERS about the project to construct a votive church at Montmartre in honour of the Sacred Heart, as a monument of atonement. When the reading finished, she decided to go into the garden, and while she was opening the door:

> "An inner voice said to me very clearly: 'It is there that I want you to be!'"* But at the same time, I saw a very high altar sparkling with lights, dominated by the Blessed Sacrament exposed in the Monstrance [ ... ]. I felt so overcome by this and by this statement that I had to lean against the door to save myself from falling. And then, I was so happy, so happy, yet I could make nothing of it. The memory of this returned every moment, with a marvellous sweetness".[17]

This state of spiritual bliss lasted 18 months. Adèle had not succeeded in confiding it to her spiritual father, and could only do so after his death to her new guide, Père Henri Chambellan, who encouraged her along this path. Despite the fact that she continued to perform her duties in Laval with joy, Adèle's heart was already in Montmartre, a place that occupied a special place in her thoughts and prayers:

> "Often in my prayers I united myself in advance to the adorations and reparations which were to be offered to the

[16] Cf. Dom Bede Camm, *op. cit.*, p. 15.

[17] *Ibidem*. * " ... article in the UNIVERS speaking about the project of a Votive Church in honour of the Sacred Heart, *as an expiatory memorial* ..." and H-15B-138 "it is there that I want you to be *as victim*. And these words are repeated a little further on in the same document".

Sacred Heart in Montmartre. Always I had the impression that Our Lord wanted all this worship to be offered in a special manner to his eucharistic Heart that had to be perpetually exposed in that place in the Blessed Sacrament, and that from there, from this inexhaustible spring, would flow out countless graces designed for the most criminal, the most obstinate sinners. Nevertheless I have not the slightest idea of how I, poor me, could reach to the heights of Montmartre".[18]

Finally, in September 1874, while she was engaged in reading the *Life of Saint Margaret Mary Alacoque*[19] she suddenly understood that the will of God was the perpetual adoration of the Sacred Heart present in the Eucharist at Montmartre and that she would have to go to the Archbishop of Paris to proclaim this message:

"I saw Jesus saying to my heart, by means of a brilliant light, that He willed his Eucharistic Heart to be the special

[18] H-15D-004, Abbé Courtois.

[19] *Marguerite-Marie Alacoque* was a mystic, a religious of the Order of the Visitation. She was born on 22 July 1647 in a tiny town in Central France (Borgogna); quite early in her childhood she showed a particular devotion to the Blessed Sacrament. At 24 years of age she entered the monastery of the Visitation at Paray-le-Monial and she was granted various apparitions and sought after the highest peaks of the spiritual life. From which she understood that her personal mission was to make known the cult of the Sacred Heart in complete harmony with the mystical experience of St John Eudes (1601-1680). He had been designated "Father, Apostle and Doctor of the Liturgical Cult of the Hearts of Jesus and Mary". She was accompanied spiritually by the holy Jesuit Father Claude la Colombière in her mystical experiences, feeling herself specially united to the suffering and agony of Christ Jesus. She died in her monastery on 17 October 1690 and was proclaimed a Saint by Pope Benedict XV, 13 May 1920.

Cf. Père Emile Régnault, *Courte Biographie et lettres inédites de la Bienheureuse Marguerite-Marie*, Hébrail, Toulouse, 1890.

object of adoration at Montmartre and that the Blessed Sacrament should be exposed there day and night. I was struck by the vehemence with which Jesus had manifested his will to me. I had no time to reflect on this when I heard these words very clearly pronounced as though around me: 'Go, find the Archbishop of Paris and speak to him!' This was a thunderbolt for me. At that moment I was certain I had received a formal order from Jesus and consequently I had to obey it".[20]

At this point, a period of great tribulation began for Adèle. On the one hand she thought that this apparition was the fruit of her imagination, on the other hand she felt the inner urgency of the responsibility of the request that had been addressed to her. When she spoke of it to her spiritual father, Père Chambellan, he considered the possibility of visiting Paris to speak with the Archbishop.

In the months following this locution, Adèle lived with anxiety and preoccupation, disturbed by what had happened and restless about what she ought to say to the Archbishop. Her spiritual father, perceiving that she was distressed, encouraged her to pursue the command – that she would not fail in this task. He said, finally, that in case of need she could quote him as guarantee of the veracity of what she would have revealed to the Archbishop:

> "Later… 'while I was going upstairs to my room, the thought of a letter of recommendation from Fr Chambellan, bearing the Society's seal, *pleased me, I welcomed it*, and I said to myself that *I definitely was going back to ask Father to do me this kindness.* My miserable self love had in this way suc-

[20] H-15D-004, Abbé Courtois.

32

ceeded in overcoming my apprehensions! And this despicable creature was going to accomplish Our Lord's command clothed in the livery of the sin of pride! I went into my room with my head full of foolish vanity. I went to the fireplace and let out a cry of grief, and fell on my knees full of sorrow and regret. A small statue of the Sacred Heart, which usually occupied the centre of the mantelpiece had been turned round and placed sideways in such a way that, on seeing it, I really believed that Our Lord had gone away and turned his back on me ... Never, never, ... will I be able to forget that sight, that impression – in a word, that light, which had opened my eyes! Perturbed, upset, I seized hold of the small statue so passionately to ask pardon, that it slipped from my hand and fell. ... The head was broken off and I had to search for a long time before finding it in the darkest and most hidden corner of my room. ... The shock I received at that moment was a grace for which I can never adequately thank Our Lord. I had relied on my vanity and not on him, and he went away.... This incident may seem of little importance, but for me it has been a source of graces and lights ever since that time.'"[21]

On 5 December, 1874, Adèle Garnier went to Paris to meet with the Archbishop, Monsignor Joseph Hippolyte Guibert[22] and despite her anguish, she felt supported by

[21] H-15D-005, Abbé Courtois.

[22] Joseph Hyppolyte Guibert born 13 December, 1802 at Aix-en-Provence, city of the South of France. Entered (to become priest) of the Order of Oblates of Mary Immaculate, being ordained priest 14 August, 1825. He was named Bishop of Viviers, city of south of France, 11 March 1842, then 15 years later Archbishop of Tours, city of Central West France. In 1871 was elected Archbishop of Paris and 2 years later was named Cardinal. He exerted himself to erect the Basilica of the Sacred Heart, where he expressed the wish to be buried. He died 8 July, 1886 at Paris.

God and was determined to do his will at any cost. Before the appointment she went to pray in the church of Saint Clotilde where she suffered a real agony thinking in some moments that she would die of suffering or go crazy. She went to the meeting and was accepted by his personal secretary, Père Reulet, who conducted her to the Archbishop.

During their meeting Adèle said to him that she believed she was obeying the will of Our Lord, and was there to inform him that it was His desire that in the future Church of Montmartre the Blessed Sacrament should be solemnly exposed day and night in the Blessed Sacrament, and that the worship offered in this Church should be quite especially given to His Eucharistic Heart. The Archbishop reacted to her words showing a certain irony and replied that the perpetual adoration was something impossible at that time at Montmartre, especially by lay people.[23] The prelate asked if there was still anything else the Lord had told her. On hearing Adèle's negative response, the Archbishop accompanied her to the door and gave her a blessing, and remarked that her journey had been unnecessary. Two days after Adèle returned to her work, with the security, confirmed by her confessor, of having done everything the Lord had requested, irrespective of the result obtained. A few years later, after the construction of the Basilica, it was the same Archbishop Guibert who estab-

---

[23] Cf. H-12-129, *Souvenirs sur notre bien aimée Mère Fondatrice par le R. P. Jean Baptiste Lémius, O.M.I., 1924.*
The good God has seen fit to mandate me to fulfil a mission. There is not even yet a Chapel at Montmartre. So, well, the thing is not possible. "My daughter, look and see what state the place of Montmartre is in and you will understand that in no way is it possible to have night Adorers, all the night: But to think of anyone up there every night! No, no, that would not be possible!"

lished the perpetual adoration, first in a temporary chapel and then in the Basilica. Then more than a quarter of a century passed before the full implementation of the work requested by Adèle to Archbishop Guibert in 1872, was realised, namely the creation of a religious community devoted exclusively to the perpetual adoration and reparation.[24]

The first experience of night vigil in Montmartre began on 3 March, 1881, fifth anniversary of the opening of the temporary chapel. On the first August 1885 adoration became perpetual and since then has never been interrupted, not even during the bombing of two world wars.

His Excellency Mons. André Vingt-trois, Cardinal of Paris, organised the Jubilee year, commemorating the 125 continuous years of perpetual adoration at Montmartre beginning on 4 June, 2010 and concluding with a solemn concelebration on 1 July, 2011.

## 1.3. The Little Nazareth

The year 1876 was important because it marked both the laying of the foundation stone of the Basilica of Montmartre and the opening of the temporary chapel. Montmartre became immediately the destination of innumerable pilgrimages from France and many other parts of the world. Adèle's desire to settle at Montmartre developed and

[24] Cf. H-15D-005, Abbé Courtois.

"Shortly before his death Cardinal Guibert approved the Association of the Eucharistic Heart at Montmartre and has also established the perpetual exposition of the Blessed Sacrament, first in the provisionary chapel then in the votive Church. A third desire, expressed by Our Lord to His poor and humble servant was to establish at Montmartre a community of Religious, vowed to the perpetual adoration and reparation".

matured. Increasingly she entertained the idea of going to live in solitude close to the Basilica, so as to be able to spend as much time as possible in adoration before the tabernacle, living as a victim set apart for sacrifice:

> "Increasingly, the thought of settling at Montmartre when Jesus Himself would be there, never left me. The call I had received since the start of 1872 never ceased to make itself heard, as a continual invitation to hold myself in readiness. [ … ] I saw myself living near the tabernacle of the Sacred Heart, spending as much time as possible adoring Him, and only living for that, as a victim destined solely for sacrifice. All that I foresaw seemed to me to be strange, impossible, madness. But nevertheless, in the depths of my soul Jesus assured me that this was His will and that He would accomplish it".[25]

She decided to share this desire with her spiritual father, who listened to her with prudence and did not give an immediate reply so as to be sure that this really would be the right choice. In his opinion, there existed some important impediments: her delicate health that would have hardly been able to bear the austerity of life as a hermit; the difficulties in moving away from family and friends; and especially the fact that Adèle did not have the economic resources necessary to sustain herself. Since her health was improving every day, Père Chambellan soon decided that she could begin this path supported by a companion, a devout woman from Laval who offered to accompany her. With regard to her family, Adèle wrote to her sisters explain-

---

[25] Cf. H-15D-005 Abbé Courtois.

ing her project, and they responded enthusiastically to her plan, fully understanding her reasons and promising to do everything possible to make her desire feasible.

Père Chambellan added a further condition: Adèle, once in Montmartre, would have to keep in contact with a religious community, which, in case of need, could be able to support and help her. This condition soon proved difficult to achieve, because Adèle hardly knew Paris and was not aware of any community that could support her appropriately. However, toward mid-February of 1876, one of her pupils, began to have health problems and Adèle had to accompany her on a visit to a specialist in a Paris clinic. Madame de Crozé indicated a community of sisters of Marie Reparatrice who would be able to give them hospitality for a week. Consulting a map of Paris during the journey by train, Adèle discovered that the religious lived at the foot of the hill of Montmartre and understood that this could be the community of support that would allow her to undertake her journey to Montmartre. The two women were welcomed warmly by the sisters and were taken to the chapel. During this visit, Adèle had the opportunity of speaking with the superior and, after having explained her intentions, without however going into too much detail, sensed her total support. During the week spent in the convent Adèle spent most of her time in prayer: she felt the irresistible attraction toward Montmartre. She prayed for a long time so that her mind could be conformed entirely to the divine will and she prayed also that her spiritual father might be enlightened, in such a way that his decision would become truly an expression of the divine will. In the future chapel she once again offered herself as a victim, sure that the mercy of God would accept her sacrifice. The journey to Paris signalled a profound change in Adèle who now felt within her soul directed toward her life project:

> When we were back at Laval, everything seemed changed around me. I was, so to speak, lifted above everything. I no longer feared anything. I no longer had any anxiety, but a complete and absolute abandonment to Jesus. I knew what he willed, and as a result I had only to allow Him to direct everything.[26]

On her return to Laval, she looked forward to 3rd March, the date on which her spiritual father had promised to tell her his decision. In his letter, Père Chambellan not only gave his consent, but also his fatherly encouragement to undertake the mission for which she felt called. And he gave her one month to make the necessary preparations.[27] The most difficult part was to communicate her decision to the persons for whom she had worked in the past eight years, establishing relations full of mutual understanding and con-

---

[26] H-15D-007, Abbé Courtois.

[27] Cf. H-15D-007, Abbé Courtois: "Arriving in the drawing-room, I found Mme de Crozé who said to me: 'Mlle, here is a letter which the Post Office had forgotten and which they have just sent me'. It was the one from Fr Chambellan, sending me, with a formal and well reasoned authorisation, his most fatherly encouragement, telling me how much he had admired Our Lord's goodness, and finally, telling me that I could make my arrangments with the least possible delay … O my Father, understand what happiness fills the soul of your little daughter! Of thanksgiving and of ardent love for the Heart of the Divine Master and for this last tenderness by which He has caused me to make the sacrifice which now I need not make effective… There remained some very painful arrangements to make, but I felt myself so strengthened that I would have braved all the forces of the world! Ah! What return can I make to Jesus for so many blessings!"

fidence. The family did not easily accept her decision and Adèle suffered greatly but she did not hesitate a moment, certain that this was the divine will. Although her companion could come to Paris only after two months, Adèle's spiritual father gave her permission to leave alone. Thanks to the help of a friend, she found lodgings in a modest house near the chapel of the Sacred Heart.[28] Her last day at Aulne was naturally very sad. On the first of May Adèle left this dear home and never again saw it. She went to Poitiers, after a brief visit to Laval, and spent a week in retreat under the guidance of Père Chambellan. It was 16 May, 1876 when she arrived in Paris to begin her solitary life there. The Superior of the Convent of Marie Reparatrice welcomed her most kindly. Adèle gave her a letter from Père Chambellan in which he entrusted Adèle to her maternal care placing her under obedience to this Superior. Adèle went up immediately on the hill of Montmartre to visit the temporary chapel, now completed. She arrived just in time for Benediction and remained there until the doors were closed for the night. She was filled with joy and gratitude:

> "The superior of Marie Reparatrice allowed me to go at once to do my first pilgrimage to the chapel of the Sacred Heart at Montmartre. I arrived just in time for Benediction and left when the doors were being closed. Oh! What a moment that was when I came to give Jesus this offering of my whole being, an offering willed and prepared for with so much care and attention! [ ...] What happiness! What love! What gratitude!"[29]

---

[28] Rue de la Fontanelle, at number 46.
[29] H-15D-008, Abbé Courtois.

On returning to the Convent, the Mother superior told her that she could remain there for a few days and go to Montmartre each day. The next day she went back and visited her lodging at No. 46 Rue de la Fontanelle. Her friend, Madame d'Evry, who handed over the keys in Laval, had prepared everything for her. Even the bed was made. Everything necessary was already there, including a small store of provisions. The room was decorated in a simple but fitting way, a crucifix hanging on the wall and some images of the Sacred Heart, the Virgin Mary and St. Joseph. Filled with gratitude, she gave her modest accommodation the name 'little Nazareth'. The next day she was allowed to sleep there and on the following morning, 19 May, Adèle awoke full of happiness because not only was it the anniversary of her First Communion, but also the day of her first communion in Montmartre. On this anniversary, Adèle offered herself once again to the Sacred Heart, ratifying in a definitive way her bond with Montmartre.

> "I offered myself without reserve to Jesus, asking him to take me as a victim, either by accepting my life, as I desired or by giving it back to me entirely consecrated to his Good Pleasure, without leaving anything for my own personal satisfaction. From that moment, I felt separated from the world. I have never lost the grace of this interior separation".[30]

However, this state of grace was quickly devastated by terrible suffering. Adèle described to Abbé Courtois the martyrdom which she endured: for several hours intense pain nailed her down, she could not move and only longed to die.

[30] H-15D-008, Abbé Courtois.

It seemed to her that she was damned and forsaken by God. She spent the entire night in agony, but still felt able to resign herself to the will of God. Next morning she was unable even to stand upright. By the evening with enormous difficulties she managed to return to the convent and asked to speak with the Mother Superior. She explained her suffering and her inability to return to Montmartre, but the Mother Superior commanded her to return, to be courageous and to resist snares of the evil one who was trying to make her renounce to the call which Jesus had inspired her to follow.

These words were invaluable and, despite being very fearful, she still placed all her trust in God and returned to Montmartre, accepting this trial as if it were a martyrdom. During the night she suffered terribly, but her will never faltered. She consented to suffer rather than to leave the place to which she knew God had called her. She was able, in spite of the unspeakable suffering, to participate in the Mass in the chapel and receive Holy Communion and at midday return in the convent, sorely tried in body and spirit. The Mother Superior received her with extreme kindness and said that the conflict which she was enduring was not finished and that it was very important for her to overcome at any cost this terrible ordeal. The suffering continued for a long time, but the certainty that she was fulfilling the will of God was an enormous support and consolation for Adèle, who was increasingly being drawn to abandon herself totally into the hands of the Lord. In this life of solitude in Montmartre Adèle found peace, serenity and joy. She experienced many marvellous graces offered to her by Providence protecting her and giving her signs that the Lord had not abandoned her, even during the time of testing:

"I had no need to trouble myself about material things – Providence provided for these in such a way that I lacked nothing, and I did not even have the worry of preparing my meals, except on Fridays. The Divine Care so arranged everything that I had only to accept as coming from God, all the help which my inexperience and lack of care made necessary. [...] For me it was an inexpressible life, a mixture of happiness, love, abandon, and also suffering, to which nothing in my past life nor in my imagination could be compared".[31]

However, the suffering experienced in the "little Nazareth", was also due to the heating system of the house located in the attic of the building, which was a severe trial for Adèle's frail health. Adèle was tested spiritually as well and only during the hours of the Mass was she able to enjoy brief moments of respite which enabled her to regain the courage to overcome. Slowly her existence was beginning to resemble a martyrdom, the memory of which continued to test her very many years later. In spite of this, she found a constant source of consolation in reading works of spirituality. In particular, during that period, she devoted herself to reading the "Imitation of Christ": the eighth chapter, taken from Book IV, relating to the oblation of Christ on the cross and to the complete sacrifice of herself, thereby obtaining the strength to continue to suffer. Especially, was she comforted by the ideal – in forming her "little work" – of the necessity of becoming a holocaust to God, in union with the Sacrifice of the Mass, so as to live to the full these sacred mysteries. Indeed it seemed to her that Christ himself, sacri-

---

[31] H-15D-009, Abbé Courtois.

ficing himself on the cross, had not asked anything else, but only the hearts of men surrendered wholly to Him without reserve.[32]

Her health continued to deteriorate visibly, so much so that she was unable to make simple movements alone, to move independently. One day, extremely tested in body and spirit, she felt an inner voice that predicted what was to be her future life: "I have not brought you here to take root, but only in heaven. Walk straight ahead like Abraham, until I show you the place of your last sacrifice".[33] So it happened. On August 23 another crisis arose, this time much more serious so that she was no longer able to move freely. Her illness continued to worsen inexorably. On the evening of August 30 the doctor was called to assess the gravity of the situation, and the superior arranged for Adèle to receive the Anointing of the sick. Nevertheless, Adèle, despite her sufferings, felt strong in God: she remained in the secure belief that she would not die at this moment at Montmartre. An inner voice had revealed to her that she would still have to follow the steps that would lead her to a martyrdom.

> "It was with deep gladness that I received the Holy Viaticum and Extreme Unction so that I felt myself already on the threshold of eternity. However, in spite of myself, the vague recollection of the words I had heard before made me think that I would not die.
> When the priest had gone, while I was praying interiorly, and my friend was praying too, I was conscious of coming back to life a little. I said to her, 'Marie, I am better, we

[32] Cf. Vincenzo Gamboso (a cura di), *L'imitazione di Cristo*, Edizioni Messaggero, Padova, 2010.
[33] Dom Bede Camm, *op. cit.*, p. 34.

must accept the will of God.' The poor child wanting all that I wanted thought that all was well, and that this truly was the will of God. The improvement continued, not that I was recovering gradually, but only sufficiently improved for the doctor to declare that I was out of danger".[34]

A few days later her condition began to improve and as soon as she was declared out of danger, her sister arrived to bring her home. On 2 September she wrote to her friend Madame Vosseaux:

> "Say with me a loving fiat to the Will of the good Master. It has pleased him to take me to the door of the tomb and to bring me back again. I have received the grace of Holy Viaticum and Extreme Unction on Wednesday morning. My happiness was so great at feeling myself in the presence of God! Oh, what an ineffable consolation! What more could I desire. May His holy and all lovable Will be blessed!... So I must leave ... Fiat! Fiat! Something tells me that I will return".[35]

Her departure was arranged for 13 September, 1876.[36] The day before her departure, Père Giroux, one of the Oblate Fathers, who had been her confessor during her stay in Montmartre, decided to bring her Communion at home from the temporary chapel of Montmartre. Adèle's joy was overflowing because on that day for the first time, the Blessed Sacrament left the chapel of Montmartre and it was to come to her:

> "The following day, a day of supreme consolation and of the greatest suffering, Jesus, my Jesus of Montmartre –

[34] H-15D-010, Abbé Courtois.
[35] H-15C-007, Madame Vosseaux.
[36] H-15F-119, Père J. B. Lémius.

wishing to show his poor child that he was not sending her away, and that she was his privileged child in spite of her great wretchedness – left the Sanctuary, which he had never left before, in order to come to her. In fact, as none of the Fathers had been ill, and no procession of the Blessed Sacrament had yet taken place, Jesus in the Blessed Sacrament had been there right from the first day, without ever leaving the Sanctuary. Also, what a consolation I was able to take away with me, when a few hours later I had to leave!

The remembrance of this favour from the Heart of Jesus has often been my dearest consolation in the years of suffering which followed".[37]

Adèle, in the face of this experience of pain, sickness and closeness to God, does not use powerful words, but assumes an attitude of humble expectation. At Montmartre, she received a mandate from God and, despite her suffering, her soul was grateful. The experience of pain and suffering, fully accepted, made Adèle more aware that it drew her closer to God, as it became for her a more intense sharing in the suffering of Jesus on the Cross.

## 1.4. Suffering and Conversion

On 13 September, 1876 Adèle returned to her home in Dijon and, in spite of her continued suffering, she remained serene because she had obeyed the will of God. Her family tried to improve her health, while her sister sought to find a priest who would bring her Communion once a week.[38] She

---

[37] H-15D-010, Abbé Courtois.
[38] This priest was Père Bizanard.

was confined to bed until 8 December, Feast of the Immaculate Conception of the Blessed Virgin. On that day Adèle received a great grace: her sufferings began to gradually diminish. Her health began to improve so much that, on the eve of Christmas, she was able to walk and even attended midnight Mass. During that period she occasionally attended daily Mass. But from the feast of the Epiphany, her condition deteriorated and she began a martyrdom of pain that lasted about seven months. Adèle, at that time believed herself to be at the point of death several times, not only on account of her atrocious physical sufferings, but also because of the agony of soul she endured. Recalling this particular period of her life, she wrote:

> "The remembrance of this terrible trial cannot be effaced from my memory, and I cannot understand how a human creature was able to endure it. The awareness of my pitiful state was always with me, and I bore all its weight with immeasurable bitterness. I said with my heart and my lips: *'O my God, may your Will be done!'* This was my only prayer, my sole prayer. I could not even recite an entire Our Father.[39]

It was in March 1877 on the advice of Père Chambellan, that Adèle accompanied by her sister and a friend went to Alise-Sainte-Reine in Côte-d'Or, a place famed for the beneficial properties of its waters. Her friend was terribly distressed by Adèle's state of health and seeing her suffering persuaded her to go to Lourdes, in spite of her great physical pain. In this situation Adèle sought counsel from her spiritual father, who encouraged her, giving her his full consent. The journey

[39] H-15D-011, Abbé Courtois.

46

to Lourdes was extremely wearing. It took them eight days because the group often had need to stop on account of Adèle's difficulty in continuing the journey and her friend often feared she would lose her "en route". They both reached Lourdes during the Vigil of the feast of the Assumption. The following morning on her 39th birthday, Adèle was taken to the Basilica and then to the grotto where, despite her extremely failing health, in front of Our Lady she did not ask the grace of healing, but of Holy Communion:

> "I could not ask for my cure, it was impossible for me to do so, unless it were for the honour of the most Holy Virgin. But I did ask, however, for sufficient strength to be able to go to Mass and Holy Communion each day, even if I had to suffer martyrdom for the rest of the day".[40]

After being immersed in the beneficial waters of Lourdes Adèle began to feel better and at once left Lourdes. Her improvement was increasingly evident, so much so that she and her friend were able to return to Dijon in just four days. She was rather saddened, once at home, to realise that the doctors and her family attributed her evident improvement to the baths at Sainte Reine rather than to the waters of Lourdes. After a short time, having regard to the notable benefits those places had had on her, the doctors advised her to move to the country in Brittany, and in particular to Bruz, a town not far from Rennes where her sister Josephine worked. Close to the home of her sister there was a small home for the elderly run by some Religious Sisters, who welcomed her willingly as a paying guest. She was given a

[40] *Ibidem.*

room overlooking the sanctuary of the chapel. So every morning the chaplain brought her Holy Communion directly from the altar. When she was in her room so very close to the tabernacle, she found she could assist at the offices, just as if she were in the chapel. During Benediction of the Blessed Sacrament she was as close to the tabernacle as if she were in the Chapel. She remained there until December 1878. She was very happy and every day her beloved sister visited her. Her health improved gradually despite the fact that she was still very weak. For this reason Adèle devoted herself to the embroidery of sacred vestments for which she showed a special talent and an enviable artistic creativity.

On the first of May 1881, Adèle had to return to Dijon because her elderly father had fallen gravely ill. The whole family met together, for the first time in ten years. Adèle was deeply saddened to see the gravity of her father's state which gave little room for hope of his recovery as it was clear that only a short time of life remained to him. Adèle decided, therefore, to stay together with her sisters in Dijon for the whole month of May. Her main concern was for the precarious state of her father's soul, for he had given up the practice of his faith many years ago.

By 18 May Adèle experienced a crushing weight of suffering when the doctor confirmed that her father's state was very critical and he was very close to death. The whole family were dismayed by the fact that he was in danger of dying without the sacraments and seemed far away from the grace of God. At this moment Adèle suffered a physical relapse and was forced to stay in bed so that her elderly father would not be worsened in his own state by his greater concern for his daughter. But even so his state deteriorated so much that the daughters decided to call a priest who was able to come only the following day.

After that meeting her father showed evident signs of a conversion to God, continually asking his daughters to pray for him. Adèle made him say with them some short formulas of prayer, just as if he were a child. The following day, the 19 May, 1881 the priest came and found their father well prepared and sincerely anxious to go to confession. It was difficult, since his mind wandered from time to time. But he did his best, and the priest was satisfied and then gave him Extreme Unction. At different times while he was fully conscious he tried to pray with all his heart. His tears, his efforts to pray, his humble gratitude for the grace that he had been granted were an immense consolation for his daughters. After the priest departed, one of his daughters helped him to make some acts of contrition, of faith, hope and charity, helping him to kiss the crucifix. One hour later he had fallen into a coma.

How great was the consolation felt by Adèle knowing that her father, after so many years, had found once more his faith and his absolute self-surrender to God. It was a further joy for her to realise this grace was granted to him on 19 May, anniversary of her First Communion Day thirty years before, when she offered her life for the conversion of her father. The following day he died in the arms of one of his daughters.

"In the midst of our sorrow we also gave thanks to God whose mercy had finally touched this soul who had strayed away for so many long years. I thought within myself that the return of this very dear soul for whom I offered my life on my First Communion Day had now been granted after so many years precisely on this anniver-

*49*

sary on 19<sup>th</sup> May. I blessed the Lord for so great a consolation. On the following day my good, beloved father breathed his last in the arms of one of my sisters".[41]

After this sad event the Garnier sisters left their old home and went to live in the town square of Saint Bénigne, close to the Cathedral, which, until the Revolution had been a benedictine abbey. Adèle was able to walk a little and about twice a week was accompanied to Mass. In the spring of 1885 she managed to go on alternate days and by the end of April, everyday, often alone. From that time on, her life became more interior, focusing on God alone. The spirit of prayer developed in her soul with more intensity than she had ever experienced (except at Montmartre), not even at the time of her first fervour. Her soul waxed strong through time spent in prayer, and throughout the day her prayer became continuous from that time. She also obtained the grace to endure with joy the problems and difficulties of daily life. From time to time her soul became so immersed and lost in God, that she was hardly aware of what was going on around her.

## 1.5. The Bridal Promise

1887 was a decisive year signalling a period of transition in the spiritual life of Adèle as she glimpsed more clearly the route she was being called to follow. Now the path of abandonment and prayer, which she had followed for so long, became more clearly defined than ever before. Adèle no longer sought her own will but only desired the divine will:

[41] *Ibidem.*

this became her only concern spurring her on to a personal crucifixion of her whole being.

L'Abbé Jules Courtois, chaplain of the Carmelite Nuns of Dijon, was the right person to guide Adèle in the road that God was preparing. With the full approval of her previous spiritual father, Adèle became spiritual daughter of this priest and was destined to remain under his guidance until his death, in 1892. One of the first counsels Abbé Courtois gave her was to urge her to write an account of all the important graces received until that time. It is due to this request that today it is still possible to know so many details of her spiritual life.

In 1873 Adèle had already consecrated herself entirely to the Heart of Our Lord in the Eucharist. Yet this did not satisfy her thirst for immolation. The vow she made on 17 June, 1887, with the consent of her spiritual father, was a vow of complete abandonment to the Divine Will. From that moment she considered herself as a small insignificant thing offered to Jesus and sacrificed as an absolute holocaust, without ever going back. After this vow, she seemed to experience a new life. She said that God from that moment watched over her as a mother who teaches her child to walk.

"… and to the degree that I said these words with all possible vigour, my soul became increasingly inebriated by the love of its God. Then, I hastened to recite a vocal prayer, even trying to do so without fervour, but the words vanished and my whole being began to be pitiably moved by this struggle. I trembled, I was troubled, my body was covered with a cold sweat, I no longer had the strength to resist, so finally I let my soul abandon itself to Jesus. And since then I always feel his ravishing presence and, at prayer I no longer have my own liberty. At least that is how it happened today.

I want to try to tell you about my day, during which my soul has been totally surrendered to the Holy Spirit, and in a manner so astonishing that I do not recall ever having received this kind of grace in such a prolonged way. But I am powerless to describe to you what took place: what I am writing to you here is so cold, so pale, that I am deeply pained to express so poorly to you this grace that Jesus grants me.

This morning, at the Mass before Holy Communion, I renewed repeatedly the acts of abandon which you have told me to make, then the acts of humility, and above all, acts of love and of union with Jesus.

I do not know what happened after I had received him. I thought I had within me, with Jesus, the Holy Spirit, all sparkling with light, all afire with love. I felt his presence like that of Jesus and *through him,* by his action within me. I adored the Father, I adored Jesus, and I adored the Spirit himself with an interior fervour that I cannot express. But all this with calm and an ineffable peace".[42]

On 2 November of this year, another great grace was offered to her. She had offered the day, in union with the Church, for the Holy Souls in Purgatory, and it had been a day of continual suffering. In the evening she was absolutely tired out. But she did not shrink from asking for more suffering, if that was the divine Will. Then she began to make the act of abandonment in these words: 'Heart of my Jesus, I offer and abandon myself entirely to Thee, in the spirit of obedience and also of love, even though I feel it not.'[43] These words were scarcely uttered when Adèle found herself suddenly ravished

[42] H-15D-012, L'Abbé Courtois.
[43] Dom Bede Camm, *op.cit.* p. 42

by the ineffable Vision of the Adorable Trinity. She felt herself actually in contact with the Triune God. And a divine light showed her that this grace was accorded to her by virtue of the Sacred Humanity of our Saviour. Then almost without realising it, she cried out in the midst of the ravishing happiness that seemed to crush her, 'My Jesus, what dost Thou want?' and then, in the midst of an outpouring of light ineffable and of divine harmony, she heard the reply which, she says, made more impression on her soul than any grace she had yet received, 'To espouse thee.'[44]

On the morrow, during the Mass, when the priest was giving her Communion, she distinctly heard the inner voice:

> "At the very moment the priest gave me Jesus, I heard the voice of my Beloved saying to me: *'This is our bethrothal feast'*, I no longer knew what to think! Love gave me absolute trust in Jesus; yet even so how can I believe that so many wonderful graces could come to me in so short a time?
>
> My thanksgiving began with a delightful adoration which Jesus himself wrought in my soul. Then all of a sudden I saw him as though on a dazzling throne in the middle of an immense hall. He was surrounded by a great number of spouses, all beautiful, brilliant, sparkling with purity and love. They were all crowned and having, *I think*, as he had, a sceptre in their right hand. As for me, I was hiding myself, entirely withdrawn in a rather dark corner of this large hall. Jesus came, and by his Will alone, fashioned around me a small room, also dark, and said to me: 'You are to remain there, and I shall come and visit you, and I myself will prepare you to become my spouse.' Then he shut me up in the room and went back beside the queens of his Heart.

[44] Cf. *Ibidem.*

Even so, I saw him as if I had not been shut up, and the ardent love that he had put in my heart made me find delightful the hidden resting place where he had placed me. In my heart I said to him: 'But, Lord, I am not doing anything for you.' He replied: 'You have only to allow me to act. It is for this that I have asked you to make the vow of abandon.' These words, without any sound, (but as if they had been inscribed within me), reassured me, and I gently continued my thanksgiving, no longer seeing anything".[45]

On 14 November Adèle related to her confessor the wonderful grace that had been granted to her. While the priest gave to her the Sacred Host, she distinctly heard within her soul these words: 'This is the Marriage.' Troubled for an instant, she returned to her place. As she bowed down humbly to adore Him, she was granted a mystical vision: she found herself as it were stretched out upon the cross, crucified with Jesus so that she was as it were fused, transformed into Him. ... Having never experienced anything of the kind before, and not understanding what was passing within her she said to Our Lord: "Oh, my God, what does it mean, what art Thou doing?".[46] The inner voice confirmed that at that moment Jesus was taking her as his bride.

## 1.6. The Meeting with Alice Andrade

After a prolonged stay in Dijon, Adèle moved with her sisters to Alise Sainte Reine. The transfer was for her a great sacrifice since in Dijon she had received such marvellous graces,

[45] H-15D-037, Abbé Courtois.
[46] *Ibidem.*

but it also meant having to separate from her confessor to whom she had rendered so faithfully an account of them.

Here it was that Adèle had the happiness of meeting her who was to become her first disciple and spiritual daughter, her chief collaborator and assistant in the work to which she was called, her most devoted companion and "my second self" as Mother Adèle said many times. Her name was Alice Andrade, known later by the religious name of Mother Agnes of the Sacred Heart, co-foundress of the Congregation and successor of Adèle as Mother General. Her father, Michel Andrade, was an old university companion of Victor, brother of Adèle. They were both naval engineers and were close friends. The mother of Alice was English. Alice was born on 20 January, 1873 and she was still an infant when her mother died. In 1879, Michel Andrade married again a young woman who became a true mother to Alice. Within 10 years the family grew, thanks to the birth of five other children. However, to please the wishes of her English mother, Alice was brought up as a Protestant, although the other members of the family were Catholics. At the age of sixteen years, after many prayers, she was permitted to convert to the Catholic faith. From that day on she devoted herself to an intense spiritual life. She organised her friends into a sort of religious community, with rules and specific practices that were observed most faithfully.

Alice was always cheerful and had a keen sense of humour. Nevertheless, in the next phase after her conversion she was tormented by scruples. She constantly had recourse to her confessor to regain peace of soul. Fortunately, she had the grace to practice absolute obedience, so this trial though prolonged, only helped her to advance in her journey of faith.

Alice experienced another difficulty, that of doubting her true vocation. For a long time she sought to know God's will for her, without receiving any clear response. The sudden death of her father in 1893, due to a bad accident was destined to enlighten her soul.

Despite the profound pain caused by this sudden loss Alice began to glimpse her path ahead. She used to speak of this awareness as the 'Ransom of the Beloved' and her desire was now fixed to consecrate herself to God in order to save the soul of the father she loved, who had been taken away from her so suddenly. When he was still alive, she had already confided to him her desire for the religious life and he had not opposed it. However, Alice was not attracted to any religious community that she knew. She did indeed, try her vocation with the Dominican Sisters, but a month was sufficient to show her that it was not there that God would have her. Furthermore, she had the conviction that God wished her to take part in the foundation of a new Congregation, but she had no idea of how to go about this.

It was Joséphine Garnier who was destined to solve the problem. She came to Paris in 1896, and her brother, who feared that the death of his old comrade, M. Andrade, might have left the family badly off (though this was not the case), had urged her to offer to the widow and children a home for the summer months in their house at Villeneuve. Joséphine soon became great friends with the Andrades, and she was specially drawn to Alice, in whom she recognised unusual gifts. She soon divined her trouble, and before long she was able to suggest to her the means by which she might find the road to which God seemed to be drawing her. They were out for a walk together one day when Alice felt herself moved to confide in this new friend her hopes of some day taking part in a religious foundation. But she felt that the whole idea seemed so presumptuous, that it was very hard for her to speak of it. It was not, indeed, until they were almost home again that she armed herself with all her courage, and suddenly blurted out, as it were:

> "The reason why I don't get married, is that I believe that I am destined to take part in a foundation, where there will be continual prayer for the Church and the Pope, but I do not know of any such foundation.[47]

Josephine's surprise and delight can be imagined. She at once began to tell her, discreetly, something of the work to which her sister Adèle felt herself called by the Sacred Heart: and when she reached the house she at once wrote to Adèle: "If it is God's will that you begin the work to which you feel He is calling you, I think that I have found you your first companion"..[48] At last the holiday season began, and the Andrades set out for Villeneuve. 'The very evening of our arrival,' wrote Alice some years later, 'we all went to dine with the Misses Garnier. They were waiting for us on the lawn. Immediately I saw our mother, I flung myself into her arms, crying out, "My mother!" "My daughter!" she replied; and from that moment I had not the slightest doubt that I was called to be with her.'[49]

Thus began a union which only death was to sever. That same year, in a letter addressed to Madame Andrade, Adèle described in this way, her link with Alice:

[47] Dom Bede Camm, *op. cit.*, p. 48.
[48] *Ibidem*, p. 49.
[49] *Ibidem*.

"We are friends perfectly united in Jesus and our affection, through charity, is more than friendship: rather it is fraternal union, the 'cor unum' will always be the ideal of christian Associations. Alas! It is not always realised. But we do our best to come closer to it, by both the goodness and holiness of our life, as this should already be for the glory of God. The Lord Jesus wants us to be 'one in Him' as He is 'with His Father' – that sublime experience, we must fashion if we want to love according to His divine model!"[50]

Adèle opened her heart to her young companion and together they discussed their future life in all its details of a possible project of common life. Adèle, had indeed, no idea of becoming the foundress of a religious order. She believed that this place of honour was reserved to another lady of great piety, who seemed to be more fitted for a part from which she herself shrank.[51]

When the Andrades had to return to Paris in October, for the beginning of the school year, there began between the 'mother' and 'daughter' a long and intimate correspondence, which is still preserved. Their project was submitted not only to the Abbé Courtois and the Abbé Sauvé who already were well acquainted for years with Adèle's aspirations, but also to the Père Balme, of the Order of St Dominic, one of Lacordaire's first disciples, and himself a founder.[52] Père Balme, in spite of

[50] H-15F-013, Madame Andrade.

[51] In fact, many writings reveal that Adèle thought that another person could fulfil this role, but not herself.

[52] See in the Letter of 18 November 1896 in which Adèle speaks of her meeting with Père Balme in H-15H-004 Alice Andrade: "Just one word, my very dear Alice, to let you know that I have already written to Père Balme to ask to see him soon and if the Religious would be able to receive me for two or three days.

old age and many infirmities, was well known as a spiritual director of souls, and was the spiritual director of Alice. Adèle came to Paris in November to consult him about the work. On 8 November, 1896 she and Alice consecrated themselves to God for His Church, through the hands of the Immaculate Mother. A little rule of life of 12 Chapters was written by Adèle, and corrected by Père Balme, and is dated 4ᵗʰ December.

> "I had no comment point by point on all your good and interesting statements. But in general I say "yes" to everything. I would add that, in the context of the readings, I would like to see the thought of Glory to the Father, which was the beginning and the end of the Incarnation and to which everything must return, added to the chapter on union with Jesus, which for us must have as its sole purpose to honour and glorify the Father. What do you think?"[53]

Right now, in 1897 began, for the fledgling Congregation, the first problems and disappointment. The person on whom Adèle counted the most, withdrew from all participation in the work, and soon it became evident that she could not trust in the others. Adèle's whole life was one of abandonment to the divine Will, and she received this cross with her usual calm nothwithstanding that this would mean an interruption in beginning the new community. Suddenly, at the beginning of March, the clouds rolled away, the third sister was found, and they could begin to think seriously of the foundation. This was Alexida Bourgeois, to be known in the future as Mother Mary of St John, and to prove herself a worthy companion of Adèle and Alice. Alexida was a woman very different from the Mother to whom God had

[53] H-15H-007, Alice Andrade.

offered her. She was then eighteen years old and came from Poitou. Very pious, very candid, she had a look in her eyes, which, as Adèle said, enabled you to read the very depths of her soul. She had, too, a heart of gold, capable of unlimited devotion to the cause.

The first meeting between Alexida and Adèle took place in October 1896 at Saint Varent when visiting her friend Mademoiselle Vivon. Alexida at this time was to enter the Congregation of the Immaculate Conception at Lourdes. One day they happened to kneel side by side at the altar-rails to receive Holy Communion. Adèle felt at this moment an inner conviction that the girl kneeling beside her was destined one day to be her daughter in religion. But she said nothing about it at the time, as the vocation of the young girl seemed to be already decided.

During the stay that Adèle made at St Varent with her friend Mlle Vivon, Alexida never spoke to her at all intimately. It was only after she had left that the girl felt herself attracted to what Mlle Vivon used to call 'the work of Mlle Garnier.' She asked eager questions about this work, and all she heard made her feel more and more that this was where God wanted her to be. She spoke of it to her director, who, to her surprise, entirely approved the idea. While this was going on, the defection of the lady chosen as Superior put a stop to the immediate carrying out of the work. As Père Balme said, 'It takes three monks to make a chapter.' Adèle wrote the sad news to Mlle Vivon, who replied:

> 'It is, indeed a pity that you cannot begin, for Alexida would have been with you.'[54] Adèle replied at once, 'But let her come and we will begin.'[55]

[54] Dom Bede Camm, *op. cit.*, p. 51.
[55] *Ibidem.*

It was then decided to begin the work in June, at Montmartre.

On 14 March, 1897, shortly before the arrival of Alexida in the small apartment near Montmartre that would welcome the nascent community, Adèle wrote to her "second daughter" a letter that clearly defines the role and the aspirations of the first Adorers of the Sacred Heart:

"My beloved daughter, [...] you are drawn by an attraction [...] to unite yourself to two poor souls, who, like yourself, have the unique desire better to serve our Lord, and accomplish His holy Will, by devoting themselves entirely and for ever to Holy Church, to its visible Head, Our Holy Father the Pope, and to the clergy. To this end we devote ourselves with all our soul, while waiting to be dedicated to it by the consecration of the Church, that is to work, pray and suffer, to immolate ourselves, if it please God, as poor and very unworthy little victims; victims, that is to say, offered to God the Father in union with Our Lord, the Divine Victim, offered by Him who is the Sovereign Priest. [...] Do you feel, my dear Alexida, that you are prepared thus to live? [...] You and Alice will be two little sisters, of whom I, on account of my age, will be the mother, and at the same time the Sister and the servant in solicitude, affection and devotion. We shall have but one heart and one soul, and thus united we shall strive to sanctify ourselves in studying our divine Model, sustaining one another by advice, example and help; in a word, by charity always and in all things. [...] Oh, my sister, how happy shall we be in our sufferings if we truly love Jesus. [...] When you arrive, we will come, your sister and I, to meet you, and bring you to our little convent, which will be ready, in its poverty, to receive you. [...] Goodbye, my very dear child, my daughter, my sister. […] Pray for your poor Mother.[56]

Once the first "cell" of the future Congregation was established, the life of Adèle – which until then seemed to be dedicated as a hermit life – become entrusted with greater responsibility to God and to her flock. She gave herself with tireless dedication and with ardent zeal in her heart, for the heart of a mother learns not to spare her own life and to allow herself to be wounded by the sufferings of others as if they were her own and also to care for each sister with the loving compassion of Christ, and finally to devote herself fully and freely to the mission she must fulfil. In this new viewpoint on community, Adèle's life expressed itself in a more total manner by assuming the condition of "servant"- servant of the Word, servant of the Cross, servant of the mission, servant of her religious family and of her daughters.

## 1.7. The Transfer to Montmartre

On 21 June, 1897 Alice and Adèle went up the hill of Montmartre in order to take up their abode there in their first dwelling: a rented apartment in a house at Rue du Mont Cenis.[57] This house was renamed 'Nazareth' just as Adèle, twenty-one years before, had named the two poor attics in which she had lived during her first stay at the foot of the Basilica. Alice, with few significant words, thus recalls their coming to Montmartre:

---

[56] H-15H-008j, Alexida.
[57] The apartment was at n. 2 bis.

"We were so happy! With what ardour we prayed at the feet of Jesus, exposed in the Blessed Sacrament in the Basilica. When we reached our dwelling, I remember that our Mother and I read together some pages of the Rule of St Benedict to which we felt attracted".[58]

"The little Nazareth" consisted of a small room, which for a few months was used as a chapel, a refectory, a community room, a parlour; and two small bedrooms plus a tiny kitchen. The furniture was rather poor and there was nothing superfluous. They had bought some folding beds in case of future postulants.[59] Alexida arrived the next day after their installation. Adèle and Alice went to fetch her from the station and, after a visit to the new dwelling, they went to the Basilica to thank the Sacred Heart. The next day the fourth sister arrived, she was called Sister Teresa. They had drawn up a little Rule of Life which they followed very faithfully. In addition, each day they went to the Basilica for Mass, Eucharistic Adoration and Benediction. So in great humility and poverty this great work began. On 29 June, the feast of Saints Peter and Paul, they all went down into the crypt of the Basilica and there consecrated themselves to Saint Peter. They tried at first to keep their project secret from the priests who served the Basilica. But this did not last long. Since they could no longer go to confession to Père Balme, their confessor, they were forced to turn to Père Vasseur. When they went to confession they had to confide their secret to him.

However, he soon became their devoted friend and

---

[58] Dom Bede Camm, *op. cit.*, p. 54.

[59] In fact two days after their transfer to Montmartre, a fourth person joined them: she was a widow from a village of the Côte d'Or, recommended by Abbé Charles Suavé.

helper. They received the chains of St. Peter from the Abbé Sauvé, who came to visit them, and wore them secretly beneath their clothing, as an emblem of their vocation.[60]

Those first few months were spent in an atmosphere of joy and thanksgiving. The sisters began a serious study of latin in order to be able to enter more fully into the liturgical life of the Church. On 21 November, the feast of the Presentation of Our Lady, Père Balme granted them another joy – clothing them with a little habit, and consecrating them in a special way to the Sacred Heart of Jesus. This "little habit" – worn under their ordinary clothes – consisted of a white scapular, having embroidered on it the Sacred Heart and the keys of Saint Peter and on the other side a cross and the monogram of Mary. The small ceremony of investiture of the four Sisters took place in great secrecy in the Dominican Convent in Levallois-Perret, in his small hospital room. The Father blessed the scapulars and placed them on their shoulders. He gave each the religious name which she had already chosen adding to each the name of our Blessed Lady. Adèle chose the name of Marie de Saint Pierre and Alice called Agnes du Sacre Coeur.[61] They were all deeply moved, as was the Father himself. Then he addressed them with words of encouragement:

[60] *St Peter's Chains* – preserved in the lower part of the Basilica of San Pietro in Vincolo in Rome – represents the most important relic of ancient Christendom. The legend tells that the chains which bound the first Pope of the Church in the Roman prison in Jerusalem, at the moment when they brought close to the one to the other they were miraculously welded together. Symbolically, the wearing of St Peter's Chains was meant to emphasise the hand of God active in the work of man: indeed when Peter was in chains the action of God emerged. Therefore the nascent Congregation intended to underline symbolically that the project of the foundation was not a human work but the decisive intervention of the Lord.

[61] Cf. H-15C-188, Père Balme.

"You are still a grain of mustard seed, but this tiny grain will sprout and become a tree, a great tree under which many souls will take shelter".[62]

These words were prophetic when read in the light of the history of the Congregation, which has developed in the shadow of "Tyburn Tree" and has produced great fruit. The Sisters spent six months quietly and lived in a hidden way. This time was necessary according to Père Balme to test their vocation and their perseverance. At this point the sisters, firm in their vocation and more and more convinced of being where God wanted them to be, decided to submit their project to the superior of the Basilica, Père Jean Baptist Lémius. They were not without anxiety because they feared that he would be opposed to their project. But soon Père Lémius began to view the work seriously, studying it closely. He prayed for guidance and light and soon found that it was time to lay the whole project before the Archbishop of Paris, Cardinal François-Marie-Benjamin Richard.[63] The Cardinal accepted the draft and placed the foundation under the charge of his private secretary, l'Abbé

---

[62] Dom Bede Camm, *op. cit.*, p. 56.

[63] *François-Marie-Benjamin Richard de la Vergne* was born on 1 March 1819 at Nantes, a city in the Nort West of France. He attended the seminary of Saint Suplice and was ordained priest in 1849 at Nantes. He was first Secretary to Mons. Jaquement, then Vicar General. In 1871 he was appointed Bishop of Belley and four years later became auxiliary Bishop of Cardinal Guibert, Archbishoop of Paris whom he succeeded on 8 July 1886. He was created Cardinal on 24 May 1889. It was he who completed the work of the Basilica of the Sacred Heart of Montmartre. He died on 28 January 1908 at Paris.

Cf. Abbé Maurice Clément, *Vie du cardinal Richard, archvêque de Paris*, J. De Gigord, Paris, 1923.

Lefebvre, who went to Montmartre on the first of March to have a conversation with the sisters. A few days later the new community received the official Act of the Foundation, which was signed by Cardinal Richard on 4 March, 1898 and the novitiate began on that day. The religious Congregation which Adèle had seen in spirit so many years before was now founded on the holy mountain. The sisters were immediately engaged in the work of preparing the Constitutions, which were discussed by Père Lémius and Père Balme together with the Mother Foundress. The latter chose as the motto of the Congregation: *Gloria Deo per Sacratissimum Cor Iesu*, motto which still remains in the Congregation.

At the end of April the small community acquired a larger set of rooms in the same house: this enabled them to be able to assign a room for community prayer, and also to accept some new postulants and on 2 July, 1898 the sisters were able to begin the daytime perpetual adoration of the Blessed Sacrament.

Together with the progress made in the foundation, crosses also began. The first was a new subject who joined the sisters about seven months after their transfer to the hill of Montmartre. This person was much esteemed by the Mother, but probably never had a genuine religious vocation. However, Adèle's humility made her fancy herself entirely unfit to govern a community, and she hoped that she would be able to hand over the reins to the new-comer.

> "This holy person is 36 years of age; to complement her gifts and her virtues, she has a sympathetic appearance which draws souls.
>
> Also, she is an absolutely remarkable Mistress of Novices, and thanks to this marvellous discovery, everything is

advancing perfectly and the spiritual joy of our little family waxes stronger, if this is possible, with the even more clear, serious and complete practice of the religious life.

Moreover, this good Mother Mistress has an organising ability which makes her capable in every way, and hence I do not have to busy myself with anything of importance".[64]

When it became clear that the Novice Mistress was not suited to the task entrusted to her, the Mother prayed earnestly for a clear indication of the will of God, and each morning during Holy Communion, an inner voice told her that she would not remain. At last she was obliged to consult Père Lémius, and it was decided that the Ecclesiastical Superior must intervene. After his visit, the Mistress of Novices herself decided to depart. She left on 9 June, 1898 in peace and cordiality.

1899 was a significant year for the small community because it was to witness the reception of the habit by the first postulants, and religious profession of Adèle Garnier and her companions. In addition, this year was also marked by the solemn consecration of the whole human family to the Sacred Heart of Jesus, made by the pontiff, Pope Leo XIII.[65] The first

---

[64] H-15D-115, Abbé Courtois.

[65] On this subject see the work of Leo XIII *Annum Sacrum. Encyclical on the Consecration of the world to the Sacred Heart of Jesus*, of 25 May 1899. In this encyclical Leo XIII arranged that in all the world, on 11 June 1899 in the principal Church in every city and of every country, after a Triduum of preparation, the Act of Consecration of the human race to the Sacred Heart of Jesus would be carried out in a public and solemn manner. This decision had been preceded by numerous official approbations of the Cult of the Sacred Heart, on the part of various popes, occurring over a period of more than two hundred years.

night of adoration was on 15 March[66] and, since the sisters did not have the Blessed Sacrament in their home, the adoration was made in turn hour by hour in the silence of their cells. On 17 March two sisters received the habit as novices[67] and the first ceremony of clothing was presided over by Mgr. Lefebvre, assisted by Père Lémius. Beside the Mother and the five other sisters in the choir, Père Vasseur, their first friend at the Basilica and Madame Legentil, who later became a great benefactor of the community, also were present.

The first profession of Adèle and her first daughters took place on 9 June, 1899, the feast of the Sacred Heart.[68] The evening before the profession, Adèle on her knees in front of her daughters, asked their pardon for everything in which she had failed with regard to them.

The ceremony of profession took place, by special privilege, in the crypt of the Basilica, in the Chapel of St Peter, which is immediately under the High Altar. Canon Lefebvre presided at the function, as Ecclesiastical Superior, and was assisted by Père Lémius. Two days later, on Sunday, 11 June, took place the consecration of the human race to this Adorable Heart. This consecration, Adèle decided, should be recited every day by her daughters in choir, and this has become one of the most cherished traditions of her religious family.

After the religious profession, the community began to

[66] It was decided that the nocturnal adoration could be repeated on the first Friday of every month.

[67] The four senior Sisters had become novices without any ceremony.

[68] Thus the first profession ceremony took place on the Feast of the Sacred Heart 1899, and also the first day of the Triduum preparatory to the solemn Act of Consecration of the human race to the Sacred Heart ordained by Pope Leo XIII.

practice regularly the Adoration of the Eucharist during the daytime, which corresponded to their fundamental desire and also was the distinctive purpose of the community itself. This practice took place from July 1899 even if the small number of sisters made it rather difficult to fulfil; but, despite the difficulties and obstacles they persevered in this practice. Throughout the day, from 5:30 in the morning until 8:00 in the evening at least one nun was kneeling for about an hour before the Blessed Sacrament exposed. At the time, the religious were only nine and it is clear that this practice certainly meant great sacrifices. This was the more so as the sisters went to the Basilica for Adoration.

Adèle felt that it was more than ever desirable to move as soon as possible to a new abode where they would have a chapel with the Blessed Sacrament and to be able to make their adoration without going outside the house. The house that seemed appropriate for their purpose was number 40 Rue de la Barre, near the Basilica of the Sacred Heart.[69] It was quite a large property, with a tree-lined park and some cottages, even if the price asked by the owner was too high for the community. However, an agreement was arrived at between the parties, as the man was anxious to sell the property to a religious community dedicated to the cult of

[69] An anecdote linked to the acquisition of this house says that the author of this acquisition was Père Lémius himself – He was saying Mass at the well-known Sanctuary of Notre Dame de la Garde at Marselles. All at once, at the offertory of the Mass (as he tells us himself), he had a distraction quite unaccountable at the time. The words '40 Rue de la Barre, the Sisters' Convent' entered into his mind with such force and such importunity that he could not drive them away What was not his astonishment when, on returning to Paris, a house-agent presented himself and offered him this very property for sale! Cf. Dom Bede Camm, *op. cit.*, pp. 60-61.

the Sacred Heart and for this reason he agreed to a more modest price. The contract was signed on 19 May, 1899.[70] In the month of November the community had to pay 50,000 francs, a sum the sisters did not have at that time and it was source of serious concern for the Mother, so, in the letter of 18 July 1899, she wrote to Père Lémius:

> Our temporal situation is – from the human point of view – very disquieting. From here in 17 months, we have to pay 150,000 francs, of which 100,000 to M. Proiert and 50,000 which we have been lent with such goodness [ ...] but we must not delay in repayment. We must find the resources to begin to build the convent, which is indispensable for the development of the Work.[71]

## 1.8. The Sufferings in the New House

On 24 May, 1901, Adèle and her daughters took possession of the new property. They occupied two cottages standing near one another, and united by a garden. One they called St Benedict's and the other St Bruno's. The installation had been long delayed by various difficulties. And now the political outlook in France was becoming very dark, as the Government was threatening new laws of persecution against the Church and more especially against the Religious Orders.

A large room in the upper story of one of the cottages became the chapel. Dom Remy came to give them instruc-

---

[70] The price agreed for the purchase of the house was of 500,000 francs.

[71] H-15F-096, Père Lémius.

tions in the Benedictine Rule,[72] and at the end of the month Père Lémius blessed the new Convent. The first Mass was said there on 1 June and on the night of 6-7 June they made their first night adoration before the Blessed Sacrament exposed on the altar of their chapel.

In spite of the moment of grace which they were experiencing, the sisters suffered great trials. These took place within the convent. There were trials defined by Alice as cases of 'obsession and diabolic possession'. The sisters maintained secrecy about these things except to their spiritual Fathers who were responsible as well for some exorcisms. The disclosure of such events, in fact, could have discredited the good name of the nascent community:

> "Except as regards our Superiors and Fathers, it goes without saying that we tried to keep the great tribulation that weighed upon us, as secret as possible. Providence helped us manifestly. Fr Lémius was able to affirm that it was a real miracle that these extraordinary facts remained almost secret".[73]

According to the account of Alice, these events were inexplicable and had to be attributed to numerous attempts by the demon to destroy the Work.[74]

---

[72] In this same year they entered into close relations with Solesmes. Their charter of affiliation to the great Abbey founded by Dom Guéranger is dated 2 July, 1901. The Solesmes nuns of the monastery of Ste Cécile were kind enough to give them a copy of their Constitutions, drawn up by Dom Guéranger, in the form of Declarations on the Benedictine Rule, and these were of the greatest possible help to them in drawing up their own Constitution.

[73] Tyburn Convent, *Led by a Star*, PartTwo, [unedited work], pp. 285-286.

[74] Cf. *Ibidem*, p. 2. "In April 1901 several times there appeared fragments of the substance used for hosts. Whatever was their origin, the manner of their appearance seems to be naturally inexplicable. The particles appeared

By the month of August these distressing attacks had not ceased to work in other and more dangerous ways. Another cruel persecution was preparing, one that would drive them

suddenly without any visible exterior agency. Once they appeared in the refectory during dinner, before all the Community; there they were on the table, on the ground, on our clothes. One day, they appeared before the Promoter of the Faith, Canon Peupertier. M. Lefebvre made the chemical analysis of several particles and declared that were similar to altar breads.

One of the Sisters persecuted by the devil received some resounding blows. The blow was heard, but without seeing the hand that dealt it.

One day, (we were then at 11a Rue du Mont Cenis) the devil said that he was going to set No. 40 Rue de la Barre on fire. Naturally we hardly paid any attention to this, the devil being such a liar. It was perhaps a simple coincidence, but, in the evening, someone came to warn our Mother that a fire had just broken out at No. 40. Our Mother and I went there. Our Mother prayed. The fire was extinguished and, as far as I remember, the damage was insignificant.

What scenes there were on certain days!

Our Mother Foundress and I had our rooms on the ground floor of "St Bruno". This was shortly after our installation at No. 40, and the keys remained on the inside, of the doors of the rooms. One morning our Mother was out, and I had gone to Adoration. A sister who returned from the Basilica, heard a great noise in our rooms which lasted several seconds. She knocked on the door, and not hearing any answer, went to seek Mère Marie de St Jean. The two Sisters tried to open the doors but they were locked, a thing which was never done. Suspecting a trick of the devil, Mère Marie de St Jean took a key at random... She opened the door. If I remember rightly, there was a door of communication between the two rooms. In any case, means was also found of entering the second room. The most unexpected sight met our gaze. In the two cells – tables, chairs, stools, crucifix, pious pictures, papers, books, toilet objects, etc. were all thrown on the ground in indescribable confusion; but nothing was broken. Meanwhile our Mother and I had returned. I still see the lamentable sight! What struck us the most was that a washstand-basin containing water was overturned, and that the water did not run out, and that the unstoppered ink bottles were on the ground and the ink was not spilt, which, naturally speaking would have been impossible. The key of our Mother's door was in a box flung into the middle of the room; after having searched well I found our key among the blankets which lay on the ground.

from the Holy Mountain whither God had called their Mother in so marvellous a manner; they were to be driven out, not merely from Montmartre, but from their beloved France. At the beginning of July, 1901, the infamous law of

One room had been reserved for Madame Auban Moet who from time to time made a day's retreat in our little monastery. The devil also made incursions there.

The clattering of dancing feet having been heard in this room we went to see. All the furniture was overturned, and in the midst, face to the ground, lay a statue of the Sacred Heart which is now at St Mary's. Although this statue was of plaster, it was absolutely intact.

These scenes recommenced one evening shortly afterwards, with variations. This time, the statue of the Sacred Heart had been thrown off the mantelpiece through the door, as far as the landing, moreover without any accident. The overturned pieces of furniture were all directed towards the door, and what astonished us the most, was that Madame Auban's two tables were turned upside down on the ground, and that the sides of the table cloths, instead of falling to the ground, were raised up in the air against the table legs, which was altogether inexplicable. As had happened in our cells some days before, the inkstand was overturned on the floor, but the ink did not flow out.

A clattering of objects dancing on the stairs has remained especially imprinted on my memory.

It was some instants after the scenes which I have just mentioned.

"I had not yet gone to bed," wrote our Mother Foundress, "when a fresh noise, loud and insolent, was to be heard on the staircase, I looked and saw fragments of earthenware toppling over with violence, knocking against one another with a great crash. I looked up, the staircase was strewn with these fragments…"

The two of us ran out on hearing the noise, and we ascertained that the broken objects were a water jug and a basin usually kept in the attic of 'St Bruno'".

"Having gone down again," continues our Mother, "I was not yet in bed when I heard a diabolical noise made by iron-ware and plates and dishes. I ran to the stairway and saw tumbling down with impossible bounds a pair of enormous tongs and a poker which the devil had gone to the further end of the garret to seek and had then thrown with force – doubtless with fury – down the staircase upon the broken crockery, which thus was more and more in atoms!"

the 'Associations' had been promulgated, which ordered the dissolution of every religious Community not authorised by the Government, or which had not solicited this authorisation within a period of three months. Every institution asking for such authorisation had to submit to the examination of the Government its Rule and also its temporal possessions, income and resources. It had thus to expose itself to the confiscation of everything it possessed.

By the end of August there remained no more hope of any mitigation of these conditions. After long examination, and many prayers, they decided that, whatever happened, they must not separate from one another, but must continue the common life, which was so dear to them. If it could not be at Montmartre, they must go elsewhere. They decided to consult a well-known Catholic lawyer, as to the risks they would run as regards their property. He examined the whole situation with the greatest possible exactitude, and concluded that it was impossible for them to remain. They could not hope to pass as an ordinary Association, there were too evident signs of their being a religious community. If they did not ask for authorisation, they would be dissolved *ipso facto*. If on the other hand, they did ask for it, he was assured that it would not be granted, and in this case they would have to depart all the same, and their property would be confiscated by the government.

In these conditions the path of duty seemed clear; and the Cardinal fully approved their determination to leave the country, much as he grieved at their departure. A friend of the Community had suggested that if they could not live together, they might separate for a time, and live two by two in lodgings at Montmartre, and thus continue the adoration.

But the Mother saw that that would be quite impossible considering it unfair to impose on the nascent community such a setback. She opted, finally, courageously, for exile; the sisters were favourable to going away despite their poverty, trusting that the Sacred Heart would come to their aid as He had already done in the past:

> "In three months, she wrote, 'we should have undone the work of four years, and there is not one of our Sisters who would not prefer exile to this, even if it had to be endured for years. As to myself, who feel my heart torn in pieces at the idea of quitting Montmartre, yet I trust not to lack the courage nor swerve from the responsibility to lead them to a foreign land. ... But to remain here under the conditions proposed would be to sacrifice the religious life to the consolation of not leaving Montmartre".[75]

The approbation of the Cardinal had brought peace and consolation to the Mother, for here, as in all the changing scenes of her life, she sought nothing but the manifestation of the divine Will. But where were they to go? They turned their eyes towards England, that Protestant land, which was

---

[75] For this decision see also H-15F-118, Père Lémius:
"Oh, Father, the Sacred Heart is there, He will provide for us, and He will not allow us to lack anything. He well knows that it is He Himself Who is taking us there, and He will watch over us as He does here. My Father, when the apostles left the Cenacle, their sorrow was great! They had to leave those places where they had lived with the Lord, where they had seen Him die. They were not rich, they had no assured income. But their good Master had said: 'Seek ye first the Kingdom of God and His justice and all these things will be added to you.' Father, I feel this, I know it, I believe it firmly: this trial will redound to the glory of the Sacred Heart, to our sanctification and *development* of our little Society".

yet receiving with such extraordinary kindness and charity the Religious Communities exiled from France. They had no hesitation as to this, it must be England, and if possible, London. Mother Adèle and Mother Agnes both knew the English language.[76] They knew that they were sure of every possible help and kindness from Cardinal Vaughan,[77] the devoted Archbishop of Westminster, and already they looked forward to establishing a house of prayer in London.

Cardinal Richard had himself, it may be added, a special devotion to prayer for the Conversion of England, and in 1897, the very year of the establishment of Adèle and her daughters at Montmartre, had ordered that a Mass should

---

[76] Mother Agnes was bilingual, having, as we have previously noted, an English mother.

[77] *Herbert Alfred Vaughan* was born on 15 April, 1832 at Gloucester, a city in the south-west of England. He came from a fervent Catholic family, where five daughters became Religious and six of the eight sons were ordained priests, three of whom also became bishops: Roger of Sydney, Australia, John of Sebastopolis and auxiliary bishop of Salford and Herbert Alfred of London. Herbert Alfred received a fine formation studying with the Benedictines at Downside Abbey, close to the city of Bath and with the Jesuits at Brugelette (Belgium). At 29 years of age, in 1851, he was transferred to Rome where for two years he frequented the Academia dei nobili ecclesistici and in 1854 he was ordained priest at Lucca (Italy). Returning to England he became the Vice President of St Edmund's College, the most ancient Catholic School of England. In 1869 he founded St Joseph's Foreign Missionary College in London, in the area of Mill Hill Park, and became the proprietor of the Catholic Weekly *The Tablet*. In 1872 he was consecrated Bishop of Salford, a small city in the centre of England; here he founded St Bede's College, which today also is an important reference centre of Christian culture and formation. In 1892 Vaughan became Archbishop of Westminster and the following year he was created Cardinal. He was the one who built the present Cathedral of Westminster. He died on 19 June 1903 in London. (Cf. John George Snead-Cox. *The Life of Cardinal Vaughan (1831-1903)*, Herbert and Daniel, London, 1910.

be said on the first Monday of every month at Notre Dame des Victoires the Cathedral Church of Paris, for the conversion to Catholicism in England.

On 8 September, the Feast of the Nativity of Our Lady, he formally authorised the transfer of the Community to the diocese of Westminster, entrusting this new mission of the community to the protection of our heavenly Mother.

## 1.9. The Ultimate Sacrifice: The Abandoning of Montmartre

Before moving to England in a definitive way, the Mother and Alice went to England in order to place their plans before Cardinal Vaughan and find a location for the community. They journeyed to London on 13 September, 1901, paradoxically, the anniversary of the day on which Adèle had had to leave Montmartre twenty five years earlier, when, after months of solitude there, she was taken away in what was thought to be a dying condition.

On reaching London they were welcomed in Saint Edward's Convent of Mercy at Harewood Avenue. On 20 September they were received by Bishop Brindle, auxiliary of the Cardinal. He was good enough at once to assure them of his paternal interest in the poor exiles, and to promise them that when they found a suitable dwelling, they would have permission for all they needed, a chapel with the Blessed Sacrament, open to the public for adoration.

They fixed, eventually, on a house in Notting Hill, 4 Bassett Road. It was not far from St Charles' college, and they knew that in case of need they could count on the ministra-

77

tions of the Oblate Fathers of St Charles. Everywhere they were received with the greatest possible kindness and sympathy. The Mother wrote to Père Lémius, that in spite of the mountain of difficulties that faced them, there was something unspeakably encouraging in their transfer to England:

> "It is the presence of Our Lord which is to me just now as sensible as it was during the first year at Montmartre. I feel myself carried along, and accompanied by Him wherever I go. Nothing alarms me, though I have no idea as to what we are going to do. We live from day to day; tired out in the evening, so much as to think that we shall be unable to move the next day; and yet we begin again without the least trouble. God is, indeed, with us. And everywhere we are received with the most touching sympathy. Sometimes we are moved to tears by it, and absolutely surprised".[78]

After all had been settled, they returned to France, on 25 September. They found the Sisters full of fervour, and already prepared for the departure. Adèle's sister, Joséphine, volunteered to come with them, and help to install them in their new home. They were touched and deeply moved here, too, by the sympathy shown them by their neighbours and friends. All kinds of people, even the poorest, vied with one another in sending them offerings on the eve of their departure. On 27 September 1901 Adèle and her three daughters made their perpetual profession and two novices took simple vows. The ceremony took place at six-thirty at the altar of St Peter, in the crypt of the Basilica. Canon Lefebvre presided, and he preached to his little flock on the Flight

---

[78] H-15F-120, Père Lémius.

into Egypt. Père Lémius and Père Vasseur were present. This solemn ceremony definitely sealed the union of Adèle and her first daughters to the Sacred Heart of Jesus.

As the house of Bassett Road was still not ready to welcome them, they arranged to stay for a week or two with relatives or friends. Adèle and some of her daughters went to Villeneuve-sur-Yonne with Joséphine.

To Adèle this parting was especially painful. All their hopes, all her prayers were centred round Montmartre, the departure was a trial far more bitter than death. Yet she endured it with an heroic constancy, a complete submission to the divine Will. Père Lémius, in his account of the birth of the Congregation, expresses these thoughts in memory of the separation from Montmartre:

> "What was admirable was the attitude of the holy Foundress during these terrible years. What did she not suffer during this year of tempest! These children whom she loved so tenderly – she saw some shaken, tormented, thrown down, crushed, others throughout days and nights helping their Sisters who were victims. She spent herself in every way. Ah! One saw in her pale countenance how much she was suffering by the tears that came into her eyes. And all the while never did she once utter a complaint; never did she depart even slightly from her calmness and confidence in God. The Spirit of wisdom hovered over her, the Spirit of Fortitude filled her".[79]

The departure for England took place in three groups. There were eleven Sisters: seven professed, two novices and two postulants. On 9 October, 1901 Mother Agnès led the first

[79] Tyburn Convent, *op. cit.*, p. 288 and H-12-138, Père Lémius.

group to England. The following day, Mother Saint John brought the second group. In the meantime Adèle went to Paris to farewell her and to take her leave from their Superior, Canon Lefebvre. She also went to visit the Father General of the Oblates of Mary Immaculate who advised her that he had recommended her in very special way to the fathers of the Congregation of Kilburn England. The night before her departure she took her farewell also from the beloved Basilica by making her last adoration on French soil.

On 15 October she arrived in England with the last group of sisters. Mother Agnès wrote down this conviction, that she was deeply aware of feeling not so much in exile, but on the mission:

> "I remember that when we disembarked at Folkstone, I wanted to kiss the soil of this dear and hospitable land, where we were going to be permitted to practise our monastic life in full liberty, according to the vocation to which the divine Heart of Jesus had called us. It was also the flame of the apostolate which enkindled our souls, under the action of the charity of Christ. We loved to remember St Augustine and the Benedictine monks who accompanied him, coming to this England to bring it the grace of the Catholic Faith. And we ourselves, little as we were, but supporting our littleness on the Heart of Jesus, we, too, were coming to labour, within the limits of our vocation, in the great work of the conversion of England... 'On the mission, not in exile,' such was the spirit that inspired us then".[80]

[80] Dom Bede Camm, *op. cit.*, p. 79.

# CHAPTER II

# THE ROAD TO TYBURN

## 2.1. From Bassett Road to Tyburn

"We are on the Mission, not in exile".[1] This reflection of Mother Agnes, which closes the first chapter of this work, is very significant since it defines the new community as missionary and not as exiled. The spirit of mission – contrary to the sense of defeat that would seem the most obvious reaction on this occasion – animated the sisters from then on, as they moved forward with a new motivation and a renewed commitment in a foreign land. On 12 October, 1901 the Congregation moved to the small house in Bassett Road remaining there seventeen months. From the outset, the sisters received numerous expressions of sympathy and charity. On 21 November, feast of the Presentation in the Temple of the Blessed Virgin Mary, they were clothed for the first time in their religious habit that they were not able to wear at Montmartre. It was a white habit with a blue girdle, a red scapular and a white cloak.[2] They had to go out for Mass to the church of the Sacred Heart at Kilburn, in the care of the Congregation of the Oblates of Mary Immaculate, who until then had served the Basilica of Montmartre. The rector of the church, Father James O'Reilly, received them with the greatest possible kindness and remained their devoted friend until his death.

---

[1] *Ibidem.*

[2] It is recalled that four years before, during the same feast day, the first sisters had received the scapular from Father Balme.

On 6 December Père Lémius celebrated Mass in their small chapel and the community made a vow to represent England before the Sacred Heart of Jesus, and to offer their adoration and prayers night and day, in a special way for this country. Cardinal Vaughan gave his approval to the formula of this vow; in fact, it was the expression of one of his greatest desires. In writing this vow, Mother Adèle was inspired by the French National Vow which was, as we have seen, the origin of the Basilica of Montmartre, and also the inspiration of her own vocation. In the Constitutions of the Congregation the Mother laid down that each convent would have a special mission of prayer and reparation on behalf of the country in which it was established. So in England the nucleus of the future Congregation was to be devoted henceforth, to the conversion of this country:

> "The present persecution raging in France, compelling the Montmartre House to seek momentarily a refuge abroad, seems to have been the occasion, which will be employed by the Divine Will to establish a second House. *This House, under the very special protection of Our Lady of Victories, St Peter, and of the English Saints, will have as its special aim to represent England unceasingly before the Most Sacred Heart of Jesus. It will work – first and above all by prayer and penance, and also by fervent and discreet zeal, and modest individual action on souls – for the return to the Holy Roman Catholic Church of this great nation called the Isle of Saints and Mary's Dowry, and which even in her error ever remains so dear to the Heart of Jesus Christ and to the heart of His Vicar*".[3]

[3] Tyburn Convent, *op. cit.*, pp. 315-16.

Once they arrived in England, Mother Adèle showed her desire to fully integrate the community into the life and customs of the land in which they lived. The community, confined in the small house in Notting Hill, were destined to fulfil a prediction[4] made more than three hundred years before, namely that there would be erected at Tyburn a sanctuary of ceaseless prayer, adoration and reparation on the site where the english martyrs were tortured and executed.

[4] It was foretold by Father Gregory Gunne, an English confessor of the Catholic faith, that a religious house would be erected at Tyburn. This prophecy was fulfilled with the arrival of the sisters in London. Below I put the translated text of the story of the prophecy: Tyburn Convent, *op. cit.*, appendix N11-16: The account in the State Papers is as follows: "The information of Richard Davison of Henley, Co. Oxon, tailor, taken before us, Sir Henry Newell, Knight, and William Knowles Esqre. at Henley beforesaid, the 8th day of June, 1585: Who saith as followeth that the 8th day of the said month, he and one William Wheteley being in a close at Henley town end, heard a couple talk, and repaired near unto them to hearken what they said. One of them he knew, whose name was Evan Arden of Henley aforesaid .... Arden said unto one Gunne that was with him, "How can you praise Campion?" and Gunne answered again that he was the only man in all England. Then said Arden, "How can you praise Campion, being so arrant a traitor as he was?" then answered Gunne, "Say not so, for the day will come, and I hope to see it, and so may you too, that there shall be an offering where Campion did suffer". Then said Arden, "What, shall we offer unto the Gallows?" "No, not so," said Gunne, "but you shall see a religious house built there for an offering". Gregory Gunne, priest, as we learn from the same State papers, was arrested on 7 June, 1585, for these 'traitorous speeches' (he had gone on to deny that the queen was Supreme Head of the church, and to affirm the Petrine claims) and there was found on him 'an Agnus Dei of silver with two consecrated Hosts within it, 11 beads of amber with a crucifix,' etc. He was sent up for examination by the Privy Council. He was born in Norfolk, studied at Magdalen College, Oxford, and had been beneficed at Elford in Oxfordshire. He had been ordained priest at Norwich in Queen Mary's reign. This is all I have been able to find out about him *(Dom. Eliz., 179, 7, ff. 10, 14).*

In fact, a little later, the community settled at Tyburn, the most appropriate place to fulfil the mission to which it had been called by the Sacred Heart.

Tyburn, for a hundred and fifty years, from the reign of Henry VIII to that of Charles II, was the Calvary of our persecuted Church. It was also a place of pilgrimage, from the time that Saint Edmund Campion would go to salute the gibbet, on which one day he himself would be hanged. Queen Henrietta Maria prayed beneath Tyburn Tree for the conversion of her adopted country, and Catholics of all ranks have ever loved to visit the spot and venerate the memory of the martyrs.

The transfer of the community to this site, so significant for english catholics, came indirectly through a layman. It was Mr. Dudley Baxter, who every time he passed near the site of the Tyburn gallows, raised his hat and prayed to the martyrs so that a religious order might be able to preserve worthily the memory of this sacred ground.[5] One day he saw an advertisement for a house for sale in that spot. He wrote immediately to the chaplain of Cardinal Vaughan, the Duke of Norfolk and the benedictine monk, Dom Bede Camm, advising them of the news and of his own wish.[6]

Adèle on that very day had written to the Cardinal to obtain certain permissions. On the same day the letter of Mr. Baxter was given to Cardinal Vaughan, and he suggested that Adèle's community could purchase the house and settle at Tyburn. When this was proposed to her, she remained in silence for a moment and then answered: "Yes, I believe that

[5] The date of this event coincides with the day in which Adele and her daughters came to England and began their life in Bassett Road.

[6] Cf. Dom Bede Camm, *op. cit.*, p. 82.

God wills it".[7] When Dom Remy Buzy heard this news he sent a letter of encouragement to urge her to undertake courageously this new challenge:

> "I am very much of the opinion that you should purchase the property at Hyde Park ... that is all I can say on that subject. I marvel wholeheartedly the visible action of the Sacred Heart in your/his work. It would take all of four pages to express my admiration at it".[8]

The house proposed by the Cardinal proved, however, to be unsuitable for a community. It was too small, and there was no garden. However, they set out immediately with the Mother to consult a Catholic solicitor, Mr Leathby. He explained that there were great difficulties against the project. If the Protestants knew of the plan, they would do all in their power to stop it, and then it was the part of London where house property was the most expensive, and the community found it hard enough to exist, already, in Bassett Road. The solicitor was charged to look out for freehold houses for sale and it was agreed that they must find a house possessing a garden. In a letter to Monsieur Charles Michel, Père Lémius describes Mother Adèle's own position and that of her community in relation to the purchase of the new residence:

> "The Cardinal (Vaughan) has written to me this morning that there is a house for sale at the very place where Saints were martyred. It is the most sacred place of London. He urges us to purchase it. The Superior of Kilburn, an apostle of the Sacred Heart (explained to me) [...] This is the Montmartre of London.

[7] *Ibidem*, p. 84.
[8] Tyburn Convent, *op. cit.*, p. 325 H-02-098

We discussed the matter. Our Sisters feel that Providence is speaking ...

We await the particulars. But cost what it may, it must be the house for us. It is the English Montmartre where the Sacred Heart will be implanted, where the National Vow will be made".[9]

A month later Mr. Leathby wrote announcing that he had discovered at Tyburn a large house more suited to their needs and that the calculated price was less than 15,000 pounds. Shortly after, on the same day, a young lady[10] went to meet the Mother. This woman had a legacy money – which corresponded to more than half of the cost of the building – and she preferred not to keep it since it was compensation for the emancipation of slaves. As soon as this lady had heard about a project involving Tyburn she had felt the desire to devote this whole sum for this great work. She was particularly touched by the idea that Tyburn would become the 'Sanctuary of hearts', in the first place because the heart of the martyrs had been torn from their breasts for the love of Christ precisely in that very place where the Sacred Heart would be adored perpetually.

However, despite the fact that the acquisition of the property – the expenses necessitated by its repairs – the modifications needed to adapt it for the use of a community amounted to almost double the donation, the Sisters decided to take this project forward. The necessary agreements for the purchase of the property were concluded in

[9] *Ibidem*, p. 325.
[10] The lady, before becoming a benefactress to Tyburn, chose to remain anonymous.

the month of August 1902. But even so the purchase underwent alternating phases and the new convent could not be opened before March 1903.

The community took possession of Tyburn convent on 4 March, 1903[11] and on 6 March the first Mass was celebrated at the Altar of the Martyrs[12] by Father O'Reilly.[13] On 20 March the first Mass was celebrated by the secretary of Cardinal Vaughan. Père Lémius, gave a sermon that received great prominence in the Catholic press. Père Lémius spelled out the true spirit which inspired the foundation of Tyburn – and that still prevails today – i.e. the glorification of the Sacred Heart and of the english martyrs in a work dedicated to the conversion of England.

## 2.2. The Sufferings in the New Community

Since coming to England the Community had grown in number with the reception of postulants, three of whom were English. This made them twenty in number. It was not yet possible with so few to inaugurate at once perpetual Exposition of the Blessed Sacrament. But even now they began by giving five nights a week to Adoration. They were able to inaugurate the Perpetual Adoration by night and day before the Blessed Sacrament exposed on their altar on 9 October, 1904. This day in France is the Feast of St Denis the

[11] Cf. H-15E-025, Monsieur Charles Michel. This date was the 27th anniversary of the opening of the provisional chapel in Montmartre.

[12] The chapel, situated on the floor above, at the time was not yet completed.

[13] Father O'Reilly was appointed in November 1901, Ordinary Confessor to religious communities and he was the direct contact for the nascent community.

Apostle of Paris, and the chief martyr of their dear Montmartre. However, although this was a period of grace for the nascent foundation, the community trials were never lacking: Adèle was often suffering great pain and weakness. Sometimes she could hardly find the strength to go down to the chapel for Mass, and had to remain upstairs for a large part of the day. In addition, the sisters had heavy trials that were difficult to bear, even though they always found encouragement in the spirit of the english martyrs whose example filled them with new strength:

> "New evils threaten us at this very moment. In spite of these crushing trials, we remain calm and full of trust in the Sacred Heart. We work ceaselessly on behalf of the Community, who happy, peaceful and fervent, have no idea of the efforts hell is making to destroy it.

> Since we will absolutely all that He wills, and desire to suffer all that it may please him to send us, since we desire that our life, our work, and our all should be totally consecrated to Him, and we have no other end than to accomplish His will, are we not assured that His grace is with us to uphold us and that, if we are faithful, it will never desert us? After all, what happens is of little importance! The Martyrs of Montmartre and those of Tyburn knew how to suffer for the glory of their good Master. Their example must help us and give us courage".[14]

And very soon afterwards, on 10 August, 1903, God asked a new sacrifice from the little Congregation, or perhaps, to put it more truly, it was asked to offer to Him its first martyr. This was Sister Mary Cécile, who was scarcely

[14] H-15E-033, Monsieur Charles Michel.

twenty years old. She was a younger sister of Mother Agnes, the Co-Foundress. In the month of May of the preceding year she had joined the Community, and her sister became her Novice-Mistress.

Her vocation had been a triumph of the Sacred Heart. She soon generously resolved to renounce all the attractions of the world and to join the Community at Tyburn. On the day she received the religious habit, she made, 'under the dictation of the Sacred Heart', as the Mother expressed it, a special offering of her life for all the intentions of the Divine Heart, for all the nations of the world, especially for England and France, or any to which she might be sent.

A few weeks later she fell ill. When the community came to Tyburn, she became confined to bed. For some months she endured great sufferings which the doctors could not diagnose. In May she received the last Sacraments, after which she had the happiness of making her vows and receiving the black veil of the professed. Yet she lingered on till the middle of August, always in a state of peace and happiness, absolutely abandoned to the divine Will. As she lay dying, her dear Mother read to her the act of offering which she had made, and though she could not speak, the expression on her face showed that she understood it, and ratified it. After this prayer, the young sister died, and on more than one occasion, the community recognised the effects of her help and intercession.

Tyburn soon began to draw devout souls around it. In May 1903, Father O'Reilly, organised the first pilgrimage to Tyburn, and it was destined to be the first of very many.

A few months later, a Triduum was celebrated in honour of Saint Edmund Campion and Saint Cuthbert Mayne. On the first two days the attendance was small, on account of the bad weather; but on the third day there was a large crowd, which greatly rejoiced the community. Mother Adèle records this truly extraordinary event in her diary:

> "The feast of Saint Edmund Campion brought us an unexpected consolation. Several priests wrote to ask leave to say the Mass of the Martyrs in our Convent. We had five Masses that day. Next year we hope we shall have a High Mass".[15]

In 1907, the Community had already so much increased that it numbered more English than French subjects. And now the pilgrims, too, who flocked to Tyburn, had so grown in number that the chapel had already become quite inadequate.

The finances of the Community were, at this time, in a desperate state. There were, indeed, other and far greater difficulties, coming. But as a Benedictine monk of La Pierrequivire, who had known the Mother many long years, wrote after her death:

> "She was endowed with the gift of Fortitude to a heroic degree. ... To be heroic on one day of one's life, is possible, to be heroic perpetually – that passes the limits of human strength. I have asked myself a hundred times if Mother St Peter ever stopped on her way one single moment to tremble before what the future might bring. When God told her what He wanted of her (and I know that He did so tell her) she went forward, she did not hesitate a moment, and at last she arrived at that which Jesus had asked of her".[16]

[15] Dom Bede Camm, *op. cit.*, p. 92.
[16] *Ibidem*, p. 93.

90

In fact, this heroic confidence was the Mother's strength, she knew that she could and must find all her support in the Sacred Heart of Jesus, who had asked this work of her. She was fully conscious of her poverty and her littleness, but this consciousness only increased her trust in Him. It will be remembered that at the very beginning of the foundation of Montmartre, she had made Mother Agnes kneel beside her in the Oratory at 'Nazareth', and pray that they might have the grace of being always poor. Nevertheless, this poverty brought to them hours of indescribable suffering. In a letter written to Abbot Columba Marmion on 23 December 1909, she gives an account of the state of her soul, sometimes troubled by financial preoccupations:

> "I hardly know how to describe it, devoured as I am by material cares of the most agonising nature, not knowing what I can do, tortured by a continual anxiety which harasses me all day and allows me very little sleep at night: and yet I feel my soul calm and more at peace than ever before, even in the midst of cruel temptations against the Faith.
>
> I have had, and I still have, much to suffer from our terrible financial trials, from my own incapacity and powerlessness, from a host of other cares, and specially that of seeing myself often cowardly and unmortified. I ought to tell you, Father, that these moments are frightful, and I hardly dare to think of them. ... And when they have passed by, the soul remains calm, reassured, more than ever God's, nailed to the Cross of Jesus, and ready to suffer all that He may will. It is the grace that flows from the tortures of Jesus.
>
> I have also had to envisage the possibility, the probability almost, of the destruction of our little Congregation; the

sacrifice that had to be made; not only for myself, but for Agnes, for all my daughters, and for each one of them, who love so tenderly their religious family. It was again terrible, but Jesus enlightened me as to each point and gave me the necessary grace.[17]

One day, in her simplicity, the Mother asked Our Lord to show them what they ought to do if the Congregation should perish; and she heard this inner response:

> "But I do not will that it should perish. How can you be so anxious? Should I allow this little Congregation to perish, which I have myself founded? I will watch over you. I will make you come safely out of all these difficulties. Have trust in me. You are working for me. Courage!"[18]

Adèle had, indeed, need of courage, and Our Lord sustained her in the trials that lay before her.

## 2.3. The House of Koekelberg in Belgium

Meanwhile Tyburn was becoming too small to house the growing community, and it became necessary to think of making a new foundation. Mother Adèle therefore began to consider doing this preferably in another French speaking country. Thanks to the intervention of Cardinal Désiré Joseph Mercier[19] and Dom Columba Marmion, his spiritual father, this soon became planned for Belgium:

[17] H-15G-023, Dom Columba Marmion.
[18] Cf. Dom Bede Camm *op. cit.* p. 97.
[19] *Désiré-Joseph Mercier* was born in Braine-l'Alleud, Belgium, 21 November, 1851. Ordained a priest on April 4, 1874, he endeavoured to spread the study of the philosophy of Saint Thomas Aquinas. He was

"We have just come out from a meeting with the Cardinal. He is a saint and a father. He welcomes us 'with great joy' into his diocese either at Koekelberg immediately if we wish or, while waiting for Koekelberg to be made ready, even at Brussels with the use of a charming expiatory Chapel where the Blessed Sacrament has always been exposed from time immemorial. The Religious who are there are obliged to leave on account of the expropriation of their adjoining land. The Cardinal was already negotiating with another Order for this Chapel but he would like us to have it and this would be a good idea in preparation for Koekelberg. We have let His Excellency know that his wishes would be the Will of God for us".[20]

The first foundation was a sign, hopeful and consoling, of the growth of the Work to which the Mother had been called. But the future was by no means so comforting, and the very next year was to prove to the Mother and her little flock to be one of extraordinary difficulty and real anguish.

On 3 January, 1909, the Mother with Mother Agnes, went to arrange about the foundation in Belgium. A house had been found at Koekelberg, a suburb of Brussels, not far from the site of the future Basilica of the Sacred Heart. The house was not too suitable for a convent, and it was clear that before very long it would become too small. But for the present it had to suffice.

On their way to Brussels, the Mothers stayed with

appointed bishop of Malines 21 February, 1906, and created cardinal the following year. He died in Brussels on 22 January, 1926.

Cf. Card. Désiré Mercier, *Cardinal Mercier's Own Story*, George H. Doran Company, New York, 1920.

[20] H-15H-028E, Mère de St John.

93

Joséphine Garnier, who had promised to give her furniture to the new Convent, and intended, if her health permitted, to live there as a boarder. But it was not to be. God called her to Himself a month later.[21] In June of the same year the nine Sisters who had been chosen for the new foundation at Koekelberg, left for Belgium. Mother Agnes was appointed Superior, but remained there only three years, returning to Tyburn in 1912. Dom Columba Marmion celebrated the first Mass in the Chapel of the new Convent, on 18 June, 1909, the feast of the Sacred Heart.

The creation of the new foundation entailed substantial costs to the new community, and this placed Tyburn in a perilous position[22] since it had been financially unstable for some time – it appeared, at a certain point that these difficulties besetting the convent were such that the property must now, be put up for sale. So during the summer the Sisters began preparing for what seemed to be an imminent move to another location:

> "To speak of Tyburn […] I am always in anguish over a situation that can only become worse each day if we do not

[21] The sisters managed to find a generous American benefactor, Mr. Buckley, who committed himself to provide the initial costs for the chapel.

[22] Cf. H-15G-065, Dom Bede Camm "I send you the letter that you so kindly wrote to me about Tyburn, setting out a plan for organising the appeal project. It seems to us that we could do (the following) […] For the ladies in addition to the Duchess of Norfolk […] we could ask the young Marquess of Bute, who is Irish […] the Duchess of Newcastle […] We also know Mrs Weld Blundell – a relative of Cardinal Vaughan. I do not know if we could invite her husband to be a member of the committee – he is religious and has an immense fortune. We are happy in thinking that we have the mission of Prayer and custodians here. That is why at all costs we will remain at Tyburn, unless the good God drives us away.

take all the steps needed to resolve it. I am speaking about the extremely disquieting financial state in which this House finds itself – a state which has urged us to hasten the Koekelberg foundation so as to give our religious family an alternative to Tyburn. [...] We do not cease to beseech the Holy Spirit to enlighten us, while we study the issue from every point of view, without being able to find any other solution than that of leaving Tyburn, given that the costs are absolutely beyond our means [...] Every year we are obliged to borrow what is needed to pay our interest, and so we are continually increasing our debts. Therefore to continue like this is to run to ruin. In addition, at the present time we do not have sufficient means to take out new loans which would be necessary".[23]

They had not yet decided where they would go, but by June had almost opted for a house in Stechford Hall, near Birmingham.[24] Then, their thoughts turned to Belgium and they explored the possibility of buying a house in Louvain. The community began soon to examine different possibilities for the sale of Tyburn. Their hope was to be able to dispose of the property to a religious community, in such a way that the site of the martyrs would be worthily guarded. In particular, they began negotiations with the community of the Cenacle

[23] H-15G-020, Dom Columba Marmion.
[24] Cf. H-15G-078, Dom Bede Camm: "We would like to transfer the novitiate from Tyburn to Birmingham. We will have great consolation and valuable help by finding ourselves closer to you, and thus our small Congregation will be able to maintain and enhance the Benedictine spirit that we appreciate so much and that we ardently desire to be like the lifegiving sap for our religious family wherever God may be pleased to send it. If you should see a house that you feel would be suitable for us I could come to see it with Mother Agnes".

Sisters. In spite of her anguish, the Mother remained calm with an inner peace that manifested itself outwardly:

> "Mother Agnes and I experience at times moments of unparalleled anguish because of our finances. We pray, we implore the Lord, we try to understand what we should do, but our anxieties are terrible both day and night and we have to be careful not to let them prevail, for then we would be swallowed up. And yet, behold, when I am at Mass, at the Office, at Benediction, everything within me is singing; I am no longer concerned, it is as if I am in heaven, loving my God, adoring Him and blessing Him in everything".[25]

However, benefactors, devout people and the catholic press took to heart the distress of the Tyburn community. In particular, Lady Mostyn of Talacre who was Irish, suggested a project of 'adoption' of each member of the community, who in turn would dedicate her prayers for the intentions of the benefactor.[26] The Archbishop of Westminster was good enough to launch a public appeal to save Tyburn. The most significant contributions were received through the idea proposed by Dom Bede Camm to Cardinal Vaughan. He suggested finding one hundred benefactors – one for each Martyr of Tyburn – who would join together to provide the amount to settle the loan owed by the community. These benefactors became officially the founders of Tyburn and their names are still displayed in the chapel precincts of the convent. During this period of crisis, the sisters lived through a time of severe deprivation and sacrifice, to the extent that their meals were scarcely sufficient to nourish

[25] H-15G-001, Dom Columba Marmion.
[26] The same Lady Mostyn had the privilege of 'adopting' the Mother.

them. Their precarious condition was publicised by a priest in the English Catholic Press[27] and this news aroused a new wave of generosity, which was expressed through monetary donations and also the dispatch of weekly food supplies to the Tyburn community.

## 2.4. The Benedictine Vocation

Since 1899 Adèle was beginning to assess the possibility of being linked to a specific religious order: in particular she felt attracted to the Benedictine Order, even if the full implementation of this desire could come only later. The Mother was in fact, incredibly impressed by the harmony which existed between the Benedictine spirituality and their own vocation and was certain that, guided by the rule of St Benedict, they would perhaps obtain deliverance from their present suffering, or at least have more grace and strength to support it. Together with her sisters she had drawn up a report on this subject with a view to presenting it to their ecclesiastical superiors. In the report they did not ask to become benedictines in the strict sense of the word but, while remaining what they were, with their own aim of life, their constitutions and special devotions, they might adopt the Rule of St Benedict as a model of religious life, while combining with its practice the modifications and additions required by the specific needs and objectives of their Congregation. On 9 March, 1901 the Mother gave her report to

[27] The first reference to the conditions in which had dogged the community were in the weekly newspaper *Universe*, but then were published numerous pamphlets and articles: *The leaves of Tyburn, Tyburn and the English Martyrs, Tyburn Speaks, etc.*

Mons. Lefebvre, begging him to submit it to the Cardinal of Paris. She also explained their ardent desire to have the Blessed Sacrament reserved among them as soon as they were settled in their new abode. On 19 March, they received the joyful news that the Cardinal had approved their report and graciously granted both petitions. They were to follow both the Rule of St Benedict and they were to have the Blessed Sacrament reserved in their new abode:

> "Regarding the Blessed Sacrament Mons. Lefebvre told me that His Eminence would grant it without doubt, when we are at n. 40. And when he will have examined our chapel. [...] Another thing much appreciated is the authorisation to take the Rule of St Benedict. His Eminence has granted willingly so much more by sharing his own views".[28]

However, after some time, once they arrived in England, there emerged some doubts as to the possibility of pronouncing vows according to the Benedictine Rule since they believed it was essential for them to belong to a Congregation consisting of various houses united under the authority of the Mother General. While looking for a solution, it was considered to be right that the sisters make their profession according to the Constitutions which, of course, included the principles and spirit of St. Benedict to the extent that they were compatible with their special vocation.

In 1903, the Mother and Mother Agnes began to work intensively on the Constitutions, inspired greatly by the benedictine spirit. So, in fact, wrote the Mother to a dear Benedictine friend, Dom Bede Camm:

[28] H-15F-103, Père Lémius.

"I am sending you today, dear father, the notebook of our Constitutions, asking you to pardon their appearance which is hardly presentable (filled with collages, corrections, additions, ...) ... You will find in them many passages which breathe the spirit of St Benedict, which will not surprise you if I tell you that the Rule of St Benedict is the foundation of our own religious life, and that as far as was possible with our vocation, we have been inspired by its spirit for our formation and in the drawing up of our Constitutions. It is no doubt a far-off resemblance, but we hope all the same that you will recognise in it a certain family likeness. For we have been anxious to follow the Rule of the Holy Father in every point compatible with our vocation. And if we have St Gertrude as our very special Patron we also look on the Blessed Patriarch as our own Father. His Rule from the very beginning, and in an ever-increasing measure, as we have studied it and understood it better, has been the ideal on which we would model our lives as closely as possible".[29]

However, this concern about belonging to a wider religious Order , was temporarily held in abeyance until about a decade later, when the Mother took up once more the question of the right religious 'location' of her Congregation. Once the sisters came to know Dom Columba Marmion the issue was thoroughly analysed from two perspectives: from the point of view of canon law and the Rule of St Benedict. It became immediately clear that no obstacles existed to prevent the realisation of their desire, and the community discovered it was possible to follow the Rule without any threat to its special charism. It was a great joy, for the

[29] H-15G-061, Dom Bede Camm.

Mother Foundress had always felt a strong attraction to the Rule. Traces of her investigation remain in the long correspondence with Dom Columba Marmion, where several times in those years Adèle questioned herself over the possible incorporation of the Congregation into the Benedictine Order:

> "Without relating the needs of our souls which will be assisted by your charity, we certainly shall begin by speaking on the issue of the incorporation of our Congregation into the Order of St. Benedict unless some notes shown to Dom Bede Camm have indicated difficulties or even obstacles to the union which we envisage or outside the aggregation as Oblates, which is not our intention. But if the glorious St Benedict really wants us as his daughters, without us having to sacrifice the fundamental things of our Congregation, we would be immensely happy".[30]

On the feast of St Benedict, 21 March, 1913, Adèle fell suddenly ill during the morning Office, and for a short time appeared to be at death's door. During a night of unspeakable suffering, the Mother saw Saint Benedict in a dream. This dream lasted a few minutes leaving her with a sweet impression of peace, trust and gratitude and at the same time a lessening of physical suffering. The day after, in remembrance of this event Adèle understood that it should be interpreted as an invitation of the saint to do everything possible to ensure that the Congregation would be incorporated into his Order. From that moment Adèle's illness improved and after a few days the doctor declared her out of danger.

[30] H-15G-041, Dom Columba Marmion.

During the summer and until the beginning of the autumn the Mother went to Belgium with Mother Agnes to take advantage of this time of rest and reflection to consider seriously the question of the possible incorporation into the Order of St Benedict. Adèle summoned the General Chapter, and in the meantime the Congregation was preparing the monastic habit proper to the Benedictines:

> You can easily understand the gratitude and joy of our sisters on receiving your letter, which shows us so clearly how God, Himself, manifested to you what He wanted of our religious family and how Saint Benedict worked for the realisation of the divine designs. Nothing could be more encouraging for us that the explicit thought of His Eminence with regard to this important initiative, where we see a powerful means for our Congregation to progress unceasingly in the good, so that in all things God may be glorified. Through you, dear Father, and through their Eminences the Cardinals, our Superiors, it is very sweet to hear "this voice of the Lord inviting us! Behold, the Lord Himself in His goodness shows us the path of life". [...] In the school of St Benedict we therefore "learn the service of the Lord" with more abundant light and assistance more powerful! The peace and joy of our hearts at this thought fill us with courage and zeal to advance.[31]

The Chapter met on 17 January, 1914 presided over by Dom Columba Marmion. It concluded by confirming that both communities wanted unanimously to become Benedictine. The General Chapter acts were immediately approved by Cardinal Mercier and Cardinal Bourne and the Congregation could at last embrace the Benedictine Rule.

[31] H-15G-049, Dom Columba Marmion.

One of the most striking consequences of this adoption of the Rule was to change the religious habit. The sisters laid aside the white tunic, the blue belt and the red scapular that had been worn up to that moment, and were clothed in the black benedictine habit, though they still retained the white cowl[32] as a sign of their eucharistic vocation. On 16 February the sisters solemnly renewed their vows according to the Rule of St. Benedict and the Constitutions of the Congregation, that were readjusted to the benedictine spirit:

> "Even if we have not yet entered officially into the beloved family of St Benedict, I am convinced that he will watch over it with the eyes of a Father and that he will not refuse his blessing that we implore under the mantle of his Rule, as Jacob did to obtain the blessing of his father Isaac. [...] Mother Agnes works so seriously and assiduously at the new redaction of our Constitutions that I would like to be able to procure for her some months of solitude and tranquillity".[33]

At this point the two communities became an integral part of one of the more ancient religious orders. The new Constitutions drawn up as a result of this change, were redacted in a definitive way and submitted to Rome shortly after the death of Mother Adèle and were approved by the Holy See on 19 July, 1930.

## 2.5. Royston: the Priory of Saint Benedict

Mother Adèle and Mother Agnes returned to Belgium in May of 1914 to see about finding a new house to replace the

---

[32] Worn in the Choir and during Adoration.
[33] H-15G-050, Dom Columba Marmion.

convent ot Koekelberg, which was already becoming too small for the growing community. But they returned to Tyburn on 21 July for the First World War was on the point of breaking out. The horrors of this Great War afflicted terribly the soul of the Mother Foundress and Tyburn became a refuge for large numbers of people fleeing the conflict. But 16 August brought a distinguished refugee: Dom Columba Marmion disguised as a dutch cattle dealer. The nun who was at the Portress's office mistook him for one of the builder's men and did not let him enter. However, he was soon recognised by the sisters. He told them that he had encountered dangers and only narrowly escaped being shot. By 26 September seven sisters of Saint Mary's arrived at Tyburn. The others remained in the Belgium convent and were miraculously preserved from the dangers of war. As Dom Bede Camm tells us, on the feast of St Thomas of Canterbury, 29 December, 1914, Mother Agnes wrote a message on the community blackboard:

> "If you hear the sound of firing (from the anti-aircraft guns), keep quite calm, which is surely easy with Jesus in our midst, and go down to the basement – except, of course, those who are at the Office or at Adoration, who will be delighted to risk something for the service of their King".[34]

In eight months of the war Tyburn welcomed dozens of priest refugees, and also a large number of religious of both sexes.

On 15 June, 1916, Mother Mary of Saint John, one of the

[34] Bede Camm, *op. cit.*, p. 115.

first sisters of the Congregation died. She had held important duties in the community and among these, that of mistress of novices. This sister suffered enormously during the last years of her life and among these sufferings the greatest was the need to live and die outside her convent. In fact she was struck by consumption after surgery and was sent to different places and nursing homes: all the treatments were of no avail. Mother Adèle was always very close to her, and she in person made decisions about this Sister's various moves. Mother Mary of Saint John died in Aubigny near Poitiers in France at just 40 years of age and in her eighth year of religious life. She received the last sacraments and in her desire for the kingdom of heaven she would often repeat: "To die what happiness! It is so good to be with the good God".[35]

Around the middle of 1915, Monsignor Barton Brown, pastor of Royston, near Cambridge, accompanied by Dom Bede Camm, went for the first time to visit Tyburn. Mother Agnes received him and the question of the urgency of a new foundation arose and Monsignor Brown suggested that it could be made in his parish. He, in fact, wanted the presence of a contemplative Order where the Lord in the Blessed Sacrament would be constantly exposed and adored. Mother Agnes was struck by the proposal and how it appealed also to Mother Adèle. A few days later Mother Agnes and Mother Hildegarde went to Royston to visit the two houses about which Monsignor Brown had written. Next, the Mother Foundress came also with Mother Agnes and Dom Bede Camm. They decided that one of the two

---

[35] *Ibidem*, p. 116.

houses would be suitable, since there was a large park beside it. The Mother decided to purchase it only if there were benefactors. Shortly after, a lady named Miss Coats, offered to purchase it at the modest price being asked for it – provided that the chapel of the convent would be open to the laity. She donated the sum necessary for the purchase of the house and also for any restoration work. Finally, when this lady learnt of Mother Agnes' desire to purchase the land adjacent to the house in order to extend their garden, she also decided to help with that purchase.

The inauguration of the new convent – called Priory of St Benedict – took place in December 1916. Eight nuns formed the community, which was presided over by Mother Prioress. In the new convent the sisters at Royston enjoyed an incredible peace after the terrible experience of the war when they were at Tyburn. In London, in fact, bombs were dropped every night and the convent was often shaken to its foundations. The daily Office continued very quietly as if all was peace around them, only at its conclusion special prayers were recited for the dead, the dying and the wounded and for those who were causing so much devastation. Mother Adèle remained calm and serene, her peaceful presence was once again a model of hope and confidence for her daughters.

It was on 29 December, 1920, thanks to the contribution of a benefactor,[36] that the novitiate at Tyburn was transferred to Royston:

[36] The sum donated was £3,000 and with this it was possible to construct a building high and spacious with a cloister annexed to the chapel and the Priory.

"I don't know if I told you that our novitiate at Tyburn will be transferred to Royston on the property of our second english convent. A benefactor gave us the sum required for this construction. Tyburn, being the Mother House, cannot at the same time contain a novitiate which will increase in numbers, and also because we lack space. If God permits, from here in three months you will have the transfer.[37]

The days from 24 June to 2 July, 1915 marked the last visit of the Mother to her daughters at Royston and also her last exit from Tyburn. Mother Adèle, now 82 years old, returned to the Priory of Saint Benedict only after her death to rest in the small cemetery of the sisters, located in a corner of their park, before returning definitively to Tyburn.

## 2.6. The Martyrdom of the Mother

As the years went by, Mother Adèle's sufferings increased and became almost continual. Her letters of that period show the difficulty she had in making even simple daily movements. She remained almost constantly in her cell, having even to sacrifice, sometimes for long months together the happiness of hearing Mass. Her daughters, found her ever ready to receive them; her serene expression and her sweet motherly smile were enough to give them peace and consolation. And, in a special way, they were aware of the face of a Mother whose spiritual authority came from a heart formed by the very Heart of Jesus, that Heart adored, contemplated and kept in view continuously in her response to the divine call. As Mother she cared con-

[37] H-15F-212, Père Lémius.

106

tinually about their small problems and about their spiritual growth. She had one great earthly comfort, and that was in the faithful devotion of her first daughter in religion. If Mother Agnes, during these last years, had to bear the greater part of the burden, on account of the Mother's state of health, it was nevertheless Mother Adèle herself who remained the heart and soul of the whole Congregation, and the inspirer of every step forward. She was informed of everything, and nothing was done without consulting her.

In spite of all, Adèle remained completely lucid and willing to give of herself, though the weight of years began to wear her down:

> "My health is holding up; I began my 83$^{rd}$ year with neuralgia that makes me really feel that I am still full of life. But as it pleases God, I am in His hands; please ask Him to sanctify me before He takes me away from this earth".[38]

Mother's eyesight began to fail increasingly, and the ophthalmologist decided that an operation was necessary to remove cataracts in both eyes.[39] She, of course, accepted this new trial with her usual abandonment to the divine will and the operation succeeded perfectly. She also suffered with greater intensity and frequency from those rheumatic attacks, especially in the right hand that already on other

---

[38] H-15F-063, Père Vasseur.

[39] Cf. H-15F-065, Père Vasseur: "Please excuse the writing. My eyes are very bad and I write with difficulty"; see also in H-15F-213, Père Lémius: "I wanted to write before, but my eyes do not give me permission to do so. I am still suffering, but I can at least trace black on white and I am glad to be able to write. [ ...] I don't know if you can read it. I don't think I could myself".

occasions had caused considerable inconvenience. Despite everything the Mother still kept up her correspondence with her daughters.[40]

The General Chapter was held on 22 May, 1922 for the election of Superior General and, shortly before this date, the Mother was intent on drawing up plans to prevent her re-election as Mother General. In fact, she was re-elected unanimously, except for her own vote. A few months later Mother Adèle began an eighteen month long agony, during which time she heard again the words that her inner voice spoke in December 1870: "It is in your heart that I will place my cross".[41]

On 14 November, 1922, she again had to receive the last Sacraments. Afterwards she rallied a little, but on Christmas Eve she seemed to be dying. The Sisters gathered around her bed and joined in the Litany for the dying. Then on 30 January, 1923 abbot Dom Columba Marmion died at his abbey of Maredsous. For the last 16 years he had been a true and devoted father. In April of that same year the Mother began to suffer as never before. Her condition continued to deteriorate and, as from the month of August, she had to endure the privation of the Mass until her death. In September she suffered fresh agonies. Her death was expected from one moment to the next, though in reality she still had much to suffer. So it was that on 16 November Mother Agnes described her state in these words:

---

[40] Cf. H-15F-209, Père Lémius: "I am suffering very much since some days [...]. Dear father, I am ashamed of my writing, my hand is still trembling so".

[41] Bede Camm, *op. cit.*, p. 131.

"She suffered more yesterday than I ever could have thought a human creature could possibly endure without dying This morning she fell into what we all thought was the sleep of death. No one could believe that she could possibly live more than a day or two. She seemed like a living reproduction of Jesus Crucified, as she lay with outstretched arms, suffocating, unable to breathe, but always smiling in union with the divine Will".[42]

On 22 November the doctor pronounced her to be dying. He said her pulse could not possibly be weaker, and that her lungs were entirely congested. The heart was worn out. Mother Agnes who was always very close, especially in these painful moments wrote:

"That morning at six o' clock, continues Mother Agnes, 'a grace-much similar to the transverberation of the heart of St Teresa appeared to be granted to her. Our Lord had Himself told her to expect it; asking her that she would let Him be crucified in her heart. Broken as it were in two, the death-rattle in her throat, her arms stretched out as if crucified begging for water, she lay, enduring the crucifixion in her heart. With very great difficulty we managed to raise her head so that the Chaplain could give her Holy Communion. It was heart-rending to watch her".[43]

When the doctor returned the next day, Adèle was a bit better, but her pulse was very weak. The doctor thought she would probably die in a state of coma. By 8 December she was still alive to the great astonishment of her doctor, but

---

[42] *Ibidem*, p. 135.
[43] *Ibidem*.

she remained almost always in a state of unconsciousness. She continued for further months in this suffering state. On 9 June, 1924 the Silver Jubilee of her Religious Profession, Mother Agnes wrote:

> "Our Mother is still with us. But it looks as though she would finish her Jubilee in Heaven. She seemed almost lifeless as she lay there in a half sleep, yet still awake. From time to time a beautiful smile would illuminate her face and those who watched beside her would see her trembling lips moving in prayer".[44]

On 17 June, the anniversary of her vow of abandonment made in 1887, Mother Adèle rendered her soul to God at 11.15 in the night. Mother Agnes, who had watched beside her bed until the end, described the last moments of Adèle as characterised by an incredible peace:

> "An immense peace hovers over the house. She is there with a little half smile on her face and her eyes will be looking at her children – 'My children' – two of the last distinct words she said on the eve. Yesterday, she was quite alone with God and unable to communicate with us at all. But I asked her if she was able to talk to Jesus and whether she was happy and she bent her head as though to say 'Yes'. The end came very suddenly and peacefully about 11.15 p.m".[45]

Her habit of thinking of others remained with her until the end, and during and after death she radiated a wonder-

---

[44] H-12-135, Mère Agnès, Letter, Mother Agnes, 9 June, 1924. Also *Tyburn Hill of Glory"*, p. 141, The Catholic Book Club, London, 1952.

[45] H-12-136, Mère Agnès, Letter 18 June, 1924. Also *Tyburn Hill of Glory"*, p. 142.

ful atmosphere of peace and joy. Those who loved her best had expected to be overwhelmed with grief at losing her, but on seeing her face, were filled with joy for she, their Mother had an incredibly happy expression:

> It was all so quick, so peaceful! She'd had her agony – or rather agonies – her end was just like her dear self, 'unnoticed'.[46]

So Mother Adèle, who had suffered martyrdom, 18 months long, was now freed from pain and in perfect peace with God and with her daughters. The sisters wrote that the body of their beloved mother remained perfectly flexible until the coffin was closed, and her face became more beautiful and more radiant, and this was the first extraordinary sign following her death:

> [...] "Our Mother's body has remained entirely flexible and there has not been the slightest change in her except that between her death and the time she was put in the coffin she became more and more radiantly beautiful. The Ecclesiastical Superiors have told us to note carefully every detail of importance in connection with her holy life and death, so that all the documents may be ready if it comes to the question of her beatification".[47]

The funeral was held on 21 June in the chapel of Tyburn, presided over by Cardinal Francis Alphonsus Bourne.[48]

---

[46] H-12-135, Mother Mary of the Angels.

[47] H- 12- 002, Letter – Mother Agnes, 22 June 1924. *Op. cit.* p. 143

[48] *Francis Alphonsus Bourne* was born in Clapham the 23 March, 1861 from english father and irish mother. At 19 years he entered the seminary of Saint Thomas at Hammersmith. Brilliant in studies, he was given the

There were many priests and the ceremony was characterized by a sense of peace and recollection. The following day
the coffin remained near the altar of the martyrs, under the
painting of Saint Benedict and the Benedictine Apostles and
English Martyrs. The following Monday Mother Adèle's
mortal remains were brought to St Benedict's Priory in
Royston, where the funeral Mass was celebrated, presided
over by Dom Bede Camm. Over the spot that had welcomed
her body was erected a modest chapel, and a few years later,
beside her was buried her dearly loved daughter Mother
Agnes. In July 1969, the body of Mother Adèle was transferred at last to her beloved Tyburn[49] and placed in a corner
of the indoor garden within the convent, accessible from the
cloister, and from the crypt of the Martyrs.

opportunity to continue in the seminary of Saint Sulpice in Paris.
Ordained a priest on 11 June, 1884, he returned to England for his pastoral
activity. In 1889 he became rector of House of Studies in Henfield Place,
teaching inter alia at St. John's Seminary in Wonersh. On 27 March, 1896
was appointed Auxiliary Bishop of Southwark and was consecrated by
the Cardinal Bishop, London, Mons. Herbert Vaughan. The following
year he was appointed bishop of Southwark. On 11 September, 1903 he
was called to London as Archbishop of Westminster. The 27 November,
1911 Pope Pius X raised him to the rank of cardinal. He died on 31
December, 1934 at the age of 73 years. Cf. Ernest Oldmeadow, *Francis,
Cardinal Bourne*, Burns, Oates & The Wheatsheaf Inn, London, 1940.

[49] Cf. Jacques Benoist, *Mg Charles et les congrégations féminines au
Sacré-Cœur et sur la butte Montmartre (1959 – 1993)*, Les Editions Ouvrières,
Paris, 1999, p. 3.

# The spirituality
of the Mother

# CHAPTER III

# FROM DAUGHTER TO MOTHER

## 3.1. Spiritual Direction

Now that we have presented the life of Mother Adèle Garnier we wish in the following pages to focus on the "Garnier spirituality". In her profound search for God the Mother always wanted to compare and support her faith experience with a spiritual guide who could assure her of the authenticity and reliability of her soul's progress.

After being accompanied in this way from her youth to respond to the call of God, Adèle discovered her profound vocation was to adore the Sacred Heart of Jesus in the Eucharist. The definitive and most significant request that she would address to her cherished and final spiritual father, Dom Columba Marmion, was that he would support her in leading her to holiness. This spiritual journey is in full harmony with the definition that the dominican theologian, Antonio Royo-Marin, gives in his treatise on *Teologia della perfezione cristiana*: "spiritual direction" referring to the art of leading souls gradually from the beginning of the spiritual life up to the summit of Christian perfection".[1]

Below we present the various spiritual fathers who helped Adèle in the path of discernment and growth in surrendering herself totally to God. We concentrate particularly on the two most significant figures: l'Abbé Jules Courtois and the benedictine monk Dom Columba Marmion.

[1] Antonio Royo Marin, *Teologia della perfezione cristiana*, Edizioni San Paolo, Cinisello Balsamo Milano, 2003, p. 976.

We will then focus on the guidance of the Spirit that the Mother experienced, with its important reference to Our Lady, from whom she received the example and help to respond promptly to the divine will with a total *Fiat*.

### 3.1.1. *Her Spiritual Fathers*

#### A. *Père Edouard Marquet*

The first spiritual father to accompany the path of Adèle, and of whom only one sole mention is made in her letters, was Père Edouard Marquet, a Jesuit. He was born on 13 February, 1822 at Port Louis (Morbihan), made his first profession on 2 December, 1842, and became priest on 2 February, 1857.[2]

The youthful Adèle, at only 23 years old, went to Nantes, and later wrote of Père Marquet: "He kindly undertook the care of my soul and arranged at once for me to receive Communion daily".[3]

Following his always firm and resolute advice, Adèle accepted to become the governess at the home of the de Crochard family. Gradually the desire for religious life awakened and grew within her, even though this had not been Père Marquet's intention.

Père Marquet's rather severe character aroused a certain fear in Adèle and she only continued with him for a short time, describing him as a "holy priest".[4]

He died on 9 April, 1912 in Paris.[5]

---

[2] Cf. Alexandre Brou, *Un jésuite bréton, le Père Edouard Marquet (1821-1912)*, Beauchesne, Paris, 1913.

[3] H-15D-001, Abbé Courtois.

[4] *Ibidem*.

[5] Cf. Rufo Mendizabal, S.J., *Catalogus defunctorum in renata Societate Jesu, ab a. 1814 ad a. 1970*, apud Curiam P. Gen., Roma, 1972, pag. 229, colonna 12, N° 723.

## B. *Père Pierre Donniou*

Père Pierre Donniou, Jesuit of Nantes, became Adèle's spiritual father and accompanied her for ten years, from 1863 to 1873. Born in Kergrist-Moelou (Côtes-d'Or) 11 November, 1825; he was ordained a priest on 15 August in 1863.[6]

His spiritual direction had a decisive influence on her, since this Jesuit father, showed himself to be a "holy, enlightened and kindly guide".[7] "Mother Adèle wrote: "In him I had unlimited confidence and blind submission".[8] In particular, Père Donniou guided Adèle in her devotion to the Sacred Heart. In 1864 he encouraged her in the decision to enter the novitiate of Conflans, in order to respond to the call of God. However for health reasons, she was able to remain there for only a few months. The following year she returned to her family in Dijon, and so Père Donniou's spiritual direction continued by letters. Three years later, in 1868, Adèle returned to Laval again as governess and was able to pursue assiduously her spiritual path under Père Donniou in the way she had followed a few years earlier.[9]

Adèle went to Nantes on 16 June, 1873 and had the opportunity to make her confession to Père Donniou. While in the confessional Adèle, among other things, advised him with great sadness and considerable embarrassment, of a divine message she had received inwardly that he had a very grave illness, which would affect him mortally and that

[6] Cf. Rufo Mendizabal, S.J., *op. cit.*, pag. 72, colonna 4, N°182.
[7] H-15D-001, Abbé Courtois.
[8] *Ibidem.*
[9] Cf. *Ibidem.*

she urgently suggested to him to make appropriate preparations to meet this situation.[10] In fact, Père Donniou died on 29 June, 1873 in Nantes, on the very day of his patronal feast. Adèle attended his funeral with intense anguish of soul that lasted several days. On the eve of her departure for Laval, the first of July of the same year, during the night, she saw Père Donniou in a dream and he reassured her: "It is me, my child, I am going to heaven".[11] Immediately, from that moment Adèle's anguish and grief of soul were changed into a great calm and serenity.

### C. *Père Henri Chambellan*

Père Henri Chambellan[12] was born on 18 January, 1834 in Paris. After having attended the seminary of Saint-Sulpice for a year, he entered the Company of Jesus on 29 September, 1853.[13] Once ordained a priest, he was sent as assistant to the residence of the Jesuits and superior of the Jesuit community in Laval in 1873. Adèle's choice to take Père Chambellan as her spiritual guide dates back to this period and to the death of Père Donniou. She very soon described him as being very "rigid, decisive and severe".[14]

In 1875, Père Chambellan was sent for three years to Poitiers as Rector of the Theological Faculty. In 1878 he was chosen as an Assistant of the Society of Jesus and subsequently as Provincial of the Region of Paris from 1879 to 1886. After

[10] Cf. H-15D-003, Abbé Courtois.
[11] H-15D-003, Abbé Courtois.
[12] Cf. Jean Charruau, *Le révérend père Henri Chambellan de la Compagnie de Jésus (1834-1892)*, Paris, Téqui, 1904.
[13] Cf. Rufo Mendizabal, S.J., *op. cit.*, pag. 142, colonna 7, N°860.
[14] H-15D-005, Abbé Courtois.

1889 Père Chambellan devoted several years to the preaching apostolate in the Province of Angers and finally became Superior of the Jesuit community in Nantes, from 1889 to 1892.

In September 1874 he encouraged Adèle to accept the interior invitation to go to Paris and communicate to the Archbishop, that: "the Eucharistic Heart was to be the special object of the cult of Montmartre and the Blessed Sacrament was to be exposed day and night".[15]

Père Chambellan was decisive in managing the attempts of Madame de Croze to prevent Adèle from going to Montmartre. In fact, as Adèle herself noted: "He gave me the formal authorisation and showed himself by his most paternal encouragement, to be strongly convinced, saying that he had admired the goodness of the Lord to me and confirmed that I could make all the necessary preparations to go to Montmartre".[16] That was on 4 March, 1876. At Laval from the first to the eighth of May, Père Chambellan made himself available to guide Adèle on the occasion of a spiritual retreat before her departure to Paris: "During the eight days I received his advice, his encouragement and his testimonies of an immense goodness and concern. She experienced a state of soul overflowing with grace".[17]

Later when Adèle was suffering terribly because of ill health, Père Chambellan wrote her several letters of encouragement and spiritual direction[18] focused on giving oneself to God as a victim, uniting oneself to the altar of Christ. Realizing that the situation was becoming critical Père

[15] H-15D-004, Abbé Courtois.
[16] *Ibidem.* See also on this point H-15D-008, Abbe Courtois.
[17] H-15D-008, Abbé Courtois.
[18] Cf. from H-15D-024 to H-15D-033, from Père Chambellan to the Mother.

Chambellan decided to go to visit her on 25 August, 1876[19] and to counsel her to return to Dijon for a certain period.[20] About twenty days later Adèle did leave Montmartre.[21]

The spiritual direction given constantly by Père Chambellan to Adèle was by letter. She expounded her problems and he replied with short and effective messages, but always encouraging and wise.

Unfortunately the letters sent by Adèle to him are not extant. However, it was possible to consult two letters of hers that he returned with some annotations, and which are kept together with his letters, in the archives of Tyburn.[22]

Père Chambellan wrote his last letter to Adèle on 28 July, 1892, just 20 days before his death, on 12 August, 1892 at Lalouvesc, a mountain village in the region of Rhône-Alpes, in the south of France, where he was recovering from a serious illness.

### D. *Abbé Jules Courtois*

Abbé Jules Courtois was born in December of 1851. He attended the Istituto di San Giovanni de la Salle and then the college of the Jesuits at Dole. Following this he entered the seminary in Dijon and then in San Sulpice in Paris, a city in which he was ordained a priest in December of 1877. He returned to Dijon and became the spiritual director of the college of the Jesuits. He also was appointed chaplain of the

---

[19] Cf. H-15D-010, Abbé Courtois.
[20] Cf. H-15D-033, from Père Chambellan to the Mother.
[21] Cf. H-15F-119, Lémius; H-15C-009, Madame Vosseaux; H-15D-011, Abbé Courtois.
[22] These letters have been catalogued as H-15C-022 and H-15C-023, Pere Chambellan.

Carmelite Convent in the same city. It was Abbé Courtois who accompanied Adèle spiritually from June 1887 and ordered her to write down her memoirs and her experience of God through the various personal stages. He aided her to entrust herself to God through the Vow of Abandon, so that she wrote: "This way of abandonment, dear Father, that the Holy Spirit helped you to establish in my soul, is a divine treasure, for which I cannot thank you even in eternity".[23]

Mother Adèle confided to him timorously but with total confidence, her most intimate and profound spiritual experiences, revealing to him that interior voice so that he could guide her toward the fulfilment of the Divine Will. Many times Adèle sought his comfort and advice on how to overcome in particularly difficult moments: "I am in great need of your holy exhortations, of your advice, of your encouragement!"[24] She learnt from him a great incentive to become "for Jesus an alabaster vase filled with a perfume of great price".[25]

Adèle, now addressed herself solely to carrying out the Will of God, beginning to feel serene in being guided by Abbé Courtois, to whom she had entrusted herself, seeing in him a Father and a judge: "whom Jesus has established for my soul and it is for you to decide when it is to disillusion me or when it is good to encourage me".[26] When she left Dijon in June 1897 to return to Montmartre, his correspondence lessened considerably, and also his spiritual direction diminished in its consistency.

He died on 31 March of 1916.

[23] H-15D-100, Abbé Courtois.
[24] H-15D-105, Abbé Courtois.
[25] H-15D-023, Abbé Courtois.
[26] H-15D-060, Abbé Courtois.

## E. *Abbé Charles Sauvé*

L'Abbé Charles Sauvé was born on 18 October, 1848 at Fontaine-Milon, in the Diocese of Angers. In 1867 he entered the Seminary of Angers and was ordained a priest on Christmas day in 1872. He devoted his life to study and to the compiling of mystical works. In 1875 he became professor of philosophy at the seminary in Dijon. When in 1903 the school was closed, he could focus more on the publication of his writings. During the last decades of his life, he did not enjoy good health, and so he spent his remaining years at Saumur in Loire, in the care of a community of women religious. He died on 11 March, 1925.

Mother Adèle, who greatly appreciated his person and his writings, did everything she could to disseminate his works and in particular the work entitled *L'Incarnation, ou Jésus Intime,* trusting that: "your book may be always in my hands".[27] Her young community at Montmartre loved to read his books as pious meditation, and as refectory reading during meals.[28]

The correspondence between Mother Adèle and Abbé Sauvé relates to the period between 1888 and 1902. Between them both there was a deep mutual understanding, and Adèle confided to him some of her intense mystical experiences on various aspects of her spiritual life.

The Abbé Sauvé frequently visited her little community at Montmartre, and sometimes stayed to preach spiritual exercises. It was to him, especially, that Mother confided: "I no longer belong to myself",[29] to emphasise her great and

[27] H-15C-165, Abbé Sauvé.
[28] Cf. H-15C-161, Abbé Sauvé.
[29] H-15C-160, Abbé Sauvé.

total abandonment to God and His will. The Mother sent to Abbé Sauvé the draft of the document, which was then the Constitutions of the nascent community, for him to highlight any corrections or to make simple suggestions. She added questions at the end to which he was invited to respond.[30]

He continued his correspondence with the Mother almost until his death on 11 March 1925.

### F. *Père François Balme*

Victor Balme was born on 10 September, 1827 at Chervreuse (Versailles). After completing his literary studies, he was ordained a priest in 1850. A year later he joined the Dominican Order and took the name of Père François. He was a disciple of Père Lacordaire, with whom he strove to relaunch the Order of Preachers in France. He was, in fact, First Prior in the new convent at Corsara in 1852 and five years later, he became one of the founders of the new convent of Poitiers. In 1868 he settled in the convent of Saint-Nom de Jesús, in Lyon, where he worked, among other things, on historical studies of the Order.

He gave significant assistance to the Dominican Sisters of Saint Catherine of Sienna while living in their own hospital for about 50 years. When he could no longer continue preaching for serious health reasons, he became an exact and qualified historian. He died on 25 February, 1900.

Père Balme was a Spiritual Director and in particular of Mère Agnes. He was also a notable adviser of the Congregation from the time of its foundation. Adèle confided to him that she desired to, and offered her life for her father's con-

---

[30] Cf. H-15C-161, Abbé Sauvé.

version[31] before his death.[32] Père Balme remained very close to the Community. He presided over the ceremony of giving the first "little habit" to the sisters of Montmartre on 21 November, 1897.[33] The Mother wrote to him with gratitude:

> "This little Society, of which you are the first and the best of Fathers [...] whom the Sacred Heart has wished, my dear Father, that you should have been our first guide and the first Father and in this, He has shown us His goodness and His care and He showed you His predilection. For, as small and poor as we are, we are nonetheless of the infinite mercy of Our Lord, a work of his Heart, destined to love him and glorify Him, to make Him known and reign".[34]

### G. *Père Louis Vasseur*

We do not have many chronological facts about Père Vasseur, but know that he joined the Congregation of the Oblates of Mary Immaculate, and was sent as a chaplain to the Basilica of the Sacred Heart of Montmartre. He was appointed confessor of Mother Adèle's fledgling Congregation by Cardinal Richard, Archbishop of Paris.

Some months before they went to Tyburn, Adèle affirmed to him that in the Community they always read "with profound religious emotion your beautiful book relating the history of the Holy Martyrs whom we invoke at Tyburn".[35]

Père Vasseur remained in close friendship with the com-

---

[31] H-15C-196, Père Balme.
[32] H-15C-096, Père Balme.
[33] Cf. H-15C-188, Père Balme.
[34] H-15C-198, Père Balme.
[35] H-15F-021, Père Vasseur.

munity, and by letter he maintained a very deep spiritual relationship with the Mother who always encouraged him to be faithful, in overcoming sufferings and in striving for holiness.[36] In a letter dated 1905, the Mother expressed her total gratitude to him for being together with Père Balme, among those closest to her religious family:

> "Dear and good father, you are tireless in your goodness and devotedness and I do not know how to thank you for all that you are for us. All that I can say to you, dear father, is that we rely entirely on you as on the best of fathers, of brothers, of friends. If the Sacred Heart has directed us to you, from the first day of our birth, it is because He knew your heart, your zeal, your charity and your absolute devotedness. He knew that neither difficulties, nor trials, nor disappointments, nor distance would be able to separate you from His little family which He entrusted to your care, even before it was born. Often we recall those first months, when under the paternal direction of the good Père Balme and your exquisite and discreet solicitude we were struggling in the dark, with the first attempts of this beloved religious life to which the Sacred Heart was calling us so clearly".[37]

Père Vasseur fostered many vocations and obtained important financial aid for both Tyburn and for the House in Belgium, so much so that the Mother, a few years before her death, thanked him again for his continued generosity:

> "I need to tell you our gratitude which always increases to the extent that you multiply your acts of charity and devotedness to our religious family which you have

[36] Cf. H-15F-045, Père Vasseur.
[37] H-15F-041, Père Vasseur.

125

helped with your prayers and with so much goodness, since its humble beginnings at Montmartre. And with every year that passes, some new testimony of your religious concern is inscribed in our debt of gratitude".[38]

Père Vasseur was military chaplain during the First World War. He died in Paris, on 11 October, 1932.

### H. *Dom Remy Buzy*

Dom Remy Buzy was born at Reims in 1856. He entered the benedictine monastery of Saint Pierre-qui-Vire on 5 October, 1876 and was ordained a priest in 1882. A few years before the foundation he met Adèle at Sainte Reine. He supported the whole Community when they moved to England, so much so that the Mother recalls that having just arrived they never felt alone. On the contrary she recognized the special closeness of Père Vasseur, Père Remy, Père Lémius and Père Sauvé to the community, and was happy to be "surrounded by a protection so sweet and strong".[39]

Dom Remy, in a particular way, helped the Community to know, study and live the Benedictine charism, through conferences, instructions, retreats and spiritual exercises at different stages of their journey.[40]

He died in Pierre-qui-Vire, September 29, 1926.

[38] H-15F-066, Père Vasseur.
[39] H-15C-171, Père Sauvé.
[40] Cf. The Mother wrote in H-15F-026, Père Vasseur: "Père Remy arrived yesterday evening. He is going to give us the retreat from Saturday, 30 August, 1902 ". And yet, in another epistle in H-15E-057, Monsieur Charles Michel: "Today, 28 August, 1904, Père Remy [ ...] and we are happy to have him and listen to his words so enlightened and strong". See also in H-15G-118, Dom Bede Camm.

## I. Père Jean-Baptiste Lémius

Jean-Baptiste Lémius was born in 1851, Montfort-en-Chalosse, in the french region of Landes. He was educated by very religious parents, so much so that in his family three sons became members of the Congregation of the Oblates of Mary Immaculate: François, Jean-Baptiste and Joseph.

He became a priest and he worked in the apostolate of preaching at Pontmain, Limoges and Angers. The focus of his apostolate was devotion to the Sacred Heart of Jesus. From 1893 until 1901 he was Rector of the Basilica of Montmartre and organised the perpetual adoration for men. In 1894 he organized the "Work of the poor" at Montmartre, which gave a practical aspect to the devotion to the Sacred Heart bringing charitable assistance to the most needy. Each Sunday at the Basilica, he met many poor people, celebrated the eucharist with them, he engaged in catechesis and shared baked bread with them. Then three times a week he organised also further catechesis, followed by a hot meal, medical examinations and the distribution of medicines and clothes.

Always at Montmartre, he also founded the "Association of priest apostles of the Sacred Heart", which aimed to live an intense priestly spirituality united to the Sacred Heart of Jesus and to pray for all priests.

While he was in Dijon, in December 1897, to preach the spiritual exercises, Père Sauvé[41] spoke to him of the small group of persons, consisting of Mother Adèle, Mother Agnes

[41] Cf. H-15F-154, Père Lémius; H-12-129, Père Lémius. The latter epistle belongs to a group of writings of Père Lémius addressed to the Congregation and preserved in the archives of the Convent of Tyburn, London.

and Sister Saint John, who had united "to go to live together on the Holy Mountain".[42] Then began an in-depth knowledge of Adèle and the work that was developing around the Basilica of the Sacred Heart and Père Lémius expressly asked Adèle to "write to him all the lights that the good God will grant me about the Work".[43] He himself went to speak with the Cardinal of Paris about the nascent Community, and also gave him two letters of submission from Père Balme and Abbé Courtois; Cardinal Richard after listening said to him:

> "You must say to your daughters that I approve of the association of Montmartre. Do follow carefully the movement of this little nascent community. I would like to appoint immediately a superior [...], he must not be a religious, because he might bring the spirit of his Order. My secretary, Mons. Lefebvre, will be their Superior. He will keep me "au courant" with everything. I want to follow this beautiful work of the Sacred Heart".[44]

Some weeks later, on 4 March, 1898, Cardinal Richard endorsed the Work. Especially in those early years, the small community felt protected and guided by Père Lémius, so much so that the Mother wrote:

> "Yes, my father, we are your daughters, very submissive but also profoundly grateful. And with the grace of God, we will follow with a filial and courageous docility the guidance and teachings that Our Lord will give us through you".[45]

[42] H-15F-170, Père Lémius.
[43] H-15F-072, Père Lémius.
[44] H-12-129, di Père Lémius.
[45] H-15F-073, Père Lémius.

The Mother referred to him, whether it was for spiritual problems or for the material difficulties which perturbed the little community (acquisitions, new donations, debts, interest, benefactors).[46] When the Community had to move to England, Père Lémius obtained permission to follow them for about a year, remaining in London.[47] He it was who presided over the solemn ceremony of the inauguration of the Chapel of Tyburn on 20 March, 1903.[48]

He himself wrote his contribution of lengthy considerations on the life of the Mother[49] and the Society of the Sacred Heart of Jesus.[50] He died on 22 July, 1938 in Talence, in the french Region of Gironde.

### J. *Dom Bede Camm*

Dom Bede Camm was born in 1864 and studied at Westminster School and at Keble College, Oxford. He was ordained as an Anglican Minister, then converted to Catholicism in 1890 and a year later became a benedictine monk in the belgian abbey of Maredsous. He was ordained a priest in 1895. From 1896 to 1912 he was transferred to Erdington (Birmingham); then to the Abbey of Downside in 1913.

He was an expert scholar of the English Martyrs. He came to know Mother Adèle in 1902, after he heard that her Community had bought a house at Tyburn. He wrote to her to congratulate her for this purchase when they were still in

[46] Cf. Letter H-15F-082, H-15F-089, H-15F-091, H-15F-096, H-15F-193, Père Lémius.
[47] Cf. H12-129, Père Lémius.
[48] Cf. H-15F-138, Père Lémius.
[49] Cf. H-12-129, Père Lémius.
[50] Cf. H-12-138, Père Lémius.

the house at Bassett Road. Mother Adèle's response marked the beginning of a friendship that lasted until her death. From that moment Dom Bede Camm strengthened his devotedness to the Sisters at Tyburn, the place of the Martyrs,[51] so much so that the Mother was pleased to have found in him "a very zealous apostle for our dear English Martyrs".[52] He wrote several works on the English Martyrs, among them are *Lives of the English Martyrs: declared blessed by Pope Leo XIII in 1886 and 1895* (1904); *A Birthday Book of the English Martyrs* (1908); *Heroes of the Faith* (1910);[53] *The Good Fruit of Tyburn Tree* (1929).

When the sisters of Tyburn found themselves in grave economic difficulties, such as caused them to think about leaving the convent at Tyburn, Dom Bede managed to obtain much assistance from many benefactors[54] and he decided to leave the copyright of his books to the Congregation. The Mother was always grateful and wrote: "We never forget the hardships, the difficulties, the efforts you have accepted and suffered for our Work".[55] So when, at the end of 1911, the situation became definitively stable, thanks to the great commitment and zeal of Dom Bede, she wrote:

[51] Cf. Dom Bede Camm, *A Sacrifice of Praise*, pp. 7-8.
[52] H-15G-060, Dom Bede Camm.
[53] On 13 August, 1909, Mother Adele wrote in H-15G-077, Dom Bede Camm: "I received your volume Heroes of the Faith. God bless your apostolate for his glory and for the glory of the Martyrs [...] When I think that our poor and tiny convent of Tyburn also has its part in this great and wonderful concert of divine praise and supplication, I cannot believe that the Sacred Heart would leave it to perish. He is preparing, I hope, a future more glorious for it on this spot where its martyrs have given the witness of their lives and their blood".
[54] Cf. H-15G-065, H-15G-066, H-15G-099, Dom Bede Camm.
[55] H-15G-074b, Dom Bede Camm.

"Dear father, you are so deserving, well beyond this last gift, to be recognized as one of the founders of Tyburn. [...] For us you are the initiator, the first to encourage our coming to Tyburn and secondly you are absolutely the guardian and with time and your tireless devotedness, the curator of this sanctuary of which the existence has been so seriously threatened and would have ended up in ruin if you had not come (as St Francis of Assisi for the church of San Damiano). May you continue to enjoy the help of the Sacred Heart, Who has chosen you, and may He grant you final success for His glory and for the honour of the Martyrs".[56]

During the Great War he was Military Chaplain with the british troops in Mesopotamia. From 1919 to 1931 he was Director of Benet House, a college for Roman Catholics students, in Cambridge. He celebrated the funeral Mass of Mother Adèle Garnier in Royston. He wrote her biography: The Foundress of Tyburn Convent (1935), reprinted in 2006. He died on 8 September of 1942 and was buried at Downside.

### K. Dom Columba Marmion

Joseph-Aloysius Marmion[57] was born on 1 April, 1858 in Dublin of an irish father and french mother. Three of his sisters

[56] H-15G-124, Dom Bede Camm; see also when the Mother writes in H-15G-176, Dom Bede Camm: "We like to think that you have been at the origin of Tyburn Convent (remember the meeting with Mr. Baxter, with the consequence of being established on the land of the Martyrs). Then for the foundation of Royston, remember the first day that it was proposed, thanks to a remark that you made to M. Agnes in the presence of Monsignor Barton Brown and how it was quickly realised. And the dear novitiate [ ...] and it is for even more than this that the Sacred Heart allows us to be indebted to you".

[57] Cf. Mark Tierney, Dom Columba Marmion, Columba Press, Dublin, 1995.

became religious at the Sisters of Mercy. He entered the diocesan Seminary in Dublin at the age of 16 years and brilliantly concluded his theological studies at the college of Propaganda Fide in Rome. He was ordained a priest in the church of Sant'Agata dei Goti, in Rome on 16 June, 1881. In this same year, he made a visit to one of his student companions and was fascinated by the liturgical atmosphere of the "fledgling" Abbey of Maredsous in Belgium. After some years of reflection, in mid November 1886, he decided to enter the monastic life in Maredsous, making his solemn profession on 10 February, 1891. In 1899, with a small group of monks, he founded the Abbey of Mont-Cesar in Louvain, where he was elected Prior. Through his apostolic activity he became engaged in the constant preaching of retreats, in Belgium and in Great Britain, while at the same time he was in great demand as a spiritual director. Very soon he became confessor of Bishop Mons. Joseph Mercier, the future Cardinal, who would invite the Adorers of the Sacred Heart of Montmartre to the diocese of Malines. As spiritual director, Dom Columba Marmion guided many different people through assiduous and voluminous correspondence of which thousands of letters are still extant.[58]

Providentially he came into contact with Mother Adèle at the end of the year 1908 and she very soon entrusted herself to his spiritual direction.

> "I seemed to understand clearly that you must be the father of my soul, that I must open myself to you in all simplicity, because Our Lord wills this so that I do not go astray by directing myself.[59]

[58] Cf. Dom Raymond Thibaut, *Union with God: Letters of Spiritual Direction by Blessed Columba Marmion*, Zaccheus Press, Bethesda, 2006.

[59] H-15G-001, Dom Columba Marmion.

I will do everything possible with his grace to be faithful in giving you an account of anything that has taken place in my spiritual state and of intimate circumstances or exterior events that produce any notable change [...]. When you first came to spend a brief time at Tyburn, I truly felt joyful in hearing you speak of the things of God as you did. While I had the desire to hear you again, I did not think that Our Lord would reserve for me the grace of being under your direction [...]. Your words entered my soul like a refreshing dew causing me great joy and raising me up to my God. I bless Jesus for this oasis where he deigned to allow me to rest for a moment".[60]

The letters which this holy monk wrote to her produced deep consolation in her soul in its search for God:

"How much I thank you, and how great is my gratitude to you for your beautiful letter which has done so much good for my soul reassuring it again that it is truly in the way of the Lord, in spite of its miseries and infidelities".[61]

Sometimes the Mother, in moments of greater difficulty for her Community of Tyburn, turns directly to speak with her spiritual director, whom she continually defines as "Father of my soul": and he helps her to find new consolation and new hope in God:

As you are so good, I thank you for everything you have done and for everything that you have been for me, during these two days of grace in my soul and of consolation for my heart! I am so profoundly grateful to Our Lord for hav-

[60]  H-15G-003, Dom Columba Marmion.
[61]  H-15G-017, Dom Columba Marmion.

ing given you to be Father of my soul in which you always foster and augment peace.[62]

On 28 September, 1909, Dom Columba was elected third Abbot of Maredsous. It would be thanks to the support of this great benedictine monk and his precious teachings, that the Sisters of Montmartre would direct their spirituality toward embracing the Holy Rule of Saint Benedict:

> "We would like to see you at Maredsous [...] we will no doubt speak of the question of the incorporation of our Congregation into the Order of St. Benedict, unless some of the annotations shown to Dom Bede Camm have indicated difficulties or even obstacles to the union that we envisage. [...] But if the glorious St Benedict truly wants us as his daughters, without having to sacrifice fundamental aspects of our Congregation, we would be very glad.[63]

We would like to ask you to give our retreat here at Tyburn [...] What a grace this would be for us and especially in that which concerns the guidance we need in matters relating to the Order and the Holy Rule".[64]

When he died, during an epidemic of influenza, on 30 January, 1923 at Maredsous his fame for holiness had already been affirmed among many contemporaries. A new monastery was soon named after him in 1933: Marmion Abbey (U.S.A.). He was beatified 3 September, 2000, by Pope John Paul II.

---

[62] H-15G-032, Dom Columba Marmion.
[63] H-15G-041, Dom Columba Marmion.
[64] H-15G-043, Dom Columba Marmion.

### 3.1.2. *The Two Masters of Spirituality*

The priests already mentioned were undoubtedly a spiritual support for Adèle's growth in God. Some of them were for her, a firm and secure point of reference to develop her spirituality in a constant and systematic way. Père Marquet guided her to daily communion; Père Pierre Donniou developed her devotion to the Sacred Heart; Père Chambellan invited her to give herself to God, as a victim, in union with Christ at the holy altar. But especially it was two of her true teachers who accompanied her closely in her spiritual life: Abbé Courtois and Dom Columba Marmion. We have already had the opportunity to present them in a general way, now we want to emphasize the direction that they gave her in an intimate and fruitful way in two different periods of her life. The first from 1887 to 1897, during which the Abbé Courtois accompanied her until the foundation of the Community of Montmartre; and then a second period from 1908 to 1915 during which Dom Columba Marmion guided her in the way of the Martyrs, toward holiness.

### A. *The Spiritual Direction of Abbé Jules Courtois*

The correspondence of Adèle with Abbé Courtois remains for us the only witness of his intense and constructive guidance that unfolds from the first months of 1887[65] to the end of 1893.[66]

---

[65] Date of the letter H-15D-001, Abbé Courtois.

[66] Date of the letter H-15D-113, Abbé Courtois. Eight other letters are preserved that were written sporadically, the most recent of which was dated 3 February, 1901 (H-15D-121), which although written at a distance of one year from another letter, does not reveal the spiritual intensity of the earlier letters.

In the first letters Adèle makes herself known to her new spiritual director, who is usually also her confessor,[67] through the precise and detailed account of her memoirs.[68] The first step that Abbé Courtois undertook was to bring his disciple to make the Vow of abandonment which Adèle did on 17 June, 1887. This interior disposition, renewed daily in prayer and adoration led the soul of Adèle to guard these divine graces, perceiving the presence of God enveloping her as a "flame of love penetrating me totally and transporting me into God".[69] Through this openness to God, Adèle discovers the joy of surrender to the divine will and has no inkling of the progress of her soul:

> "Ah, if you knew what a change has taken place within me after the Vow of abandonment. It is something inconceivable, it is like a new life where suffering, joy and love are

[67] Cf. The Mother writes in H-15D-019, Abbé Courtois: "At confession yesterday you gave me as a penance, the grace of making an act of absolute abandon morning and evening". Another letter highlights – H-15D-044, Abbé Courtois: "As usual Our Lord permitted that I receive from you a new and treasured gratitude in my confession". Finally, another letter says – H-15D-085, Abbé Courtois: "I have abundant gratitude to you for all your charity at my last confession. And therefore what consolation and what gratitude I felt for your goodness and for the very great lights that the Holy Spirit seemed to give to my soul".

[68] By the letter H-15D-001 (H-15D-011), Abbé Courtois.

[69] Note the full quotation in H-15D-012, Abbé Courtois: "I am preparing for the Act of donation that you have asked me to make as soon as possible to the Sacred Heart and it is almost a duty for me to show you how Our Lord Himself deigns from His side to supply what I lack, by the many favours He lavishes upon me. I have been so spiritually inebriated during these days, that yesterday evening I wanted to resist and sought to escape, by vocal prayer and even to distract my spirit somewhat during prayer. Oh! I can do no more without an order from you… I come to recollect myself to adore my God, when I am enveloped by this flame of love penetrating me wholly and transporting me into God, to heaven".

inseparable, and your poor daughter has to live a supernatural life, despite the miseries and weaknesses from
which she is still totally distressed. But with what care
Jesus watches over me".[70]

"It seems to me that Jesus fashions my soul to have neither
inclination nor choice, but to take everything that He
sends me as the most sure and best way to glorify Him, by
detaching myself from my poor personal tendencies. So
for the future, Jesus wants me to abandon to His Heart my
own ways of acting. I will take as the most excellent provision whatsoever He will decide for me, following my own
attractions only when He will place nothing else before
me. Oh the power of abandonment! What transformations
you effect in the soul! I cannot believe, apart from it being
some marvel, the astonishing change that it has brought in
my soul for 15 days and the fruit of peace and detachment
that the Holy Spirit seems to produce".[71]

Adèle lived such intense moments, which reached sublime spiritual heights, such as moments of ecstasy, of intimate union, thanksgiving, visions, and all the other "divine
operations within my soul"[72] which one needs to verify by
due comparison. Several times she asks her spiritual father
to enlighten her about her mystical experiences, to help her
to understand if they were an illusion or if they really were
God's work. This attitude of being very scrupulous and
timid in the face of the experience of God does not indicate
uncertainties in her soul; on the contrary, it shows an attitude of complete trust and obedience in the one she consid-

[70] H-15D-017, Abbé Courtois.
[71] H-15-D-019, Abbé Courtois.
[72] H-15-D-014, Abbé Courtois.

ers to be the fundamental guide for her soul, for the upbuilding of a faithful relationship with God:

> "Oh my Father, kindly tell me if you wish, to believe that I am under an illusion, but for me it is impossible to say this myself. [ …] Oh my Father, either I am mad, or these radiant splendours are the only truth, the true life, the beginning of the blessed eternity".[73]

> "My self-love makes me think that you may laugh at me and think that I am the plaything of my imagination. Well, so be it. It does not matter and it is better that you consider me foolish and that at least I act wisely in letting you know what my poor discernment believes to come from Our Lord".[74]

> "If you think I am under an illusion do not be afraid of upsetting me by telling me so. I know that my distress will not last long, because nothing will prevent me from loving Jesus and from being loved by him, and all the rest is nothing".[75]

This spiritual direction was characterized by the complete trust of Adèle vis-à-vis Abbé Courtois and the direction he wishes to give her soul: a total abandonment to God

---

[73] H-15D-012, Abbé Courtois.

[74] H-15D-030, Abbé Courtois.

[75] H-15D-041, Abbé Courtois. See also other expressions that have the same attitude of great prudence and that show her need to confirm through her guide the authenticity of her experience of God, as in H-15D-062, Abbé Courtois: "My Father, I really think that all this that I have told you here seems to belong to dreams, but even if I am speaking so poorly, I must not for that reason remain silent out of self-love". And again in H-15D-068, Abbé Courtois : " Sometimes I am afraid of judging too audaciously the spirit that leads me, and I ask myself if this deep peace and this continual contentment of the will, this feeling of habitual and intimate union with God are not the height of illusion. My fear does not last long because I would humbly submit myself to your judgment and I desire only to be in the state where I want my God ".

that passes through her complete obedience to her spiritual father, whom she calls "my Father and judge that Jesus has established for my soul":[76]

> "I know that I must surrender myself blindly to your guidance so that, if you say 'yes' today and "no" tomorrow, I should act today as a result of the 'yes' and tomorrow as a result of "no". If, after examining all, judging that my aspiration are illusions and you will tell me that it is wiser and more secure for me not to dream of a degree of love which is incompatible with my nature, I will obey you without anxiety and without pain, in the firm conviction that the Holy Spirit will enlighten you in a special way so as to guide me.[77]
>
> I submit myself with all my heart to your judgment, not desiring any other thing but only to know the divine will and to abandon myself to it so as to fulfil it".[78]

It was not always easy for her to speak of her spiritual experiences because of the difficulty in finding the best way to express the intensity of divine revelation,[79] as well as her

[76] H-15D-060, Abbé Courtois.

[77] H-15D-023, Abbé Courtois; see also H-15D-025, Abbé Courtois: "My father, I do what I can without anxiety, or concern to control gently the too lively impulses of my soul, as you have told me; and it seems to me that Jesus is blessing my obedience, [ ...] I really feel that an efficacious grace accompanies all your advice". Or later the Mother says in H-15D-013, Abbé Courtois: "If you give me a refusal, I will submit myself with the same contentment to your decision as if you had granted it. ".

[78] H-15D-060, Abbé Courtois.

[79] Cf. The Mother writes in H-15D-012, Abbé Courtois: "But I am powerless to tell you what has taken place. What I have written to you is so cold, so pale, that I grieve greatly at having expressed so poorly to you what Jesus has granted to me". And also in H-15D-085, Abbé Courtois, explains: "How can mere words convey any idea of the marvels into

embarrassment in overcoming a certain self-love.[80] For this reason she felt that in addition to continuing correspondence, this spiritual guidance needed to take place in actual meetings in which by direct dialogue in personal encounter her soul would be able to grasp the most fitting dispositions to continue her path of self-abandonment to God.

> "I am so confused and shamefaced about all I have dared to write to you that I do not know what I will do tomorrow in your presence.[81]

> It seems to me, my Father, that it would be very helpful to see you, so that you may revive my poor soul which is very languid and enervated; and if it were possible I believe it would be good to make a kind of retreat with you".[82]

After some years of spiritual direction, Adèle manifests greater serenity and not only receives from her director his ongoing sure guidance but also includes him in her experience that God is at work in her soul:

> "It must be said that you now know my soul so well, its way, its miseries, its dispositions that I no longer go into details, as I used to do when I needed to let you know me better".[83]

which He plunges the most unworthy of His creatures when He so pleases".

[80] Cf. H-15D-063, Abbé Courtois.
[81] H-15D-013, Abbé Courtois. See also in H-15D-085, Abbé Courtois.
[82] H-15D-112, Abbé Courtois.
[83] H-15D-083, Abbé Courtois. In H-15D-085, Adèle writes: "I think that now you know me better and you have a clearer view of my misery, my pride and my carelessness".

This guidance would lead Adèle to understand her own vocation within the Church, drawing her into the intense experience of Adoration of the Eucharistic Heart of Jesus, which would then become the Charism of her new community gathered at the foot of Montmartre:

> "What it will be for the future, does not really matter since it only behoves me to do the will of God at each moment [...]. He leads me by the hand, here or there, becoming for me the true sun illumining my whole life and thus fashioning it entirely according to his heart. [ ...] to live for Jesus, to desire his glory and his kingdom, pray for souls and finally to abandon myself absolutely to his eucharistic Heart, to his love, such is my goal, my sole attraction".[84]

In front of her profound experience of God, Adèle spontaneously felt very great gratitude toward her spiritual father. She continually expressed this with words of sincere thanks, sometimes preferring to write rather than to express it directly to him.

> "I prayed for you [ ...] at least this is an opportunity which presents itself to thank you a little; because I do not know how to do that normally, whereas I am really touched by your zeal and your care for my soul".[85]

> "This way of abandonment, dear Father, that the Holy Spirit helped to establish in my soul, is a divine treasure, for which I am powerless to thank you even in eternity".[86]

---

[84] H-15D-063, Abbé Courtois.

[85] H-15D-014, Abbé Courtois. In H-15D-088, Adèle writes: "My life so different from the past, where your holy direction brought me, my dear Father. May the Lord reward you".

[86] H-15D-100, Abbé Courtois.

## B. *The Spiritual Direction of Dom Columba Marmion*

When Adèle, in 1908, came to know the benedictine monk Dom Columba Marmion she had become Mère Marie de Saint Pierre, Superior of *Soeurs Adoratrices du Sacré Coeur de Jesús de Montmartre*. Her Community was still living in the unsettled conditions of the transfer from Paris to London – from Montmartre to Tyburn – and this responsibility kept her totally occupied: "so much work, so many demands and concerns that I have almost been beside myself".[87] But she was always supported by her unconditional abandonment to the Divine Will and the grace received in prayer and the sacraments. Her meeting with Dom Columba and listening to his words awakened in her an admiration and an immense spiritual joy, so that she felt he should become "the Father of my soul"[88] to give a new impetus "lest I become lost by directing myself".[89] For her it did not suffice only to have a religious vocation, or to play a role in the Church, but she saw the value of a holy spiritual director who could guide her along the path to the perfection of the evangelical counsels. The Mother, in fact, recognised that it was not easy to find someone who could accompany the spiritual depth of souls:

> "You know that our good and pious confessors are not always spiritual directors. I have to say that, in the ten years that I have been a Religious, my soul, for what intimately concerns its path, has been almost without counsel".[90]

---

[87] H-15G-001, Dom Columba Marmion.
[88] *Ibidem.* Cf. H-15G-032, Dom Columba Marmion.
[89] *Ibidem.*
[90] *Ibidem.* See also in H-15G-004, Dom Columba Marmion: "I have a need of renewed direction, since more than 10 years I have lacked this".

After a few months the Mother, ever faithful to render an account to him of the intimate or external circumstances that produce some change in her soul,[91] guesses the great value of his spiritual direction, both profound and safe, even in spite of her weaknesses, imperfections and mistakes:

> "You have the charity of kindly wanting to direct me, or at least to watch over me, so that I do not stray from the path where the good God has kept me for some time. And also
>
> I need to be reassured by you every so often, in this state of prayer that is so little in relation to all my miseries and imperfections".[92]

In this new spiritual accompanying Dom Columba's guidance does not therefore focus on the disposition of abandoning herself to the Will of God, as much as on the need for a review of her attitudes and thoughts, in order to reach a state of purification that makes the soul more transparent in God:

> "My prayers are spent calmly and lights that I receive are above all on the awareness of my baseness that is like a weight preventing me from contemplating my God in his goodness and his splendour as I would like. This is a state of purification, from which I would like to profit so as to love Our Lord better".[93]

The spiritual experience of the Mother, focusing on eucharistic adoration remained intense and Adèle felt increasingly transformed by the divine presence, in which

[91] Cf. H-15G-003, Dom Columba Marmion.
[92] H-15G-004, Dom Columba Marmion.
[93] H-15G-014, Dom Columba Marmion.

the Divine Master and the power of the Holy Spirit continued to allow that "unspeakable union with my God"[94]
source of light and joy. By sharing these sensations from the
Holy Spirit that were part of her more mystical experience,
Mother Adèle was greatly comforted and encouraged by her
spiritual father, and wrote to him:

> "How much I thank you, as I am so grateful to you for
> your beautiful letter which has done so much good for my
> soul, assuring it again that it is well integrated in the way
> of the Lord, despite its miseries and infidelities, and
> despite the crushing that it experiences in its tortured, so
> anguished nature".[95]

Gradually Mother Adèle Garnier assumed the task of
spiritual direction in regard to her spiritual daughters and to
her spiritual family. So that she became the first person in
the work of the spiritual guidance of the community and its
future. She was delighted to learn that, although Dom
Columba Marmion had been elected Abbot of Maredsous –
mandate that could remove him from the community – he
would remain "our Father and my Father".[96] Thus, while the
financial events of Tyburn deteriorated more and more, to
the extent that her life was "devoured, so to speak, by the
most distressing material concerns",[97] the Mother opens her
wounded heart to her father. She tells him of her firm intention to live "in intimate union with Jesus on the cross",[98]

---

[94] H-15G-016 Dom Columba Marmion.
[95] H-15G-017, Dom Columba Marmion.
[96] H-15G-019, Dom Columba Marmion.
[97] H-15G-023, Dom Columba Marmion.
[98] *Ibidem.*

without the consolation of visions or ecstasy as occurred in the past, but with the certainty of living a total abandonment, almost up to renouncing her own small Congregation:

> "I had to consider the possibility, the near probability of the destruction of our small Congregation".[99]

In spite of the increase in the number of commitments due to his new position, the new abbot, in this situation also was very willing to give her attentive guidance and firm support. He continued to follow his daughter disciple and the entire community through letters, meetings, visits and preached retreats.[100] In a particular way, he even supported Tyburn with material aid,[101] which enabled the Sisters to recover greater serenity in their community life. In this way, at a time of dire suffering, he was able to unite strongly, his support to the Mother with practical help to the community:

> "I would like to thank you very warmly for all your advice and decisions about our business at Tyburn and Koekelberg. Acting in accordance with your direction, we have the peace that fulfilling the Divine Will confers".[102]

---

[99] *Ibidem.* See also another letter in which is highlighted the same fear of leaving Tyburn in H-15G-028, Dom Columba Marmion: "We have to consider whether to leave Tyburn is the will of God and accept it with all our heart as being the only thing to do. We will make any decision in this way, and Our Lord Jesus will help us and will deign to bless us, in any place we would go".

[100] Cf. H-15G-118, Dom Bede Camm, which refers to the visit of Dom Columba Marmion at Tyburn.

[101] H-15G-031, Dom Columba Marmion: "Reverend Father, I would like to thank you for the great love that inspired you to send our poor Convent of Tyburn such a generous offering".

[102] H-15G-032, Dom Columba Marmion.

The most decisive support that characterized Dom Columba Marmion's spiritual direction was his assistance to the community in accepting the Benedictine Rule adapted to their charism.[103]

The Mother had by now, complete confidence in this monk who guided not only her soul, but also the whole Community to the will of God, in this matter.

> "Your decision, made before of God, having taken all possible care to examine and consider the conditions and circumstances, seems to be for us the manifestation of the divine will and the encouragement to guide, as you say, the Congregation in the way indicated. It is a great thing to have worked and at the same time to have searched carefully and laboriously for the solution to the practical difficulties without deviating unduly from the Holy Rule. Certainly there will be points that will give some difficulty to arrange and to settle. But what is important is that God wants this and He will bless our work, our research and our good will and if there are obstacles, they will be overcome because with Him nothing is impossible. [ ...] We know, my dear and most reverend Father, your support, your protection and your paternal devotedness toward us are assured, may God blessed!"[104]

The Mother, forced to stay in her room on account of her fragile health, seemed to have completed her spiritual journey, carrying with her also, her daughters. Now there remained only the last, important request to her director: to lead her to holiness. After having abandoned herself to God

---

[103] See in this respect the already mentioned H-15G-041, Dom Columba Marmion and paragraph 2.4: *The Benedictine Vocation.*
[104] H-15G-043, Dom Columba Marmion.

to do His will and for the good of her Community, there opened for her the path to perfection, by sanctifying herself, thanks to the holiness of her beloved spiritual father:

> "When you speak to us you impart to us some morsels of your spiritual banquets. My poor soul is in real need of your great spirituality, since I am almost always deprived of daily Mass and Communion. It seems to me that I am vegetating and that, if the Lord is pleased to let me live longer it is only to profit a little by sanctifying myself. Pray that I may love him, serve him better and that if my life is useless for work, it may do a little something by love and abandonment to the divine good pleasure".[105]

### 3.1.3. *The Invocation of the Holy Spirit*

"I feel also the guiding of the Holy Spirit as accompanying me, sometimes tangibly, which gives me interior jubilation".[106] This consideration that the Mother shared with l'Abbé Courtois, in her letter of 9 August, 1887, expresses well how her soul, received and fulfilled the action of the Spirit, letting herself be led with docility and joy. It was this that imparted strength to deal with the daily difficulties, to cope with the unexpected things and fatigue, to experience moments of prayer and adoration even when she felt less motivation and was more inclined to distraction. Little by little she discovered within herself a capacity to give herself to Almighty God, which left her, as she recalled: "extraordinarily surprised, so that I could only see the action of the Holy Spirit. Therefore I do all I can to remain open to his

---

[105] H-15G-047, Dom Columba Marmion.
[106] H-15D-025, Abbé Courtois.

147

guidance".[107] This became her commitment, to be ever decisive about letting herself to be guided by the Holy Spirit, the "teacher of her soul": "Oh what a life is that when the Holy Spirit makes himself master of the soul to the point that it no longer feels its own will, but only the will of the Father".[108]

In fact, if on the one hand, the spiritual personalities, whom the Mother had met and who led her toward important milestones, have had a relevant role, on the other hand her willingness to allow herself to be led by the Spirit indicates an attitude of complete trust in God, through the action that the Spirit inspires in her life. It would belong to her spiritual father to encourage her in letting herself be guided by this "intimate direction":

> "Your last letter, so reassuring, has done me so much good, so that I no longer doubt this intimate direction that the Holy Spirit gives to my soul, while Our Lord is pleased to uproot my attractions, aspirations, and wants of my soul".[109]

Not only is she reassured by her spiritual father, but she herself invokes the Holy Spirit for him since she is so convinced that the Holy Spirit will guide the mind of her director in such a decisive manner as to lead her toward the design of God.

And so, addressing Abbé Courtois, she exclaims: "I unceasingly beg the Holy Spirit to enlighten you in a special manner in order to guide me!"[110]

---

[107] *Ibidem.*
[108] H-15D-084, Abbé Courtois.
[109] H-15D-068, Abbé Courtois.
[110] H-15D-023, Abbé Courtois. See also what the Mother writes in H-15F-089, Père Lémius: "All these concerns which so oppress you my father, do know that I bear them with all my heart and that I would like to

The Holy Spirit will become the one who prompts her in her praise of God, her prayer of thanksgiving and petition to her good and merciful Father: "The Holy Spirit prays in me, he forms my intentions, my desires, my petitions".[111]

The invocation of the Spirit became her prayer to ask the Almighty for wisdom, so as to be able to take the right decisions to remain faithful to the divine plan. And it is precisely with this attitude that she will advise her daughters, above all when the financial difficulties seemed to lead to great sacrifices, such as the most extreme and painful one, that of leaving the beloved convent of Tyburn:

> "We must continue to pray to the Holy Spirit, so that He will grant us what we need and supply everything that we lack, and make us become and want everything that God wants, and only that".[112]

spare you. But nevertheless you are the only one to whom I can turn for help and advice. The Sacred Heart for Whom you expend yourself with indefatigable zeal and devotedness will not remain deaf to your prayers. [...] I will beg the Holy spirit to inspire you as to what must be done. And, if you see ways of proceeding, I am prepared to do anything to retain the property of the Sacred Heart according to His intentions"..

[111] H-15D-012, Abbé Courtois.

[112] H-15H-042C, The Sisters. Three days later, with this same confidence in the invocation to the Holy Spirit, she wrote to her spiritual father in H-15G-020, Dom Columba Marmion: "The financial situation of Tyburn is very disquieting. At the present moment it is absolutely grave for us and full of difficulties. [...] We live always in the anguish of a situation that can only become more grave each day. [...] We do not cease to implore the Holy Spirit to enlighten us and we study the question from all points of view, without being able to find any other solution that that of preparing for our departure from Tyburn". See also what the Mother wrote on the occasion of the first General Chapter in H-15F-194, Père Lémius: "After having been ill in Belgium, I had to wait to return to London, so that Mère Agnes (and I) came for the General Chapter. Two dele-

In sharing the divine graces with her spiritual father, the Mother – aware of the difficulty in speaking of her extraordinary experiences – habitually invoked the Spirit in order to assist her in finding the most appropriate words: "I pray at every moment that the Holy Spirit of God may come to my aid so that I may not be impeded in writing".[113] The Mother was fully aware that if the Spirit enkindled the grace, the same Spirit would suggest the best way to share his action:

> "I would really like to be able to explain to you what Our Lord has made me understand this evening about the treasures of grace enclosed in the Eucharist, but it would be necessary for the Holy Spirit to guide my pen, because in spite of the light in which I saw these things, I feel incapable of expressing them".[114]

Abandoning herself to the Spirit and surrendering herself totally to him, the soul of the Mother received unexpected divine graces, that, though on the one hand created a certain uneasiness, on the other hand caused an inexpressible "interior fervour":

> "I will try to tell you how my soul has been surrendered totally to the Holy Spirit, and in such an astonishing manner that I do not remember ever having received before such a grace, with this sort of continuity. [ …] After having received Communion, I do not know what took place and

gates from the Brussels Convent also came. I was somewhat fearful of this first Chapter; but we prayed so much to the Holy Spirit to guide and direct it all that everything transpired admirably".

[113] H-15D-033, Abbé Courtois.
[114] H-15D-053, Abbé Courtois.

I believed I had within me, with Jesus, the Holy Spirit sparkling with light, all burning with love. [ …] I felt the presence of the Holy Spirit like that of Jesus and through Him I adored the Father, I adored Jesus and I also adored Him with an interior fervour that I am powerless to express, but all of this with a calm and ineffable peace".[115]

The Mother, living this serene abandonment in God, in his "good will", contemplates the work of the Holy Spirit within her, with the firm deliberation of remaining faithful: "I have only to be faithful to His action".[116] Guided by the Holy Spirit, she would be led toward ever more sublime mystical experiences: in the act of abandonment, the Spirit produced in her fruits of peace and detachment,[117] in the state of the divine union the Spirit purified her soul,[118] in the experience of ecstasy the Spirit led her to an inexpressible love.[119]

[115] H-15D-012, Abbé Courtois.
[116] H-15G-009, Dom Columba Marmion.
[117] Cf. H-15D-019, Abbé Courtois: "Oh power of abandonment what transformation you work in the soul! I could not believe that without a prodigy such a marvellous change could have taken place in my soul in just 15 days, as well as the fruit of peace and detachment that the Holy Spirit seems to have produced".
[118] Cf. H-15D-025, Abbé Courtois: "Both at Mass and in prayer, during these days, I am not always, but most of the time, in a state of union that causes me at the same time, a great joy in God in my soul and a kind of suffering, of a very painful constraint. This union therefore does not depend in any way upon me, and it seems to me that I am not only the thing that is suffering which is like a struggle between the sensitive part of myself and the supernatural. This is not easy to explain, but I think that I must tell you, because it is the almost habitual disposition these days and I think that this is a work of purification that the Holy Spirit carries out in me".
[119] Cf. H-15D-035, Abbé Courtois: "I felt as if I were elevated on high the same way as I have already described a few days ago, and it seems to me that a supernatural force raises my spirit and makes me ascend by

It was especially during the Eucharist that the Mother would live more intense spiritual moments, sustained by the Spirit of God:

> "I found myself adoring this divine prescience and little by little, adoration, admiration of my God, love, thanksgiving, also the confusion so penetrated me that I strongly felt that the Holy Spirit wanted my soul exclusively, high above the things of earth. Since I was not yet sufficiently mistress of myself, I promised the Divine Master, according to the command that you have given me, to lay aside completely and entirely during the Mass every preoccupation, every anxiety even legitimate; I promised Him, with His help, such a confidence that I was not afraid of anything and such an abandonment that I accepted everything [...]. And then what an inexpressible union with my God, what happiness contemplating His glory, what love adoring His goodness. [ ...] The Holy Spirit poured out in my soul streams of light and inexpressible happiness".[120]

This sublime grace that the Mother obtained during the Sacrament of the Eucharist was not the result on her part of any desire or disposition of soul or even praiseworthy effort, but was clearly and uniquely the fruit of the Spirit of God:

> "I understand that very well, and I see clearly that neither desire, nor application, nor effort could obtain this grace; it is the gratuitous action of Holy Spirit and I even perceive

degrees. [ ...] my God transports my soul in this state of love and ineffable adoration, to where the earth and creatures could not even appear, except in the intervals between this kind of ecstasy. Then the Holy Spirit formed in my soul certain acts, prayers, gratitude and visions that all became absorbed into an inexpressible love".

[120] H-15G-016, Dom Columba Marmion.

also [ …] the Holy Spirit begets the union with Our Lord in the soul".[121]

The Mother always lets herself be led by the Holy Spirit even when passing through times of great spiritual and physical trials, intensive labour, in which she would feel put to the test by "great crucifixions of spirit":

> "I had throughout this last month, some great crucifixions of spirit, but also of powerful relief in my soul. The Lord has been pleased to increase every day the anxieties and anguish by making their causes more and more harrowing and pressing. Sometimes I wonder how my mind can withstand such tests. And if it resists it is, I believe, because my divine master keeps my soul in an inexpressible peace: which seems to me as 'an ocean without shores' that is like an immensity of love and peace. It is a very comforting vision for me this tableau that I interiorly contemplate and which seems to be shown to me by the Holy Spirit so as to give me the courage and strength to withstand the great evils from which I am threatened if God did not come to my aid. The more I suffer from these inexpressible torments, the more I feel the love of God grow within me, and a need increasing each day to adore, to bless His Holy Will, to bless the hand that strikes me and that I cherish with all the ardour of my soul".[122]

### 3.1.4. *The Reference to the Blessed Virgin Mary*

In studying the spirituality of the Mother one cannot prescind from her special devotion to Our Lady, as an important reference for feeling accompanied in the fulfil-

---

[121] H-15G-005, Dom Columba Marmion.
[122] H-15G-025, Dom Columba Marmion.

ment of the divine will. In this regard we emphasize that, by analyzing her letters, we are quickly struck by the fact that her decision to make the vow of chastity at the age of 35 years of age was made precisely on the day of the Feast of the Immaculate Conception. Her choice of this date shows her total entrustment to Mary, the *Tota Pulcra*. This Vow would be renewed annually, until her perpetual profession, as she recalls to her spiritual father: " Today, Saturday, 8 December (1888) Feast of the Immaculate Conception, I will renew the vow of chastity made 15 years ago".[123]

It is known that, due to her delicate health, the Mother did not seem to be able to realise her vocation of total self-giving to God within a religious order. In 1877, in particular, taking into account her serious health condition, she decided to make a pilgrimage to Lourdes, to ask the help and protection of Our Lady, invoked at the Grotto as the Immaculate Conception. She began her pilgrimage on 6 August, accompanied by her friend Maria Laval and, after eight days of travel arrived at the Marian Shrine. Her soul, already deeply devoted to the Eucharist, asks God, through the intercession of the Blessed Virgin Mary, not so much for healing, but "to be strong enough to be able to go to Mass and Holy Communion".[124] Great was her happiness when at the end of that same month, she went to Brittany near her sister and, as a guest of a home for the elderly, she was able to receive Holy Communion every day:

> "My room overlooked the sanctuary of the Chapel and every day I received Holy Communion. Our Lady of Lourdes did not wish to heal me, but had accepted my prayer.

[123] H-15D-078, Abbé Courtois.
[124] H-15D-011, Abbé Courtois.

My sufferings, my weakness, the impossibility of busying myself with material things, all this was easy to bear since I had the joy of Mass and Holy Communion".[125]

This link between the Holy Communion and the Blessed Virgin Mary is also evident in other circumstances, where Adèle herself recalls that "preoccupied by the desire to receive Jesus with a pure heart, I felt myself to be with the Virgin Mary".[126]

This great devotion to the Blessed Virgin Mary was to increase more and more in her soul. The heavenly Mother would become the reference point and constant support in her journey of faith so that Adèle also felt the need to make her own personal "heroic act" to the Madonna, entrusting to her every satisfaction:

> "On All Souls' Day (2 November, 1888), without your permission, I have, in all humility and poverty, and also with a great deal of confusion, placed into the hands of the Blessed Virgin Mary all the satisfactions that I could receive or be attributed to me so that she may dispose of them as she wills. I followed the manner indicated under the name of the heroic act".[127]

The protection of Our Lady,[128] united to the help of the Sacred Heart, will always be perceived as being very close,

---

[125] *Ibidem.*

[126] H-15D-037, Abbé Courtois.

[127] H-15D-074, Abbé Courtois.

[128] Cf. H-15D-121, Abbé Courtois: "The devil is fuming against us and pursues us; but the Sacred Heart and, the Blessed Virgin Mary protect us wonderfully". See also the letter H-15H-055, to the Sisters: "The more we are drawn to exert ourselves to be fervent and virtuous, the more it

part of her spiritual experience, but also very real and living, as when she prayed during the novena to the Immaculate one to obtain a house for the Community,[129] or to cancel their debts.[130] Then, when she began to draw up the Constitutions for the nascent community, the Mother turned to Père Lémius to make sure they emphasised devotion to the Blessed Virgin Mary:

> "Also if you can insert, as a necessary component to the holiness of our life, devotion to the Blessed Virgin Mary".[131]

will attract graces and blessings on the Institute and at the same time on each one [...]. With the blessing of the Sacred Heart and the protection of the Blessed Virgin Mary, we walk with confidence, humility and courage: our efforts will be blessed by God".

[129] Cf. H-15C-152, Abbé Sauvé: "We have had a series of touching graces on account of which Père Lémius was beside himself and could only go excitedly to tell this miracle to the Archbishop at which the good Cardinal and Monsieur Lefebvre marvelled. It is true that we were very moved by what happened during a threefold novena to the Sacred Heart, to the Immaculate and Saint Michael. We entitled this novena "Irresistible". We asked in the first place for very important spiritual graces and three temporal graces: the Sacred Heart for material resources, the Immaculate for a House and Saint Michael for good postulants. The novena finished on 10 October (1898). Now, that day, I received the communication of the decision of the Reverend Mother General of the Cenacle regarding the postulant and Père Lémius tells me to take her. Being close to him, I told him of our novena saying that Saint Michael had heard us, first sending us this excellent postulant. He was astonished and said to me, but today, the Superior of the Cenacle has offered me a House for you inasmuch as it depends on her. They wish to give it to you, if the donor is in agreement with this. The Superior General wishes very much to do this. As regards the third grace of material resources, this certainly will be comprised in the second grace if the Blessed Virgin does give you this house".

[130] Cf. H-15F-093, Père Lémius: "It was to Mary Immaculate that I had confided individually the debts of the Sacred Heart for the House and on his feast we find already this is wonderfully answered".

[131] H-15F-073, Père Lémius.

Of course in the personal prayer of the Mother the custom of reciting the Rosary is not lacking, which sometimes together with the Holy Mass became the only moments of recollection during her busiest days:

> "My time was so completely taken up today that despite my good will I have not been able to find, outside of the Mass, more time to devote to prayer, than to say a rosary".[132]

Our Lady truly was for Mère Marie de Saint Pierre la *Mater Magistra*. Her spirituality contains a wealth of Marian references, in particular that of abandoning herself to the Will of God, with the same expression of the Mother of God: *Fiat*.[133] In many letters, especially in the final part of the greetings, Adèle had recourse to the intercession and to the memory of Our Lady. She, therefore, earnestly wished that veneration of Holy Mary would remain a stable element for her religious family. She entrusted the new foundation at Koekelberg in a special way to the Blessed Virgin Mary, where the presence of the Heavenly Mother would reign and guide her devoted daughters as if she herself were the "Mother Superior":

> "Whatever the difficulties we encounter, we have the confident hope that Our Lord will help us to overcome them. We prayed to the Holy Virgin to be willing to be Superior of this foundation and we are sure that she has accepted. Therefore she, herself will help, guide and govern us

---

[132] H-15D-065, Abbé Courtois. See also the reference to H-15E-057, Monsieur Charles Michel: "I send you the photograph that you asked me [...]. I am posing while reciting the rosary that my hands are fingering".

[133] See in this connection the following paragraph and in particular the references to the expression *fiat*.

according to the intentions of the Sacred Heart of her divine Son".[134]

## 3.2. The Route through Suffering

Adèle, on her journey of faith addressed in a direct and decisive manner another reality that would mark, I would say almost indelibly, her spirituality: suffering. Her delicate health tested her in different situations, but she never lost her complete trust in God, to Whom she abandoned herself in a state of Victim, united to Christ, sent by the love of the Father "as a victim of expiation for our sins" (1 Jn. 4.10 ). She found a compelling attraction towards those who had paid with their blood for their fidelity to Christ. This was the beginning of her mission on the Hill of the Martyrs, in Paris, and then dwelling at Tyburn, the place of the English Martyrs, and then becoming herself a fragrant offering, a "Martyr among the martyrs", in perpetual adoration of her beloved Heart of Jesus.

### 3.2.1. *Acceptance of Suffering and the Cross*

Adèle's fragile health was the first suffering she had to face. In fact, it was precisely on account of her weak and delicate physical state that she had to waive, twice, the pursuit of those divine designs to which God seemed to be directing her. First of all, while still a young 25-year-old because of her illness she had to leave the novitiate of Conflans. Then, on 19 May, 1876, in the wake of her first day in Montmartre, a place that represented that long-awaited and yearned for spiritual goal, she recovered, but with extreme pain, from a

[134] H-15F-199, Père Lémius.

state of "terrible terror ... and frightful agony"[135] that presaged immediate death: "what I have suffered exceeded everything I have suffered in my life".[136] Her condition deteriorated significantly, until it left her immobile in bed, with the prospect of leaving Montmartre. Adèle's attitude was always one of complete availability to the divine will, by adhering to God with a ready and profound: *Fiat*:

> "I am always in bed, nailed by weakness, but above all by the Good Pleasure of Jesus this adorable nail is full of graces. It imparts to the soul strength and gentleness: *Fiat*. [...] He wills that I leave here, therefore I go on Wednesday. [ ...] Pray that this departure He wants may be a pure offering by His poor servant. *Fiat! Fiat!* Oh sweet and dear word. I would like to have it written in my heart in letters of fire!"[137]

Even when the Montmartre experience ended on 13 September, 1876, Adèle, rather than being defeated or disillusioned, was reconfirmed in the same openness to God's plan:

> "Will I return to the heights of Montmartre? This is the secret of the good Master. Oh *Fiat, Fiat, Fiat,* I need to say this word that unites me with Jesus".[138]

The evidence of her unstable health continued and Adèle spent another "seven months with an intensity, a violence and a diversity of extraordinary suffering",[139] abandoning herself especially to the crucified Christ, so as to feel herself

135 H-15D-009, Abbé Courtois.
136 *Ibidem.*
137 H-15C-009, Madame Vosseaux.
138 H-15C-010, Madame Vosseaux.
139 H-15D-011, Abbé Courtois.

"with her hands tied, separately, and stretched out on the cross".[140] Faced with these painful hardships, she was conscious of being able to serve and be more united to Jesus, Who was "preparing her to bear her suffering with love",[141] and so finally feel herself crucified with Christ:

> "I bowed down (my head) humbly to adore my Saviour, and then something completely extraordinary took place: I tremble with joy every time I think about it. I found myself as stretched out on the Cross, crucified with Jesus and in such a way that my limbs were penetrated by the members of Jesus in a fashion that experience alone can make clear: it was like a fusion, a transformation of myself in Jesus; my soul was lost in his and my whole being lightning-struck, melted away in His".[142]

This experience would bring Adèle to reinforce her love for the cross, to see in suffering an opportunity for greater union with Christ, a teaching to desire suffering so as to be a little more conformed to Him.[143] Her awareness of living her suffering of the presence of Jesus was to become emphasised more and more; the pain would not only represent a physical situation, but would become an opportunity of sublime spirituality, of a body that gives itself wholly to its Creator, in an offering pleasing to Him:

> "The physical suffering is of an order less elevated than moral suffering. But when the physical suffering is supernaturalised by the supernatural disposition of submission, con-

---

140 H-15D-014, Abbé Courtois.
141 H-15D-017, Abbé Courtois.
142 H-15D-041, Abbé Courtois.
143 Cf. H-15D-055, Abbé Courtois.

formity and loving abandonment to the divine good pleasure, it becomes very sanctifying for the soul and gives God a glory that often heroic work does not procure for him".[144]

The acceptance of the Cross became so profound in Adèle so as to make her feel mystically a disconcerting, but at the same time wonderful, divine message: Christ's own voice announcing to her that He would imprint on her heart a cross and on this cross would be revealed the very face of Christ Himself:

> "When the Cross I have placed in your heart has hollowed out its position truly well, that is to say, when it makes only one with your heart, then I will engrave My Face on this Cross and on your heart at one and the same time. I will do this in such a way that if you tried to displace the Cross in order to be less bruised, you would at the same time, obliterate My Face, or else rend it".[145]

This mystical experience strengthened in Adèle the awareness to see suffering as a privileged moment of grace and divine predilection, where she not only accepted the pain with a confident Fiat, but she yearned to remain with it in view of a total union:

> "Here I am by the merciful predilection of Our Lord nailed to my bed, since yesterday. [ ...] Pray for me so that I might be faithful to love the Cross always and not desire to be freed from it".[146]

---

[144] H-15E-060, Monsieur Charles Michel.
[145] H-15D-061, Abbé Courtois.
[146] H-15C-142, Abbé Sauvé. See also this same situation of 1 October, 1888, described in H-15D-070, Abbé Courtois: "Today I am nailed to my

Her journey of reflection and research would continue, until she reached the spiritual insight that later would become the charism of her new community: to sacrifice themselves in union with Christ, the perpetual sacrifice of the altar and to live an interior apostolate where prayer, suffering and abandonment all represent the guidelines:

> "Not only does Christ Jesus want me to be immolated in union with him, in the perpetual sacrifice of the altar, as priest and sacrificer through his divine action, but He also calls me to an interior apostolate. [ ...] He showed me how this interior apostolate could, like the immolation, be continued through prayer, suffering and the conformity of abandonment, and that each moment of my life, united to him, would be an act of the priestly ministry, if I am faithful. And for this I must attain such a purity of which I have not yet any idea; to the extent that my soul will be reclothed with a higher degree, it will work more effectively to the glory of God and the salvation of souls, above all and very especially for the sanctification of the clergy".[147]

Later, in her life, Adèle, after becoming Mère Marie de Saint Pierre, sustained not only the physical pain and suffering caused by an eye infirmity,[148] by rheumatism in her right hand[149] and shoulder,[150] but above all by the anguish and

bed... when I get up, I must be supported and for a few steps pains are so violent throughout my body, that I must immediately go back to bed. I have no doubt it is the spinal cord that is impaired. But I must confess, with all sincerity of my soul that I really feel a complete indifference, abandonment".

[147] H-15D-080, Abbé Courtois.
[148] Cf. H-15C-165, Abbé Sauvé. See also: H-15F-095, Père Lémius.
[149] Cf. H-15E-062, Monsieur Charles Michel. See also: H-15F-182, Père Lémius ; H-15G-074, Dom Bede Camm.
[150] Cf. H-15E-064, Monsieur Charles Michel.

anxiety of a community that was not likely to have sufficient material means to go forward. Then too, her soul was no longer so enlightened by visions or ecstasies, but intimately united to Jesus on the Cross, at the most awesome moment and the consummation of his love for us, the cry of pain, in the forsaken heart of Christ, at the pinnacle of love. Here Adèle lived, here the disciple dwelt, "nailed to the cross itself", in the "grace that comes from the torture of Christ":

> "Dear Father, I do not have the visions, nor the ecstasies of my soul into God through those raptures that I had from time to time in contemplation. [ …] When temporal anxieties lay hold of me in an excessive way, then my recourse is in intimate union with Jesus on the Cross, at the most awful moment of his life, his very Passion, when he uttered this terrible cry: "my God, my God, why have you forsaken me"! There, my Father, I plunge myself, in the forsaken, heart of my Jesus and dwell there. It is the pinnacle of his love that he wanted to know, to suffer, to desire the abandonment by his Father! Then this cry that I utter with Him; it seems that I have no more faith, but I know that it is faith alone that makes me utter this cry! It is faith in Jesus, in his love, in his total devotion to his Father. I understand vaguely that this is the culminating point of the suffering of Jesus and at that moment he saved us from despair and made us make with Him the most perfect act of love, the act of the most complete abandonment. And I have to tell you, my Father, that these moments are frightening and I do not even dare to think of them [ …] and when they have passed, my soul feels calm, serene again, more than ever, in God, nailed to the Cross of Jesus and through Him completely ready to suffer everything that He wills, and however much He wills. This is the grace that comes from the torture of Jesus".[151]

[151] H-15G-023, Dom Columba Marmion.

*163*

That is why the Mother matured in the awareness that the more there are difficulties and sufferings, the more the Lord expresses his providential grace and its sweet consolation, because He never leaves us alone, but "the heavier the Cross, the more Jesus will bear it with us":

> "My good Father, the heavier the Cross, the more Jesus will bear it with us, and our pains and our travail will become our consolation, even when we are exhausted and overwrought. In my humble and small sphere, I have proved this in an intense manner! Sometimes it is like having to walk on shaky ground, strewn with briars and thorns, with burning coals and crevices everywhere, yet I find myself as it were, carried by Christ crossing without danger and without fear these many obstacles. I also feel completely penetrated and impregnated with a peace that small moral and physical disturbances do not trouble. [ ...] Sometimes I also feel my faith somewhat weakened, and that it revives by recalling certain favours which have helped me greatly at other times to became detached and disengaged from everything so as to fix myself in God".[152]

### 3.2.2. *The State of Victim*

To be defined as "victim" must be included in the spiritual terminology of Adèle, especially in the first part of her life. In fact, already from 7 December, 1874, when she encountered the Cardinal of Paris, Mons. Guibert, in order to speak of eucharistic devotion to the Sacred Heart in the future church of Montmartre, she felt and described herself as "a victim destined" for adoration of the Sacred Heart:

---

[152] H-15G-035, Dom Columba Marmion.

"I saw myself living close to the tabernacle of the Sacred Heart, passing all the time possible adoring him and only living for this purpose, as a victim destined solely for sacrifice. Everything that I felt as premonitions seemed strange, impossible, absurd; and in spite of this, deep within of my soul, Jesus assured me that it was his will and that he would accomplish it".[153]

A year and a half later, Adèle, who was no longer so young at 38 years, took cognizance of the fact that this desire was realised in her "small Nazareth", exactly on 19 May, 1876, anniversary of her first communion and the day on which for the first time she received Holy Communion in the Basilica of the Sacred Heart of Montmartre:

"It was the anniversary of my First Communion and it was also my first Communion at Montmartre. I offered myself to Jesus without reserve asking him to take me as a victim either by accepting my life as I desired, or by rendering it entirely consecrated to his Good Pleasure, without leaving anything for my own personal satisfaction. From that moment, I felt separated from the world. I have never lost the grace of this interior separation, for the world no longer held any attraction for me, in any way".[154]

Immediately after this offering, in the same evening, Adèle suffered terribly: the feelings of anguish, sadness, agony invaded her soul, with pain so strong that she was left petrified. The thought of an immediate end to her life, lent her, however, the strength to voluntarily offer her life to

[153] H-15D-005, Abbé Courtois.
[154] H-15D-008, Abbé Courtois.

the Sacred Heart, with the certainty that God "from the first day deigned to take his victim".[155] From that moment she felt herself to be the "poor little victim",[156] in the hands of her God, completely prepared to fulfil his Will.

Adèle continued to grow spiritually, disengaging herself from immediate interests, from material concerns, from passing projects and interests. Separating herself more from the things of this world, Adèle was at 50 years of age a mature woman, who, sought only one project in life: "My soul is united to Jesus as a victim for the glory of his Father; it no longer belongs to me".[157] A further step in this divine union would reveal her vocation: participation in the "interior priesthood", to which God had been preparing her for a very long time and by which her soul aspired to immolate herself at all times with Jesus:

> "Jesus made me understand that his altar would be in the centre of my soul, that there he would unceasingly immolate me with himself, and that I would immolate myself by abandon. He showed me that for this I had to attain very great purity of heart, soul, mind and body, so that the victim – who would also be priest with Jesus, would not be defiled".[158]

Increasingly, in this journey of abandonment and unconditional trust, Adèle left herself to be governed by God, disposed to become "all purified and consumed as a victim".[159]

---

[155] H-15D-009, Abbé Courtois.
[156] H-15C-006, Madame Vosseaux.
[157] H-15C-143, Père Sauvé.
[158] H-15D-078, Abbé Courtois.
[159] H-15D-094, Abbé Courtois.

After an attentive and meditative Lent, Adèle made a comparison between herself and the Prioress of the Victims of the Sacred Heart of Marseille. Then, experiencing within herself the full disponibility to offer herself entirely to God by the Vow of Victim, her spiritual father, l'Abbé Courtois, agreed that she make this vow. She did so on 31 March 1893, Good Friday, at 15:00 hours, the time the Church celebrates the memorial of the death of Christ, the Victim sacrificed to God the Father for the salvation of the world:

> "The Vow of victim, even if it is comprised implicitly in that of abandonment, can include a special generosity that calls and draws to the soul a greater sharing in the sufferings of Jesus".[160]

### 3.2.3. *The Offering of Martyrdom*

In the writings of the Mother, that we have analyzed, it is interesting to note that the first time that there is the term "Martyrdom", this is inserted in a context of suffering when Adèle had just arrived in Montmartre, in her "little Nazareth" and she already experienced terrible moments of pain. Recalling these events Adèle speaks of a "Martyrdom without name":

> "A dreadful terror seized hold of me. A hideous anguish overturned my entire moral and physical being. The most bitter gloom penetrated my entire being. A convulsive trembling shook my body.. I felt as if I was in my death agony and it was a terrifying agony. The excess of the suffering nailed me to my place and I remained for hours a prey to this nameless, desolate martyrdom".[161]

---

[160] H-15D-099, Abbé Courtois.
[161] H-15D-009, Abbé Courtois.

In fact this anonymous adjective of her martyrdom, "nameless" is striking, almost as if indicating that the martyrdom of the Mother and her daughters would know, as we emphasise later, a name and a place: "Tyburn". In this anonymous martyrdom, albeit Adèle found herself in "a ghastly desert, tortured by the most abominable thoughts during the night, and by anguish and indescribable terrors during the day",[162] while meditating on the *Sacrifice of Christ* in Chapter IV of the *Imitation of Christ*, she received "the grace to continue my martyrdom of heart, soul and body".[163]

When the vocation to "interior priesthood" was revealed to her, she realised that she would not only share in a state of victimhood, but it would be an offering of true martyrdom, where grace triumphs in every situation:

> "The Lord made me understand that he is calling me to this interior priesthood. He showed me all the rending asunder and the despoliation he had wrought in me for a considerable time so as to attain this. Now, he wills that I no longer be attached to anything, neither to myself nor to any creature, but to him alone. It is he who breaks my heart with an intensity which appears to me to be a martyrdom wherein his love always wins the victory".[164]

Also in the new Community the Mother, sharing her anxieties and prayers with Père Lémius, reveals that their only interest was to become faithful to the divine will

---

[162] H-15D-010, Abbé Courtois.
[163] *Ibidem.*
[164] H-15D-078, Abbé Courtois.

through that "continuous Martyrdom"[165] that would sanctify their religious life.

Once transferred to Tyburn, the Community again would pass through great trials, and bitter anguish. Faced with this suffering, the gaze of the Mother was enlightened by a new reality: a new testimony had come to assist their martyrdom. Having started their offering to God on the French "Mountain of the Martyrs" actually Montmartre, they can now turn to the English Martyrs of Tyburn with complete confidence that these martyrs would confirm and protect their work.

> "The martyrs of Montmartre and those of Tyburn were able to suffer for the glory of their Good Master. It is necessary that their example will help us and give us courage. After all, the tests of this life are short for each one; and if a work is to see its ongoing, unceasing succession bearing fruit, each one has only to play his part and the grace will not only be sufficient, but superabundant".[166]

And when the situation of the Community became so serious, that the Mother envisaged, the "taking into account the possibility, the almost probability, of the destruction of our small Congregation"[167] and having to leave the Convent of Tyburn, she interpreted this as a further opportunity to

---

[165] H-15F-080, Père Lémius; see, all the citation: "Because, my father, if I pray to the Lord to grant us the things that seem necessary to practise the religious life and to facilitate the development of our society, I do not need to tell you that my spiritual life is spent entreating him to make us faithful, make us what he wants us to be, and we can only become that by a continuous Martyrdom".

[166] H-15E-033, Monsieur Charles Michel.

[167] H-15G-023, Dom Columba Marmion.

169

feel more united to the atrocious sufferings endured in this same place, in previous centuries, by the same English Martyrs, becoming herself "a Martyr among the martyrs":

> "Our troubles are like the suffering that the martyrs came to seek at Tyburn: should we be surprised that we have our part and ought we not consider ourselves happy with the grace that is given? We cannot aspire to the glorious witness of blood, but we ought to rejoice, as you say, to carry the Cross with the Divine Master. I seem to myself to be more united to these martyrs since we are suffering so much".[168]

## 3.3. Her Spiritual Guidance

Adèle, as daughter, chosen and protected by God, accompanied by the breath of the Spirit, responding to the call of God, places herself in complete readiness to share the charism received, together with all her daughters. She will become the Mother, the guardian of the Work of God. But above all, she will be the courageous Mother in the face of the suffering of the weakest, and she showed those at the moment of death how to accept words of truth, full of hope; she would help them unite themselves to Christ and together with Him cry out: "Father, into your hands I commend my spirit" (Lk. 23:46).

### 3.3.1. *The Leadership of the Community*

> "My incapacity, my inability, my absolute ignorance concerning the things of the religious life lead me to renounce the place of being the first person in the Community. For

---

[168] H-15G-093, Dom Bede Camm.

ten years, the few skills that I could have had to deal with works or business, etc. have completely disappeared. [ ...] From the point of view of the Work, I believe that my mission is finished with regard to the activity. It is clear that the Sacred Heart has wanted to use me to begin, to open the door. That is done, now I do not feel called to anything else. I no longer have more light, nor grace for doing something else. Perhaps it will be necessary for a few months to remain in appearance the director or superior, because of my age and of what I started. But when our situation has been rectified, and our community seriously established, it would be good to permit me to retire on the sidelines, to live the common life to the extent of my strength and devote myself exclusively to prayer and recollection. Our Lord knows that I would like to ask him every day that he would be well pleased to accept my life for the work; it will be when he so pleases. In the meantime He will grant me the life of prayer in front of the Sacred Heart living in the Blessed Sacrament".[169]

These words, written to l'Abbé Courtois, 4 February, 1898, bear witness to the fact that Adèle once at the foot of the Sacred Heart, together with a small nucleus of daughters, now believes she has completed her mission. In fact it was just eight months since she arrived at Montmartre to respond to the divine call, in the presence of his Eucharistic Heart and already she had offered him her life, but above all she wished that others might guide the nascent family. However, this did not happen, because she was still to be the Mother to guide her daughters, until her last day on earth. She would be the Mother because she would bear wit-

[169] H-15D-115, Abbé Courtois.

ness to and transmit the charism which God had placed within her. But above all, she would be the Mother, because all her disciples would recognise themselves to be daughters of that spirituality which she cherished in her soul entirely abandoned to God.

Through her writings, in particular the letters sent to distant sisters who lived in the other monasteries of England or in Belgium, we can grasp the great authority and kindliness of Mother Marie de Saint Pierre.

The Mother, not only received numerous letters from her daughters, but she herself loved writing and was able to express herself with great simplicity. Indeed she showed some self-irony at the age of 82 years, by writing jokingly to one of her Sisters: "I am a very poor writer, you know! I'd love to write to each of my dear daughters".[170] It was not always possible for her to find the time, on account of her many and multiple duties[171] and as well, her poor state of health did not always permit her to use easily her right hand, which was chronically affected by rheumatism[172] or to see clearly, for her eyes, were very weak and tired.[173]

---

[170] H-15H-180, Mère Génévieve.

[171] Cf. H-15H-137, Mère Myriam: "I absolutely lack time to write. I am disturbed every minute". See also in H-15H-157, Mère Thomas: "My dear child, see, for how long a time I have wanted to write, but here (Sante Marie), as at Tyburn, I am often late for things more urgent and are thus obliged to postpone those that are less urgent, despite the fact that they are more pleasing".

[172] Cf. H-15H-090, Mère Gertrude: "I cannot answer at length because my hand is infirm".

[173] Cf. H-15H-123, Mère Hélène: My dear daughter, my eyes are not so good to write to you, but I want to send you my best wishes for the feast and thank you for your dear letter". See also H-15H-127, Mère Hélène: "It is a true sacrifice not having been able to write again, I am

All her letters normally begin with a tender expression of greeting, for example "Very dear Child," (in french: "Ma bien chère enfant"), when it does not contain the name of the nun. In certain special circumstances she underscores her affection and maternal role with the formula: "My beloved daughter" or "My well-beloved small daughter" (in french: "Ma bien chère Fille", "Ma bien aimée petite Fille"),[174] and even repeats this several times in the letters, as when she writes, on 29 May, 1922 to Mère Hélène: "my dear daughter, so truly loved in Corde Jesu, for you my daughter, may everything be as follows: God only in view".[175]

She was always present and caring, encouraging gently weaker and more suffering sisters with her loving attention and maternal advice. For example, as when she writes to Mother Dominica: "Courage and great confidence in Our Lord [ …] no fasting for you and take everything that is necessary to sustain yourself",[176] or again, when she showed the same concern, feeling the sisters needed to take all precautions against the cold, in order to avoid bronchitis, during the winter.[177] She showed a similar concern by sponta-

sure that you understand. But for three weeks my eyes have been very bad and I was not allowed even to write a few lines".

[174] Cf. H-15H-069, Mère Dominica: "Abide in peace, my beloved daughter"; or also in H-15H-120 and H-15H-122, Mère Hélène: "My well-beloved small daughter" and H-15H-124, Mère Hélène: "O my daughter, we love God". See also in H-15H-154, Mère Louise: "My dear Daughter"; finally in H-15H-171, Mère Raphael: "My beloved small Daughter".

[175] H-15H-125, Mère Hélène.

[176] H-15H-065, Mère Dominica. See also in H-15H-085, Mère Gertrude: "Above all be careful to take sufficient nourishment and do not fail to advise M. Dominica or M. St. Thomas if there is something you may not have or that can do you good".

[177] Cf. H-15H-154, Mère Louise.

neously sending to Mère Myriam a small box of chocolates: "I sent yesterday a small box of chocolates; it was all that we could do. But tomorrow we will send you chocolates and biscuits, since there is no need to leave you hungry".[178]

Clearly Mother Adèle's attitude, profound and intimate that she manifested in her spiritual guidance of her daughters who continually sought her advice and approval, was an attitude of complete self-giving to God:

> "My very dear child,
> I should have answered your good letter if it were not so difficult for me to write in English. But I think you have in your heart, understood that I am ready to help you as much as I can – to be quiet and happy in your vocation".[179]

When it comes to turning our gaze to Christ Jesus, the invitation of the Mother is insistent. She invites her daughters to have only Jesus as the sole and constant model of life; without stopping to look at themselves, and without closing themselves up in their own limitations:

> "Do you think a bit too much of your mistakes, my dear little daughter, and under this impression you fall back on yourself and you concentrate in a vague fear and anxiety. Try not to scrutinise yourself so much, my good daughter; immerse yourself in the merciful love of God. [ …] Think of him, love him, strive to do everything for him, and little by little, he will attenuate your failures and put in their place in your soul the virtues that he loves. May you always desire to imitate this Divine Model who has said to

[178] H-15H-142, Mère Myriam.
[179] H- 15H-159, Mère Marie Emmanuel.

us through his word and example: "always do what pleases my Father".[180]

It is precisely in the footsteps of Christ that complete adhering to the fulfilment of God's will is sought after and accomplished as the only satisfaction and joy:

"My very dear daughter,
May the holy and adorable will of God be our only satisfaction and joy! In this will we are assured of finding the true good, that alone is able to satisfy our love. Everything else merits not even a desire, nor any regret. Never forget this".[181]

Discipleship of Christ becomes intensified especially in moments of suffering and pain, in which the Mother continually encouraged her daughters to feel particularly united to the sufferings of Christ and to understand that not only is this a privilege of grace, but that Christ himself still takes up the cross, our cross, continuing his Calvary for the sanctification of our souls:

"Abandon yourself to this agony, in union with Jesus in the Garden of Olives, on the Cross. He himself, God, willed to work in his Holy Humanity, to suffer because of our sins, the weariness, the fear, the disgust, the horror. Is it not a predilection to be chosen to suffer these same weaknesses! Rejoice therefore, my daughter, to have such a participation in the Passion of Our Lord, bear humbly and

---

[180] H-15H-173, Mère Marie Claire.

[181] H-15H-133, Mère Myriam. Similar thoughts are found when the Mother writes to Mère Hélène, reaffirming that her sole intention is to lead her daughter to do the will of God in H-15H-121, Mère Hélène: "Maternally I come to you to help you prepare your heart to accept and carry out the will of God".

valiantly this ordeal that will purify you like fire [...] in infirmity, in weakness, in incapacity, there is a new life, a life in Christ, renouncing what pleases you as nothing, aspiring to please him, through your resignation, your submission, a total abandonment and a filial trust and without limits, in him. Let nature physical and moral, cry out whatever it will. But subdue it through the humble contrition of your sins, the firmness of your faith and sure hope that he wants to, and is doing everything for your greatest good. Therefore abide in peace, my beloved daughter. I see you climbing your Calvary – Jesus climbs it with you, even if you cannot see him nor feel him".[182]

The Mother then invited her daughters to allow themselves be led by God, adoring the Sacred Heart of Jesus who will transform the soul of his faithful ones:

"I thank the Lord for the transformation that he has effected in you little by little, and that I have witnessed. Tomorrow, the feast of the Transfiguration, I will pray our resplendent Saviour to make his love sparkle so radiantly in your heart that you no longer will be able to live except only for him, to love him, to adore him, to unite yourself always to his Divine Heart who will transform you into his image".[183]

Courage, confidence and patience[184] are the terms that are repeated in the writings of this Mother, eager that her

[182] H-15H-069, Mère Dominica.
[183] H-15H-187, Mère Rose.
[184] Cf. H-15H-070, Mère Dominica: "Take courage, patience and trust. Remember how much Our Lord had continuously to work hard forming his apostles [...] and it finally made of saints and martyrs of them". See also in H-15H-124, Mère Hélène: "I would like to respond as much as I can to your filial trust [...] encouraging you to have patience

daughters should be formed and should help one another, united in the one ideal: to adore Jesus Christ in the Eucharist.

A Mother, as she herself says, loves her daughters with "a mother's heart that thinks of you frequently, and recommends you so often to Jesus".[185] Indeed, as a Mother her prayer is ever active even when she could not write letters, and she herself was inactive; she was constant in prayer, ever concerned, resourceful in ideas and reflections, abandoned and trusting in the Heart of Jesus:

> "You know how much from afar I take part in all your anxieties and I pray to the Sacred Heart to help you bear them and to reward you with the best thanks".[186]

> "In prayer I offer to Jesus your soul, your spirit, your heart, your entire life".[187]

---

[...] take courage, confidence and patience"; or in H-15H-202, Mère Marie: "Have then, courage and confidence. But do not sink into sadness and moaning".

[185] H-15H-100, Mère Eucaristie.

[186] H-15H-082, Mère Gertrude. See also in H-15H-080, Mere Gertrude: "I pray for you to the Sacred Heart. I ask him to help you and strengthen you and give you light and courage in the face of the difficulties that you will meet and that your delicate conscience makes more arduous". Or still in H-15H-085, Mère Gertrude: "I pray for you every day and I have full confidence that the Sacred Heart will help you in your office and also strengthen your health". See also in H-15H-101, Mère Eucharistie: "As you pray for us, we do the same for you, quite often".

[187] H-15H-119, Mère Hélène. See in H-15H-163, Sisters of Royston: "If I could write everything that in my prayers today I have offered as consolation for you, you would bless the Lord and his tender love for you which has brought me so much joy". And yet particularly significant is the letter H-15H-173, Mère Marie Claire: "Being prevented from writing, I am committed with all my heart to pray for you all and for you, in particular, my very dear daughter, for I see both your good and serious voca-

The Mother was always grateful for the letters that her daughters sent her and, even apologised when she was not always able to respond, inviting them, especially when they had difficult moments, to write "every day".[188]

Adèle's style of concluding letters is significant. After having encouraged, exhorted and guided her daughters toward God, she takes her leave of them mostly by greeting them with an affectionate, simple and heartfelt sense of belonging to her disciples, defining herself as "Your loving mother", Mère Marie de Saint Pierre.

### 3.3.2. *Her Support of Those Who are at the Point of Death*

The spirituality of the Mother is so profound and transcendent, that she is not afraid to accompany people even in the most difficult moments, when their lives are now coming to an end, when we perceive inexorably that their hours are numbered, when they are living their last moments. In fact, in the presence of those who are at the point of death, words for the most part are stilled in a silence and it seems we are incapable of counselling or leading toward God the one who is suffering. The Mother, on the contrary, strong in her abandonment to God and her personal experience of pain, was enabled by faith, to support and encourage, with words full of hope, whosoever found himself in extreme suffering. Her spiritual counsels were efficacious in leading the

tion and the fears or discouragement that make you sad sometimes and I pray earnestly that our good Master would lift you up and gladden your heart".

[188] H-15H-128, Mère Hélène: "Here, every day, we await a letter from you". See also in H-15H-136, Mère Myriam: "Send me your news every day [ …] a postcard is enough, when there is nothing special".

soul to find a christian identity in suffering, in which also the preparation for death became an experience of grace.

The first person that the Mother so accompanied to the eternal meeting with God was her father, Nicolas Garnier, for whom, since the day of her first communion, she had offered her life to God in exchange for his conversion.[189] This accompanying was in fact, only a few words, but carried out with so much spiritual care, counselling him to take care of his soul, which for a long time had neglected God. Thanks to her attention and loving care and the constant commitment of her sisters, their father accepted the visits of their priest, Père Bizanard. When the situation worsened, the day before his death her father made his confession, and received Holy Communion, and also participated in the rite of the Anointing of the Sick. His christian attitude in the face of his imminent death was a source of great comfort and gratitude to Adèle, happy that the soul of her father had been prepared for the meeting with God:

> "In the midst of our sorrow, how much I gave thanks to God, whose mercy had finally so touched this soul estranged for so many years. I thought within myself that the return of this soul so dear, for which I had offered my life on the day of my first communion, had now been granted after so many years, on the day of the anniversary, 19 May; and I blessed God for this great consolation".[190]

Nicholas Garnier died the next day, 20 May, 1881.

---

[189] Cf. H-15C-196, Père Balme: "Then on 19 May, 1850, I made my First Communion begging Our Lord to let me die that day and to grant the conversion of my father who was far from his duties as a christian".

[190] H-15D-011, Abbé Courtois.

Another person very close to the Mother, who was accompanied to the meeting with God was Sister Cecilia. Sister Cecilia was clothed with the religious habit on 20 November, 1902, at Tyburn, along with Sister Hildegarde and Sister Genevieve.[191] She placed in the hands of Sister Marie Agnes her offering and her consecration as a victim to God for the salvation of souls, for the Church, the Holy Father, and for Priests.[192] Sadly just six months later she fell gravely infirm, so seriously that she was constrained to remain in bed for long periods.[193] In the early days of June 1903, since her health was always precarious, with acute pain, she received the Anointing of the Sick.[194] Already at the end of the same month the doctors warned that there was nothing further that they could do for her.[195] Mother Adèle remained always close to her daughter, imparting courage to her. In the last few minutes of her life such was Sister Cecilia's faith in God that she had no fear in preparing for a good death, renewing her offering as Victim to the Lord:

> "Half an hour before her death, since she seemed to be fully conscious, I read for her the act of offering as a victim to the Lord, with a loud voice, slowly, and she manifested sufficiently by the expression of her face that she ratified it and united herself with it. For us it was deeply moving, this first! Thus accepted! She gave her last sigh, just as I spoke aloud this prayer: *'Wound of the Heart of Jesus, open now to receive this soul'".*[196]

---

[191] Cf. H-15C-172, Abbé Sauvè.
[192] Cf. H-15E-034, Monsieur Charles Michel.
[193] Cf. H-15F-028, Père Vasseur.
[194] Cf. H-15E-029, Monsieur Charles Michel.
[195] Cf. H-15E-031, Monsieur Charles Michel.
[196] H-15E-034, Monsieur Charles Michel.

In the presence of a soul with such suffering, there was not despair, nor anguish, but the awareness of living moments of grace and of an offering made, to enter worthily into the eternity of God, abandoning herself definitively to him.

Sister Cecilia died on 10 August, 1903, after great sufferings[197] and on 10 October, 1904 her mortal remains were translated to the Cemetery of San Vincenzo at Montmartre.[198]

But the spiritual accompaniment even more detailed and intense, as we find in her letters, was what the Mother undertook with Monsieur Charles Michel. He was very close to the Congregation and toward him Mother Adèle had such confidence that she not only gave him the management of their material goods as administrator of their house at Montmartre, but foresaw also of having the opportunity of forming together with him the Society for the Sacred Heart.[199]

A few months after the Mother, together with her daughters, left Montmartre, Monsieur Charles Michel her friend and supporter began a prolonged Calvary. In fact, already on 29 November, 1901, Adèle wrote a letter full of apprehension, confirming her entire spiritual solidarity with him to emphasise that he needed to entrust himself to God, with "the surrender of what is most active in ourselves":[200]

> "I feel everything that you are suffering under those repeated blows. But I feel no less this depth of love and abandonment that makes you immerse yourself in God more and more, giving and sacrificing everything and

[197] Cf. H-15E-053, Monsieur Charles Michel.
[198] Cf. H-15F-161, Père Lémius and H-15E-060, Monsieur Charles Michel.
[199] Cf. H-15E-095, Monsieur Charles Michel.
[200] H-15E-016, Monsieur Charles Michel.

despoiling yourself of everything for his sake, so as to live only for him! Dear friend, this is the true life, this is the secret of heaven brought down to earth! He will give what is needed to achieve his plans. But first of all, what must be required by him is the entire handing over of ourselves to him, the renunciation of that which is most active in ourselves. I do not know if you feel this – but I believe it firmly, as this renunciation and this detachment impart freedom to the soul, while at the same time assuring it that it must then live for Jesus alone because it is he who has made it enter and then walk along this way".[201]

Slowly the Mother led her friend toward reflection on the path of abandonment, giving the testimony of her own experience. Self-abandonment to God, throughout various sufferings of our life, even the most terrible, allows us to feel, despite appearances, the hand of God leading us; it predisposes us to know how to recognise gently the joy of letting ourselves be led entirely by Him, the only one capable of consoling us and guiding us "according to his ways":[202]

> "I find that the way of abandonment is at the same time the most terrible and the most consoling. It is the most terrible because Our Lord is strewing fearsome crosses, of dangers that return unceasingly and the path always seems to lack solidity. And at the same time, we feel that the hand that sustains us, the heart that encourages us belong to this gentle Master who is so eager to undertake guiding us himself. When we look back and see the path, we remember trembling, past torments, our heart is moved at seeing everything that the Lord Jesus has done

---

[201] *Ibidem.*
[202] H-15E-044, Monsieur Charles Michel.

for those who only want to live for him and who abandon themselves to his guidance. All the events that arise, looked at from the human point of view and even very reasonably, presage consequences which, dreadfully, we must take into account. But the Lord is there, he watches over and leads mankind and arranges everything according to his plans".[203]

Mother Adèle was always attentive to follow her friend, letting him feel all her companionship. She suffered increasingly on account of his illness, even to telling him that "I suffered greatly in knowing that again you are suffering even more".[204] In this help and sharing of life and of suffering, the Mother came, therefore, spontaneously to make a comparison with her own personal experience, where for ten years she had lived in an extremely uncertain and precarious state of health,[205] and she herself refers to this in order to encourage him and show him all her understanding:

[203] *Ibidem.*

[204] The same terminology is used by the Mother in the letters that follow and which show this suffering of increasing deteriorating health of Monsieur Charles Michel. In fact in the letter of 22 January, 1904 she expresses this, in H-15E-044, Monsieur Charles Michel: On 19 October, 1904 she adds in H-15E-060, Monsieur Charles Michel: "I feel deep sorrow knowing you are so suffering". By 10 June, 1905, already her own words are more intense, in H-15E-068, Monsieur Charles Michel: "It is a very great sorrow for me to know you are suffering so much"; then, when the situation is worse, on 21 October, 1905 the Mother writes, in H-15E-075, Monsieur Charles Michel: "I am very sorrowful to learn that the progress in your state of health has not continued".; On 1 February, 1906 she resumed in H-15E-080, Monsieur Charles Michel: "I am suffering greatly to learn that you have had again more suffering".

[205] Cf. H-15E-067, Monsieur Charles Michel: "So often I compare your physical and spiritual state to what I went through in the last few years I

"Take courage! [...] I do understand, I know from experience, having spent ten years in a state worse than yours. [...] I suffered sometimes very long periods of sadness and terrible discouragement. Everything was black and dark; I felt no consolation in my suffering and during long months I could only resign myself saying no other prayer than that of the *Pater*. These years were without walking, without reading, without any occupation – this time was so painful! I regard it as a preparation for the life that was reserved for me at the end of my existence. Then if someone had told me that I would return to a state of being able to work for many years, I would have proclaimed it to be a miracle".[206]

Mother Adèle did everything she could to find time to write and to make Mr Michel feel her companionship, in spite of her various commitments and many occupations.[207] Together they certainly prayed for an improvement in his state of health, but even more than that, to be able to do the will of God, to rely on the salvific designs of the Sacred Heart, saying, "not only *Fiat*, but an *Amen* full of love and gratitude":[208]

spent in the world". See also H-15E-086: "During ten years my state of health was truly frightful, desperate and was considered incurable by competent doctors".

[206] H-15E-092, Monsieur Charles Michel.

[207] Cf. H-15E-044, Monsieur Charles Michel: "If you knew what variety of duties and cares devour my days. It is incredible"; then still in H-15E-056, Monsieur Charles Michel: "In my desire and my hope to write to you, I finally took a sheet of paper and I closed my door, because I am sorry only to write promises of letters, without ever writing them. Finally! You understand that my silence does not depend on me and you always excuse! ".

[208] H-15E-056, Monsieur Charles Michel. See also in H-15E-071, Monsieur Charles Michel: "I am very moved by your letter and you can well

184

"I believe that we should desire to do a great deal of work for the Sacred Heart, and if we lack the health, let us ask, and try to obtain it. If Jesus does not want it, he will show it by the ineffectiveness of the treatments and He knows well that we will say not only *Fiat*, but an *Amen* full of love and gratitude".[209]

It was within this perspective of making a self-offering to the Sacred Heart and to his Good Pleasure that the Mother tried to direct her advice, so that he may feel truly "the friend of the Sacred Heart" and "a sharer in his Work", even when Monsieur Charles Michel, tired and discouraged, manifested in a disconsolate manner that he felt himself now to be totally useless:

understand that. What will the Sacred Heart do for you? It will be what the future will soon show us. But what he wants first of all, is your formal consent, absolute, full of love, supernatural joy and acceptance of all the sacrifices that He can give you. How far this will extend and to what in particular will it lead, this is his business and you must not have any anxiety, nor fear. Your acquiescence is complete, he will draw to you all the graces and first of all humble and trusting fidelity to follow all the divine lights in the measure that they will be given to you".

[209] H-15E-056, Monsieur Charles Michel. See also in H-15E-068, Monsieur Charles Michel: "It is so great, so extraordinary that the events here below, are such tiny things in comparison to the grandeur of eternal things! So, starting from this point of view, I can only thank God for everything that He sends us. But also, his tenderness invites us to pray, to beg him to obtain not only spiritual graces, but also the temporal goods useful for our sanctification, health, that we ought to employ for his glory. And it is for this reason, my dear good friend, that we do not cease to ask health for you, with the reservation that this be the Divine Good Pleasure". And again in H-15E-087, Monsieur Charles Michel: "Believe me, my very dear friend, that we are wholly united to your holy dispositions, asking that the Divine Will be done in you, in this as in all other things. Even though my desire to see you regain your health is so ardent, I only ask our Good Master, for what his love and wisdom reserve for you, because

"You are the friend of the Sacred Heart, and He has so few friends who carry the cross with Him with a good heart. We must thank him because He lets you carry it. He needs good and affectionate Cyreneans to comfort him amidst so much outrage, ingratitude, abandonment".[210]

"Therefore, if you are reduced to a state of physical and also often intellectual powerlessness, which implies an immensity of sacrifices of every kind, there is here ample reason to rejoice, my dear friend, because it is precisely so that you would be labouring in the work of the Sacred Heart. You consecrated yourself to him, giving him your heart, your body, all your being and he is taking everything to dispose of it according to his Good Pleasure, and your desire, and all your ambition".[211]

He knows what can glorify God the most and better sanctify you. But I have the fond hope that our desires are in accord with his plans".

[210] H-15E-092, Monsieur Charles Michel. See also in H-15E-085, Monsieur Charles Michel: "I ask for you abundant and precious graces from the Sacred Heart and I thank him for all those which he has poured out and never ceases to pour upon you in every way. So there is no doubt that the very painful state in which he leaves you is one of the greatest signs of his predilection. He has so moulded you to his will during this long ordeal, that now you only want to live with Him and for Him. He has brought you to this source of living water where suffering and anguish are such a sweet relief". Let us now see H-15E-097, Monsieur Charles Michel: "Since we have known you, you have become the best of brothers, and the most devoted of friends. And for the last five years you have, not only taken our place at Sacré Cœur, but you have shouldered the responsibilities, troubles, difficulties and misunderstandings of every kind out of devotedness toward us, in honour of the Sacred Heart [ …] the Sacred Heart, has set us on our path through one of his best friends with the most devoted and faithful heart we could have desired".

[211] H-15E-075, Monsieur Charles Michel. As regards the feelings of uselessness see in H-15E-083, Monsieur Charles Michel: "You told me to

The Mother knows that to bear pain is a great sacrifice, especially because it is not sustained by one's own forces, which become more and more feeble, and increasingly weak; it helps to meditate on how the acceptance of suffering is also a great act of love of God, since it is a sincere gesture, made in the privation of any other self-interest, and our test also of how much we love God with total confidence. Such love never ceased to make him feel his deepest support and deep encouragement, urging him not ever to abandon God. Mother Adèle constantly repeats, even several times in the same letter: "courage and confidence, my dear friend",[212] inviting him to see and accept his illness as a sign of predilection in God's mysterious plan:

> "In any case, my dear friend, what I know as you too know it, is that our Divine Saviour, by the cross that he keeps on your shoulders, shows you very well his predilection and that its power is with you and gives you his grace so that you can obtain its great fruits".[213]

While his illness became increasingly grave and now that he had the full awareness that his time on this earth was

ask the Sacred Heart not to let you remain on earth in the midst of almost useless things. And to whom have you told this bit of news? To us! Ah! certainly, you do such and such things for God and the least of them is not your meritorious state of suffering, privation, of dependence. Who knows everything that you will obtain through this state of abandonment to the Sacred Heart in these conditions?"

[212] H-15E-100, Monsieur Charles Michel. See also H-15E-101, Monsieur Charles Michel.

[213] H-15E-093, Monsieur Charles Michel. See also H-15E-091, Monsieur Charles Michel: "Be happy therefore, because you have the privileged gift of love that gives without ceasing since it receives without ceasing". And also compare H-15E-100, Monsieur Charles Michel: "My dear friend, we trust in

almost over, the Mother helped him to follow from the depths of his heart and right to the end, "the road to Calvary".[214] Now he not only had to embrace the Cross, but to cling to it. And her friend Charles Michel accepted this further challenge marking it with a new identity, which was emphasised by his choice of a new name: "Paul of the Cross".[215] The Mother, would accompany him to the very end, greeting and encouraging him in this new dignity, with the final words of hope that praise and thank God for the graces received:

> "Dear brother, Paul of the Cross, willing victim, full of love and tenderly united with the Divine Victim, the Lamb without blemish has been pleased to summon immediately to eternal happiness, we thank him without end for having chosen in you, the foundation stone upon which he would build the work dear to his Heart. May the divine Heart keep you in himself, in the most intimate and deepest abyss of his love and may he be praised and thanked for all the graces that he has conferred on you".[216]

God, and we know how to see as a sign of his love and his predilection the trials and sufferings that he sends us to unite us more closely to himself. These are the daily crosses, these privations, powerlessness, through which above all we can prove our love by accepting them with a good heart and with a filial abandonment". See also H-15E-109, Monsieur Charles Michel: "As you well know, the Sacred Heart loves you with a love of predilection and your prolonged trial is for you the witness that He gives you and by which He allows you to prove your love for him".

[214] H-15E-094, Monsieur Charles Michel.

[215] H-15E-095, Monsieur Charles Michel: "Already this cross was on your shoulders. You have agreed to be called Paul of the Cross and you have to continue to fully implement this beautiful name that recalls the crucifixion. Every day the cross becomes heavier for you and through it your union with Christ becomes closer, more intimate to the point that it could not become by any other way, even by that which we had imagined to be the most desirable".

[216] H-15E-110, Monsieur Charles Michel.

Finally, a moving letter also remains that the Mother wrote on 22 November, 1908, to accompany her sister Josephine who was seriously ill, drawing close to her holy death that took place a few months later on 13 February, 1909:[217]

"We are in the hands of God in death as in life, and nobody knows what will be tomorrow. But in reading (your letter) and seeing the graces that you receive, the gentle and maternal blessings that the Holy Virgin bestows on you and the profound peace which has penetrated your soul, I think with you that the day of the Lord could be close and that he is announcing it to you through this gentle glow of dawn, in which it appears to be enfolded. Reading your letter, I felt very much aware of the grace in which you are clothed, coming to touch me [...]. In recent days it has been a sacrifice not being able to be close to you at this moment. But after your dear letter I look at this deprivation as a precious grace for both of us. We would not be able to rise above the natural pain, our hearts would be broken. This is so much so that the supernatural keeps our souls in an upper region where we are more intimately united to the very Heart of Our Lord who, at this moment, fills us with far more precious favours".[218]

[217] Cf. H-15G-008, Dom Columba Marmion.
[218] H-15F-006, Josephine Garnier.

# CHAPTER IV

# THE INNER JOURNEY

## 4.1. The Fulfilment of the Divine Will

The pages that follow linger more on the inner journey of Mere Marie de Saint Pierre. God called her to begin this journey by abandoning herself to Him.

In total obedience to God, Adèle, dwelling before of the altar, in adoration, renewed the prayer which Christ taught us: "Father, may your will be done" (Mt. 6:10). And God did not abandon her, but continually made her feel "his voice", finding in her a complete readiness to listen: "Speak Lord, your servant is listening" (1 Sam. 3:9).

Her "call" was toward the Eucharist, and in the Heart of Jesus she found the place in which to remain and adore Him, who loved us infinitely and who has redeemed us with his blood, testifying that "No one has greater love than this, to lay down one's life for one's friends" (Jn 15:13).

Adèle chose to remain at the centre of this love, making a spiritual journey beginning from abandonment to God and attaining to the sanctification of her soul, since, as recalls Royo-Marin: "The perfect conformity with the will of God is one of the principal means of sanctification".[1]

---

[1] Antonio Royo-Marin, *op. cit.*, p. 937

### 4.1.1. *The Vow of Abandonment*

In the spiritual experience of Adèle numerous forms of trust in God are mentioned in her letters. Sometimes there are personal vows, at other times there are simple acts that open the soul to God, but all these she lived with intensity and fervour.[2]

The crucial experience for Adèle, which impressed on her soul the authentic spiritual attitude to welcome and strengthen the divine plan for her was her self-abandonment to God. She expressed this first of all, in the constantly renewed *Act of abandonment*,[3] that then matured definitively to become her *Vow of abandonment*.

It was her spiritual father, Abbé Courtois, who accepted the first desire of Adèle,[4] (already expressed to Père Cham-

---

[2] In Adèle's spiritual journey we find the *Vow of Chastity* that she made on 8 December, 1873, Feast of the Immaculate Conception (cf. H-15D-078, Abbé Courtois) and then there was her custom to repeat several acts invoking the Spirit of God as *acts of humility, or love or union with Jesus* (cf. H-15D-012, Abbé Courtois; then Adèle speaks to us of the *deed of donation to the Sacred Heart,* May 1887 (Cf. *Ibidem)*. In the same year June Adele writes of her experience of the *Act of Consecration to Jesus in the Eucharist* (Cf. H-15D-017, Abbé Courtois). In January 1888, she speaks of the meaning of the *Act of Consecration to the Will of God* (Cf. H-15D-061, Abbé Courtois). Again in a letter dated November 1888, she speaks to us of the *heroic Act* (cf. H-15D-074, Abbé Courtois). The *Vow of the Victim* was made on Good Friday 1893 (Cf. H-15D-099, Abbé Courtois).

[3] For example, already before she visited the Cardinal of Paris, Mons. Guibert, Adele felt drawn toward complete abandonment to God, as she writes in H-15D-005, Abbé Courtois: "During all the meditations Jesus urged me more and more, he asked me or rather he proposed to me an act of abandonment that would have led to that, without knowing whether I would be able to live it, that in poverty and oblivion, and that separated from everything, I would be absolutely faithful to his love".

[4] Cf. H-15D-014, Abbé Courtois.

bellan), and then accompanied his spiritual daughter toward the *Vow of abandonment*, made on 17 June, 1887:

"Finally, O Sacred Heart of my Jesus,
I acknowledge myself totally incapable of fulfilling this
vow without your help;
if I make it, it is because you urge me to do so,
and because I hope that you will deign to do in me
that which I cannot do myself.

The only thing that I ask you very humbly,
O Heart full of mercy and power,
is that you would never permit me to place any obstacle
nor make the least voluntary opposition
to your action or to your operations within me".[5]

The words expressed in this vow highlight the link between it and the devotion to the Sacred Heart, an aspect that will also emerge in numerous other reflections.[6]

This vow, which would cease only at the request of her confessor or spiritual father,[7] transformed the soul of Adèle, and made it ever more detached from everything and to be

---

[5] H-15D-016, Abbé Courtois.

[6] Cf. H-15D-063, Abbé Courtois : "To live for Jesus, to desire his glory and his kingdom, to pray for souls and finally to abandon myself absolutely to his Eucharistic Heart, to his love, this is my end, my sole attraction". See also in H-15D-025, Abbé Courtois : "I continue to renew frequently the donation of myself to the Heart of Jesus, both with the acts of abandonment, and by throwing him one glance or rather an upsurge of love that completely transports me into Him". See also in H-15D-026, Abbé Courtois: "And so indigent and wretched that I am, I unite myself with the Heart of Jesus in the Eucharist, abandoning myself totally to Him".

[7] Cf. H-15D-023, Abbé Courtois.

united only to God.[8] This attitude of constant abandonment promoted the work of God in such a way as to "mould her soul with the greatest ease".[9] She thus became ever more attentive and able to accept the words which God spoke through the inner voice that pervaded her soul,[10] as when she heard the words: "you have only to allow me to act, and that is why I have asked you to make the vow of abandonment".[11] In fact, it was God who had called her to fulfil it and to renew it continually, so as to grant her further experience. Her spiritual situations were changing for her in their intensity of sentiments: at times more strongly at other times less intense: "Everything seems to lead me to the same purpose: union with God, in love and abandonment".[12] So, in the soul of Adèle "love and abandonment", "heart and desire" are united with a similar significance and the same spiritual intensity, for, as noted by the Franciscan theologian Fr. Hildebrand: "Abandonment leads to the perfection of

---

[8] H-15D-019, Abbé Courtois. See also in H-15D-017, Abbé Courtois: "Ah, if you knew what a change there was in me after the vow of abandonment. It is something inconceivable, it is like a new life where suffering, joy and love are inseparable, and it makes your poor daughter live a life wholly supernatural in spite of her wretchedness and weaknesses by which she is even more bruised".

[9] H-15D-025, Abbé Courtois.

[10] Cf. H-15D-030, Abbé Courtois.

[11] H-15D-037, Abbé Courtois.

[12] H-15D-084, Abbé Courtois. See also in H-15D-076, Abbé Courtois : "For some time my state has been usually more arid than comforting. But I receive from my good Master the grace not to be affected and continue to abandon myself to him in this as in all the rest. If It pleases him to let me find only poverty and wretchedness in myself then I am content also and I only wish to come out of it to the extent that even he himself wants".

194

holy love, and at the same time allows the soul to express its love. We can affirm with reason that we must love to abandon ourselves and surrender to love. Abandonment is the most complete expression of perfect love".[13]

In this spiritual exercise Adèle arrived at such a point that Our Lord truly was "the initiator and inspirer, and at the same time, the aim of all my acts",[14] far beyond all her miseries and infidelities.

Called to eucharistic adoration, Adèle experiences also how through this way of 'abandonment her soul feels a special participation in the *interior Priesthood*:

> "The Lord made me understand that he is calling me to this interior priesthood and that this priesthood is to be the crowning of his blessings, and for this he has been preparing me for a long time. He showed me all the rending asunder and despoliation he has wrought in me for a considerable time so as to attain this. Now, he wills that I no longer be attached to anything, neither to myself nor to any creature, but to him alone. It is he who breaks my heart with an intensity which appears to me to be a martyrdom wherein his love always wins the victory. [ ...] Jesus again made me understand that his altar would be in the centre of my soul, that there he would unceasingly immolate me with himself, and that I would immolate myself by abandon".[15]

This provision was truly crucial in leading the soul of Adèle to know and do the will of God. In this regard, recalls

---

[13] P. Hildebrand, *Dictionnaire de spiritualità ascétique et mystique, doctrine et histoire*, Beauchense, Paris, 1949, Vol I, col. 10.

[14] H-15D-052, Abbé Courtois.

[15] H-15D-078, Abbé Courtois.

the theologian Royo-Marin: "Conformity with the will of God is a loving, whole and intimate submission and harmony of our will with the will of God in all that he disposes and permits. When it is perfect, it is known better under the name of Holy Abandonment to the will of God".[16] Strong in this certainty Mother Adèle desired that the path of "Holy Abandonment" should become not only the basis of her personal experience, but also that it would be reflected fully in the foundation of the new fraternity that would be formed by her according to the design of God. Planning together with her 'daughter' Alice, the future of their communion, Adèle expressly recalls this path of "Holy Abandonment":

> "Holy abandonment: what God wants, as He wants and when He wants. It is a duty to make it a reality and, for us far from being difficult to adopt, it must enter into our souls as into its home and reign there, more than by its right, but above all because of its attractiveness".[17]

This spiritual wealth was fully shared also with her friend and collaborator, Monsieur Charles Michel; Adèle recommended to him, who was seriously ill, filial submission, loving abandonment, which incomparable treasure leads to God.[18]

After many years of intensive following of Christ and of religious life the Mother confides to her spiritual father,

---

[16] Antonio Royo-Marin, *op. cit.*, p. 937.

[17] H-15H-008c, Alice Andrade. See also in H-15H-008 and Alice Andrade.

[18] Cf. H-15E-091, Monsieur Charles Michel. See the pages dedicated to the spiritual guidance that the Mother gives to her dying friend, in 3.3.2 . *The support of those who are at the point of death.*

Dom Columba Marmion, that her way was "always a serene abandonment, in a loving conformity with the good pleasure of God".[19] Her soul now had learned to live and grow in a state of serene trust in God:

> "Most Reverend Father, I would like to speak to you a little of my soul that lives always in the peace of abandonment. It seems to me that Our Lord Jesus makes my soul advance greatly in this path, detaching it increasingly from earthly things to see and do everything with purity of intention, in view of God alone".[20]

During Mother Adèle's life, she always lived intensively this abandonment, because she had requested, more than once, to accept new and painful situations, that seemingly occurred so as to open a path to embark on another like situ-

---

[19] H-15G-009, Dom Columba Marmion.

[20] H-15G-014, Dom Columba Marmion. See also in H-15G-027, Dom Columba Marmion: "And so, my Father, I feel my soul so serene, so abandoned to its God, receiving from him the grace of an invincible confidence, not to stay or to go here or there, but not to be abandoned by him, to remain faithful increasingly. In the midst of my anguish of spirit, I find my soul filled with love, I bless and adore my God, I cherish his holy Will, I know that it is infinitely perfect, I rejoice in accepting and fulfilling it if he gives me the grace, as I cannot doubt, because of his goodness. I cannot prevent the spirit of anguish, of nature, of being tormented, but what is in me belongs only to God, what he gives me by his grace is peace in his love; it seems to me that he increases and strengthens my confidence in him, as the difficulties multiply, of that, the evidence is growing. So, I never cease to thank him for such help, while all the human hope fades…My spiritual state in the midst of these temporal concerns remains that of an habitual union with Jesus, a union which seems to augment day by day and a strength that only God could give me, an "habitual elevation of my soul to him, a detachment greater than ever from all that is not himself, a total abandonment in view of glorifying him by a filial trust in his guidance".

ation. Paradoxically abandonment to God, becomes more robust, in these cases, when life choices are undertaken. From this point of view, therefore, it is possible to say that, as well as abandonment, as a spiritual dimension, the path of Adèle was strewn with "materials of abandonment", that is, by renunciation and loss of expectations, situations or places. First, in fact, Adèle had visited the novitiate at Conflans, feeling called to religious life, only to abandon that community for health reasons. With great enthusiasm she was brought to Montmartre to live in the shadow of the great Basilica, in adoration of the eucharistic Heart. But she also had to abandon this experience. Then again, once she formed the Community of Adorers of the Sacred Heart of Jesus, she was forced to abandon Montmartre once more on account of the repressive laws of the french Government. Having arrived at Tyburn, it seemed that she would have to abandon even the place of the martyrs because of enormous economic difficulties. Furthermore, as you have seen, she very much loved to write, but had to desist several times due to severe rheumatism, especially in her right hand. Finally, she who had dedicated her very existence to the adoration of the Blessed Sacrament, had to spend the last period of her life unable even to receive Holy Communion.

Her whole life was truly a state of abandonment to God, rich in grace and holiness. Certainly, when Mère Agnes had the opportunity to emphasize this, she wrote it in the letter communicating the news of Mother Adèle's death. She wrote that even Divine Providence, at the most extreme moment of her earthly existence, was pleased to call their Mother one final time to abandon herself into the arms of eternity on the day of the anniversary of her Vow of abandonment:

It is a delicate attention of the Heart of the divine Master to call her to the eternal wedding the same date as 17 June in which she had made her vow of abandonment.[21]

## 4.1.2. *The Search for the Will of God*

Since her youth Adèle had never acted on her own initiative, but, as we have had the opportunity to stress in the previous chapters,[22] she acted with the intention of always doing the will of God. She had this disposition in her dealings with her spiritual fathers. She practised moments of intense prayer and loved to let herself be led by the Holy Spirit in the favourable or unfavourable situations which Divine Providence gave her opportunity to experience. That to do the Will of God was her only desire was also the opinion of her spiritual fathers who guaranteed for her the authenticity and the possibility of choosing the Good Pleasure of God.

This strong desire to do the will of God was rooted in the attitude of abandonment. Abandonment and will combined profoundly in a single spiritual experience by which Adèle renewed her trust into the hands of the merciful God who creates, forms and saves: "Into your hands I commend my spirit: thou hast redeemed me, O Lord, faithful God" (Ps 30:6).

We can see this spiritual momentum in the firm attitude by which she rose above feelings of anxiety and anguish in the face of difficulties and relied on divine support. In so

[21] H-12-091, Mère Agnès. [citing a letter from Dom Raymond Thibaut OSB].

[22] Cf. Chapter III of this work and in particular the section *From Daughter to Mother*, in paragraph 3.1.1 . *The Spiritual Direction.*

doing she repeated the words uttered by the same Master, at the pinnacle of his own abandonment to the Father, as when he felt that his last hour had come, he prayed: "Father, if you so will, remove this cup from me! However not my will, but yours, be done" (Lk 22:42).

> "Despite my anguish I felt supported by Our Lord and I was determined to do his will, at all costs: 'My God may your will be done'".[23]

The pairing of "abandonment-will", therefore, appears to be lived by Mother Adèle with conviction and became a source of renewed strength impelling her to seek a path of holiness, feeling her own soul more and more conformed to the divine call.

God guided her toward the Mountain of the Martyrs, Montmartre in fact, to adore and pray intensely to the Sacred Heart of Jesus. But when, after years of discernment, at just 38 years of age she had to leave that place, Adèle was clearly convinced in her soul that God, who had desired her to be close to this holy hill, had then by his will taken her away again. This conviction that the necessity of leaving Montmartre emanated from God instilled into her the necessary enthusiasm to continue to praise, bless, fulfil and love his Will:

> "I left Montmartre on 13 September, 1876, after having received graces and trials in an incalculable number. I had come there by the Will of God, and have left it to obey this same adorable Will. May it always be praised, blessed, accomplished and beloved everywhere".[24]

[23] H-15D-005, Abbé Courtois.
[24] H-15D-010, Abbé Courtois.

She would pass through years of suffering on account of her delicate health and the insecurity of her vocation, with moments of terrible anguish. Despite this deep travail, when even the strength to pray was removed, Adèle revealed a significant link that united her to the Will of God. In a letter, in fact, she reminds us that if her infirmities prevented her from being able to recite the whole of the *Our Father*, the strength of her soul impelled her to repeat only: "Your will be done! It was my one and only prayer".[25] Her soul grew in humble abandonment to God, the only one able to activate in her that absolute disposition to overcome even the aridity and the absolute sense of uselessness. It was he who disposed her to pray with trust and love with strength of will:

> "My God, My God, even in the midst of my aridity of my absolute powerlessness, I see, I point out to my soul your divine operation that always disposes me to love and bless your adorable Will".[26]

At the moment when she senses that God is asking her to give herself totally to Him, to be his bride, she accepts this desire with her soul ready to correspond and return his love. She does so with the same attitude of availability shown by the Blessed Virgin Mary, ready to be "the handmaid of the Lord. Be it done to me 'according to his Will'"[27] (Lk 1:38).

In her spiritual experience Adèle understood that God

---

[25] H-15D-011, Abbé Courtois.

[26] H-15D-029, Abbé Courtois.

[27] H-15D-037, Abbé Courtois; here is the whole quote: "Then ... I cried out with all my soul, and still in the same ecstasy of bliss which was overwhelming me: 'My Jesus, what do you want of me?' Then, amid the ineffable light shining in my soul and the divine harmony gladdening it, I heard these words which made a greater impression on me than any

was calling her to a further step of profound self-abnegation; it would no longer be enough to entrust herself by the vow of abandonment. No, God was inviting her to consecrate herself to His Will:

> "of him. ... (When I awoke) ... scarcely had I begun to pray, having *offered* my prayers as usual for the Pope, the Clergy, and France, when I was interrupted in my vocal prayer (I think it was the Creed), by these words, solemn, gentle and having the formal tone of a command: *'Consecrate yourself to my Will.'* I thought I was dreaming, I was frightened for a moment, and I said: 'Lord, I consecrate myself to your holy Will, but am I not entirely consecrated to it by the vow of abandon?' Then, no longer did I hear words, but an interior invitation to keep myself at the disposal of the Divine Will. He made me say these words to him while dictating or inspiring me with them himself: *'I unite myself to Jesus and I consecrate myself to the Divine Will, for the Church, the Pope and the Clergy; I give myself with all my heart to whatever this adorable Will shall do within me or through me.'*
>
> Then, at the moment when the priest, showing the Sacred Host, says: 'Behold the Lamb of God', I made my first daily consecration to the Divine Will, with great gladness. ..."[28]

other grace has ever produced: *'To espouse you!'* ... That voice so full of majesty and love caused such a delightful wound that I thought I was going to die. I said to him: 'Lord, it is impossible! You know what I am!' But then through an interior impression that I received I understood him as saying to me: 'It is no longer the time to speak to me like that, but only of your love.' This reply removed all misgivings from me, for it made me see in the twinkling of an eye, that the love of Jesus, wishing to unite itself to a soul, could restore it to perfect purity. So I abandoned myself to him ... So adoring the designs of my God and humbling myself before him, I said to him with all my heart: 'Behold the handmaid of the Lord. Let it be done to me according to your Will!'...

[28] H-15D-060, Abbé Courtois

Adèle was aware, furthermore, that this new consecration must be renewed every day in front of the Blessed Sacrament.[29] This revelation implanted in the soul of Adèle deep serenity and created the conditions for a charism which signifies the foundation of the spirituality of the Adèle's "Work". Now Adèle, without worrying about the future, focuses on this "since it only belongs to me to do the will of God".[30] And to live this fully she mapped out the conditions and the guidelines for the future Community:

> "... To live for Jesus, to desire his Kingdom, to pray for souls, and finally to abandon myself entirely to his Eucharistic Heart, to his love, such is my aim, my sole attraction ..."[31]

To do the Will of God meant for Adèle to remain united to Christ, who obedient to the Father, always fulfilled his will. His greatest expression of conformity to God is his sacrifice on the altar of the eucharist and on the Cross. Adèle thus offers herself in the state of Victim, living in "an ever more intimate union [ ...] sacrificing myself at every moment with Jesus"[32] and especially feeling herself participate in the " intimate and universal Priesthood"[33] of Christ, in whom, as she recalls, "the altar of Jesus would be in the centre of my soul".[34]

---

[29] Cf. *Ibidem*.
[30] H-15D-063, Abbé Courtois.
[31] *Ibidem*.
[32] H-15D-078, Abbé Courtois.
[33] *Ibidem*.
[34] *Ibidem*. We will deepen in the pages that deal with the centrality of the Eucharist this important relationship between "Cross and Eucharist", between the participation in the 'Priesthood of Christ" and the state of

Feeling herself led by the Holy Spirit, albeit through both moments of grace and moments of dryness, she experienced a new reality, a new life where she "no longer felt any will but that of the Father":[35]

> "I am in God, I live for him; his glory, his will, his kingdom and my annihilation: this is what gives me a new life in him, and no longer in my foolish and wretched person".[36]

In this new life of total self-offering and fulfilling of his Will, Adèle embraced all the sufferings as an occasion of union with Christ, who, until his death on the Cross, carried out the Will of God.[37] This new life delineating the fulfilment of the divine will, became realised completely in her new Work. In this Work, her spiritual experience would become the charism of her religious Family, in which the fulfilment of the Will of God would remain a cardinal point. Thus, writing to her 'daughter' Alexida she postulates this total abandonment to the divine will:

> "For this end, we are vowing ourselves with the whole of our soul – while waiting to be vowed through the consecration of the Church, to pray, to work, to suffer, to immolate ourselves, if it pleases God, as the poor and most

"victim" because we see in these specific points the significant 'Garnier' spirituality that reveals to us the absolute timeliness of her message. These concepts are among other things, emphasized strongly in the documents of the Second Vatican Council and also by other authors who develop these issues, such as the theologian François-Xavier Durrwell or Ratzinger himself, today our Pontiff, Benedict XVI.

[35] H-15D-084, Abbé Courtois.
[36] H-15D-095, Abbé Courtois.
[37] Cf. H-15D-108, Abbé Courtois.

unworthy little victims. Victims, that is to say, offered to God the Father in union with Our Lord the Divine Victim and through him, the High Priest. So here we are saying: O my God, we are yours, to do your Will. Grant that we may love and fulfil it in everything".[38]

In ten years Adèle truly became the Mother, the spiritual guide of the family of the Sacred Heart of Jesus, who before the altar of the Lord constantly worshipped the Lord in the Blessed Sacrament. There were great joys, but also profound sorrows; they lived sisterly community life first at Montmartre and then at Tyburn, always allowing themselves to be led by the holy will of God. Later when the Mother opened her heart to her new spiritual father, Dom Columba Marmion, she made a review of her life, making it very evident that seeking God's holy will was her only concern and her unique strength:

> "I have to say that, in the ten years that I have been a Religious, my soul, for what intimately concerns its path, has been almost without counsel. It is true that during almost all this time, I had so much work, commitments, concerns that I almost lived outside myself. However I was always sustained by the disposition the Lord maintained within me that of only wanting to seek him and his holy will and of abandoning myself totally to his Good Pleasure, accepting it with great love when I knew it, and searching for it when it was not evident".[39]

[38] H-15H-008j, Alexida. See also another epistle sent always to her friend while reflect on spirituality to pursue, in H-15H-008b, Alice: "Live from this holy Will, in the love of the Most Holy Trinity and the Holy humanity of Jesus, and in anticipation of heaven".

[39] H-15G-001, Dom Columba Marmion. See also how the attitude remained well balanced as a result, in particular in H-15G-003, Dom Columba Marmion: "I so need to abandon myself completely to the good

Enriched by this spirituality, the Mother would address the journey of her community, a task with heavy trials and responsibility, but firm in her fulfilment of his will, "moulded increasingly" to the Will of God:

> "More and more, my most reverend and dear Father, I feel in the hands of God, not only for our Congregation, but for my own soul. It seems to me that he is moulding it more and more according to his good pleasure, shaping it to his will, in such a manner that it does not feel itself in a special way unless it is on the sculptor's turn-table of self-renunciation as much as possible in order to take the whole form that Jesus is pleased to give it. I try with his grace to unite myself unceasingly to him with my whole heart to all that he sends or asks".[40]

### 4.1.3. *The Inner Voice*

Royo-Marin speaking of extraordinary mystical phenomena, in the context of locutions, says: "In themselves locutions do not enter into the normal growth of sanctifying grace, and therefore of their nature they presuppose a favour occurring gratuitously. Thus, they belong in themselves to *graces freely bestowed, gratis datae,* and when they occur we align them reductively to the prophecy. However, many of these locutions cause great good to the soul that receives them, especially those substantial ones which reproduce the good that they signify [ ...] St John of the Cross himself, severe as he was in rejecting all these species

pleasure of God, to the guidance of Jesus on my soul and my whole life, that I do not feel any other desire than that for total union that will make me live from God, for God, in God, always".

[40] H-15G-033, Dom Columba Marmion.

of extraordinary graces, did not hesitate to write about the word substantial: "Happy the soul to whom God speaks!".[41]

Mother Adèle in her great and profound spiritual experience welcomed the "divine voice". Her inner attitude, which is evident from her writings, was always docile and attentive to remain united to God, to his holy will. This capacity for meditation and interior openness gave her the ability to listen to the divine voice that was manifested both in some moments of her life, and in the spiritual steps which were decisive for her choices. This voice which imprinted itself in her soul, was "felt inwardly" during spiritual reading or during prayer or in her participation in the Mass, and also in deep spiritual moments, such as visions or ecstasy. Her experience of locutions over a period of time can be summarized in three key moments: the first includes the years ranging from 1872 to 1887; then the period from 1887 to 1888, and finally the last in 1909. Certainly this dating does not synthesise all the dialogue between the disciple Adèle and her divine Master, but they are taken from the documentation in which there remain throughout her writings, locutions shared privately with her spiritual father Abbé Courtois, as regards the first two periods and, in 1909, with Dom Columba Marmion.

In accepting this inner voice, the Mother manifests her great prudence and obedience in sharing them with her spiritual director and asking him confirmation of these messages, so as not to fall into illusion or suggestion, but remaining always anchored in her profound journey of faith, where God speaks and listens to the disciple.

[41] Antonio Royo-Marin, *op. cit.*, p. 1074.

The intent to collect and record these testimonies, already reported in other parts of this work, allows us to have a precise enough summary of her journey of faith. It also assists us to glimpse the spiritual "style" that God had in conducting the soul of his disciple to complete a journey of faith, service and holiness.

The first words that Adèle welcomed interiorly already signalled her vocation. It was in fact, toward the end of February 1872, when she read an article in the newspaper *L'Univers* that spoke of the project to build in Paris a Church dedicated to the Sacred Heart. Adèle at that moment felt strongly an inner voice that revealed to her: "It is there that I want you!";[42] this voice was accompanied by the vision of herself in adoration at the altar in front of the Blessed Sacrament.

After about two and a half years, she had the opportunity of seeing Jesus in front of her: he wished his eucharistic Heart to be the special object of the Cult at Montmartre, with the Blessed Sacrament exposed day and night, and she felt a voice saying: *"Go and find the Archbishop of Paris and speak to him!"*[43] This mission Adèle fulfilled in December of 1874.

[42] H-15D-002, Abbé Courtois.
[43] H-15D-004, Abbé Courtois. Here is the whole quote: "The thought of Montmartre always remained with me. Patienntly I waited until it pleased Jesus to show me what he willed me to do in this matter. I was occupied one evening in holy reading. It was the life of blessed Margaret Mary. ... At that moment ... I saw Jesus saying to my heart by means of a vivid light, that he willed his *Eucharistic Heart* to be the special object of the worship at Montmartre and that the Blessed Sacrament should be exposed there day and night. I felt these words very clearly pronounced as though *around* me: 'Go and find the Archbishop of Paris and speak to him.' 'Sometime after this I saw Fr Chambellan, and after hearing the details which I had given him, he thought that most probably I had received an order which I should carry

Later Adèle felt called to go out, to seize hold of the presence of God who sets out on a journey, which leads from her own will to his will, as he did with Abraham: "Go from your country to the land that I will show you" (Gn 12:1 ), with Moses: "Go back to Egypt" (Ex 4:19 ); with the great prophets Isaiah, Jeremiah and Ezekiel (Cf. Is 6:9 ; Jer 26:2 ; Ez 3:4 ) and with the minor prophets Jonah and Amos (cf. Jon 1:2 ; Am 7:15 ), and finally with all those who have been redeemed by Christ: "Go; your faith has saved you" (Lk 17:19).

Adèle continued her spiritual journey with intense prayer and a serene abandonment. On 9 June, 1887, solemnity of Corpus Christi, while she was in adoration in the Carmelite Church in Dijon, abandoning herself to the Heart of Jesus in the eucharist, she had a vision where Jesus touched her hands and when she asked him what this gesture meant, Jesus replied: *"It is for love and for works; later I will take complete possession of you!"*.[44] Through this message

out. Towards the end of November (1874) a new call made me understand that the moment had come to act. In all this I felt like a sleep walker. I hardly knew how these things were happening and being arranged. It was as though I was being led by the hand ".

[44] H-15D-014, Abbé Courtois. Here is the quote included in a broader context: "Abandoning myself anew to the Heart of Jesus in the Blessed Sacrament, I suddenly saw my heart like a vast field, untilled and unfenced. It was open to everything, like a forsaken land. At the same time I felt my hands were being bound, separately, and outstretched on a cross. I was unable to move them, it was as though they were dead. Then I saw Jesus in his Sacred Humanity his entire adorable Person an ineffable whiteness. He bent down as if on his knees on this untilled land of my heart, then he touched very lightly each of my hands. Then he carried out an activity incomprehensible to me, on the vast field of my heart. He seemed to be gathering, plucking or pulling up little things. I do not in the least know

Adèle contemplated immediately the idea that her relationship with God would be an intense one of love. Repeatedly the Mother would speak of love, the experience of love, the close presence, loving and attentive of God and her brethren. Indeed it is precisely in the love of God and one's neighbour, which consists the whole essence of the spiritual journey, of devotion, of the whole of the christian life: *"You shall love the Lord your God with all your heart, with all your soul and, with all your mind.* This is the greatest and first commandment. The second is like it: *You shall love your neighbour as yourself.* On these two commandments depend all the Law and the Prophets"* (Mt 22:37- 40).

In the letter of 23 June, 1887, addressed to her spiritual father, Adèle says that during the Mass she received another interior message: she felt Jesus say: *"I will separate you absolutely from every creature!".*[45]

---

what they were, but from all this I experienced inexpressible well-being. [...] I told you that I saw him, but it was not in the least the way one sees created beings. It is a way of seeing that belongs exclusively to the interior senses, and which is a thousand, thousand, and again a thousand times more ravishing than the most inebriating sights here below ... I was not able to see my Saviour's face, the splendour of which was like a veil between myself and him. [...] Then I asked Jesus why he had touched my hands and my heart with his divine hands. Then, I really believed that it was he himself who answered me: 'It is for love and for works; later on *I will take complete possession of you.'* [...] He does not want me to be troubled or preoccupied about doing more or undertaking who knows what thing. He himself will send the occasions when he wishes to employ me – and the evidence of this and his grace will accompany them. [...] I had not to become preoccupied about anything except to love him, and to love him always more and more, with all the tenderness, all the confidence, all the abandonment of which I was capable, that I work more for him in love than by doing greater and edifying works in the world".

[45] H-15D-018, Abbé Courtois.

On 13 September before falling asleep, on her knees beside her bed, she completed the act of abandonment; and in the solemn silence perceived the divine voice encouraging her: *"Fear nothing my well-beloved; I will raise you up and I will crown you!".*[46]

Comforted by her spiritual father, Adèle continued to welcome these divine messages with great humility and confidence. While on 10 October of that same year, she took part in the Mass she felt her Master saying: *"Do not be troubled, I will come to your aid!".*[47]

Jesus continued to call her to himself in a mystical manner and on 2 November, 1887, while Adèle kneeling at her bedside makes a further act of abandonment to God, asking of him explanations about a vision of the Holy Trinity, the divine Teacher reveals to her his intention: *"To espouse you!".*[48]

[46] H-15D-030, Abbé Courtois. Here is the whole quote included in a broader context: Before going to bed, [...]. A moment later I was on my knees making the act of abandon I began by surrendering myself to Jesus with a fullness that I did not recognise. [ ...] "My Jesus, nothing, nothing will separate me from you, I am yours, donated, abandoned, without fear, without reservation; awaiting from you the highest degree of love or the last place among those who love you. I do not know. I know nothing other than you; your joy makes me at the same time, live and makes me die. I was lost in love and overflowing with delights. Suddenly a solemn silence made itself felt within me, and Jesus said to me: 'Fear nothing, my well-beloved; I will raise you up and I will crown you.' I was in an ecstasy of happiness, without, however, understanding these words. [ ...] My spirit was carried away, ravished, torn away from myself and transported into indescribable splendours which I had never ever foreseen".

[47] H-15D-032, Abbé Courtois.

[48] H-15D-037, Abbé Courtois. Here is the whole quote included in a broader context: "I was on my knees beside my bed [ ...] I began my act of abandonment; I had so little desire and fervour that I said to my Lord: "Heart of my Jesus I offer and abandon myself entirely to you in a spirit of

The next day, during Holy Mass, at the time of Communion Adèle heard the voice of her Beloved saying: *"This is our betrothal feast ... You are to remain there, I shall come to*

obedience and of love, although I do not feel this.' [ ...] Now, my Father, I am obliged to stop a little to pray before recounting what happened because just alone to recall this grace causes me such a profound emotion that I do not know how to write it down. Oh, that the Holy Spirit would deign, that the God of light and love would guide me in this duty of obedience to you, my Father, and of gratitude to God. At the very moment that I had pronounced the words that I have just told you [ ...] I was suddenly ravished by an ineffable, indescribable sight of the most Holy Trinity! With an illumination, a splendour that I had never contemplated, and with unimaginable wonder! It was no more only my interior sight that enjoyed this blessedness! I felt that I was in contact with the Adorable Trinity! [ ...] I am unable to describe what happened, it is an ineffable mystery! My soul was as if set ablaze by her God, and such was my ecstasy that I cried out: 'My God I love you! I love you my God, I love you!' I could not restrain myself. A torrent of peace, of love, of inconceivable blessedness flooded my soul, enraptured me. [ ...] My soul was as if embraced by God and I was so overcome that I cried out, 'My God, I love you! I love you! My God I love you! I could not contain myself. A river of peace, of love, of inconceivable felicity flooded my soul, transported me. I was obliged to bury my head in my bed so as to stifle the cries that escaped from my breast, and which I could not restrain. [ ...] Then I cried out with all my soul, and still in the same ecstasy of bliss which was overwhelming me: 'My Jesus, what do you want of me?' Then, amid the ineffable light shining in my soul and the divine harmony gladdening it, I heard these words which made a greater impression on me than any other grace has ever produced: *'To espouse you!'* [ ...] That voice so full of majesty and love caused such a delightful wound that I thought I was going to die. I said to him: 'Lord, it is impossible! You know what I am!' But then through an interior impression that I received I understood him as saying to me: 'It is no longer the time to speak to me like that, but only of your love.' This reply removed all misgivings from me, for it made me see in the twinkling of an eye, that the love of Jesus, wishing to unite itself to a soul, could restore it to perfect purity. So I abandoned myself to him. [ ...] So, adoring the designs of my God and humbling myself before him, I said to him with all my heart: 'Behold the handmaid of the Lord. Let it be done to me according to your Will".

212

*visit you and I myself will prepare you to become my spouse; You have only to allow me to act, and it is for this that I have asked you to make the vow of abandonment".* [49]

After ten days, on 14 November, again during Holy Mass, while receiving Communion, Adèle felt inwardly these words: *"This is the marriage!"*.[50]

---

[49] *Ibidem.*

[50] H-15D-041, Abbé Courtois. Here is the quote included in a broader context: "While he was giving me the Sacred Host, I distinctly heard these words interiorly: *'This is the marriage'* I was troubled by this for a moment and did not dare to swallow the Sacred Host. Finally Jesus came down into me while I was returning to my place, having already forgotten the words I had heard. I bowed down humbly to adore my Saviour, when something altogether extraordinary took place within me. I tremble with happiness every time I think of it. I found myself stretched out on the cross, crucified with Jesus, and in such a way that my limbs were penetrated by the limbs of Jesus in a manner only to be grasped by experience: it was like a fusion, a transformation of myself in Jesus. My soul was lost in that of his, my whole being melted, poured out into his. Never having experienced anything like this and not knowing what was happening, I said to the Lord: 'O my God, what is happening? What are you doing?' 'I am taking possession of you, you are mine, you are my bride.' There, clearly once more, was the reply I received from Jesus. A few minutes later, as I was abandoning to him out of love, all the graces with which he was overwhelming me, it seemed to me that he said to me: 'You will again appropriate many things to yourself.' At that moment there appeared in front of me or within me, I do not know which, the face of Jesus crowned with thorns. But this sight which enraptured me, lasted no more than a flash of lightning. I immediately knelt down for the elevation. (She was making her Thanksgiving during a second Mass.) While the priest was elevating the Sacred Host, I saw Jesus once more, but as risen and all glorified yet entirely veiled by a light cloud which only allowed me to perceive him. [ ...] Then I heard again the same interior voice saying to me: 'Today I have espoused you in faith.' Many times during the past few months I have heard these words interiorly: *'I will espouse you in faith.'* But I dismissed them, not understanding them. It was then that I received as it were an assurance that a higher grace was yet

Disorientated, Adèle remained in adoration, full of fear and joy, when suddenly she felt herself stretched out on the cross, crucified with Jesus, as in a single fusion, a mystical transformation and heard Jesus explain: *"I am taking possession of you, you are mine, you are my bride! [...]. Today I have espoused you in faith"*.[51]

This spiritual state marks an important stage for the soul of Adèle: it is considered by the mystics the *ninth grade of prayer: the transforming union or spiritual marriage*. In particular Royo-Marin recalls that: "The last degree of prayer classified by the mystics is that of *transforming union with God*, also known by the name of *spiritual marriage*. It is the seventh mansion of the *interior Castle* of Santa Teresa, and is also designated by the names of *consummated union* and *deification* of the soul. It is the final degree of perfection classifiable within what can be achieved in this life and

---

reserved for me but I was not yet ready for it. The very great surprise I felt was something which made me happy. I wanted to doubt, and asked myself whether the devil could not work similar prodigies so as to lead a poor, weak ignorant soul astray. But I received what was like a sorrowful complaint from Jesus who asked me whether I doubted his power or his love, and whether he would permit the devil to deceive in such a way a soul who had abandoned itself to him. Jesus also made me see what marvellous effects all the favours he is granting me are producing in me, and that this alone ought to reassure me. Then he seemed to invite me to ask him for a proof that it really was he who was the originator of all that was happening to me. 'Lord, I beseech you to let me die of love for you!' He replied: 'Well, I will grant you this proof.' Jesus said to me: 'To die for love of me is to live for love of me. Do you not understand?' My Father, if you think that I am under an illusion, do not be afraid that I will be upset if you tell me so. I know well that my distress would not last long for nothing can prevent me from loving Jesus nor being loved by him, and all the rest is .nothing to me".

[51] *Ibidem.*

constitutes a prelude and immediate preparation for the blessed life of glory. St John of the Cross defines it: *a total transformation in the Beloved, in which both the parties cede to each other, the mutual transferring of each one's whole self-possession, with a certain consummation of loving union, in which the soul becomes divinised and God by participation, as far as possible in this life"*.[52]

Adèle continued her journey of total confidence and intense abandonment to God, willing to accept his holy will.

During a moment of prayer in the Chapel of the Good Shepherd, 29 January, 1888, after making the act of consecration to God's will, Adèle heard again the voice of Jesus say: *"I want you to be entirely holy, I will sanctify you [...] I will do whatever I want in you!"*.[53]

On 25 September, 1888, Adèle witnessing a vision, where she was suspended in a deep pit, felt God reassuring her: *"Do not be afraid, I will raise you up strongly and I myself will save you from falling!"*.[54] Already other times God had invited

---

[52] Antonio Royo-Marin, *op. cit.*, page 897.

[53] H-15D-061, Abbé Courtois.

[54] H-15D-069, Abbé Courtois. That is where the quote included in a broader context: "This morning [ ...] Before going home, I went to the Church. Scarcely had I placed myself in the presence of God when my soul felt enraptured with love and adoration at the feet of the Jésus-Hostie [ ...] I suddenly found myself as it were, suspended in a kind of circular well. It was so deep that I could neither see the bottom nor its opening. I could only see something like a light above it which drew my attention yet even so I was not able to gaze at it.

The divine might raised me gently, gently, but even so I wished to reassure myself or to recover my breath, by leaning myself on the rough places which were in the form of hooks bent back below; these appeared on every part of the inner wall of the well. The (hook) shapes were *things* and *persons*. I realised that by supporting myself I was slowing down my ascent. But at the same time when I wanted to detach myself from my

Adèle not to "have fear". This announcement further, therefore, was not only a spiritual reassurance, but the confirmation that Adèle had received the same mystical experience that the great biblical figures experienced: from Abraham, who felt the angel of the Lord, saying to him, "Fear not, Abram. I am your shield; your reward will be very great". (Gn 15:1), to his son Isaac: "I am the God of your father Abraham: fear not, for I am with you, and will bless you, and make your offspring numerous for my servant Abraham's sake" (Gen 26:24); to the prophet Isaiah: "fear not, for I am with you; do not be afraid, for I am your God. I will strengthen you, I will help you, I will uphold you with my victorious right hand" (Is 41:10), to the prophet Ezekiel: "Do not be afraid of their words" (Ez 2:6); to Mary: "Do not be afraid Mary: for you have found favour with God" (Lk 1:30), to Joseph, her husband: "Fear not Joseph to take Mary your wife" (Mt 1:20); to the apostle Peter: "Fear not, from now on, you will be fishers of men" (Lk 5:10), to the apostle Paul: "Fear not Paul" (Acts 27:24). But above all, the welcoming of the words of Christ who instructed his disciples: "Do not fear those who kill the body [ ...] rather fear him who is able to destroy both soul and body" (Mt 10:28).

supports, I felt my hands and my clothing being grasped by a certain number of persons, above all by several priests some of whom I recognised.

Other persons were attaching themselves to (my hands and clothing), and the upward movement, instead of slowing down as before, became rapidly faster. I was seized with terror, and I cried out: 'My God, draw only me alone! For I am afraid and am ready to drop!.' But with infinite gentleness giving me absolute reassurance, my God answered me *without words:* 'Do not be afraid, I will raise you up strongly, and I myself will save you from falling.'

The soul of Adèle was totally directed to doing the holy will of the divine Teacher who reassured her to continue to walk for Him without fear.

Finally, during a vision, which took place in the same year 1888, on Christmas day, Adèle felt herself transformed by the participation that Jesus gave her in his priesthood and she perceived Christ's voice saying to her: *"It is in me and through me that you live, that you give yourself, that you sacrifice yourself. Your soul is all mine, and I render it sacerdotal: offer yourself at all times with me, and offer me to my Father, with yourself"*.[55] It is pointed out here that this is a clear call to become ourselves a living offering, to accept the same invitation that the apostle Paul addressed to the Romans: "I appeal to you therefore, brethren, by the mercies of God, to offer your bodies as a living sacrifice, holy and pleasing to God; this is your spiritual worship" (Rom 12:1 ).

In Adèle's letter of the first of August 1909, she shared with her new spiritual father Dom Columba Marmion a mystical event where she heard the divine voice. With embarrassment and humility the Mother spoke to Dom Columba of her vision in which she saw her soul, united with God in the most perfect dispositions.

Contemplating the harmony and beauty of this work of God within herself, Adèle heard the Lord saying: *"Behold, this is what I can do in a soul!"*.[56]

---

[55] H-15D-081, Abbé Courtois.

[56] H-15G-015, Dom Columba Marmion. Where the quote is given in its full context: "My Father, I am somewhat embarrassed to tell you what happened this morning in my soul during Mass. [ …] Suddenly on high in a shining light I saw my soul unite itself to God, in dispositions so perfect, so conformed to the desire for God that I believed, that I would die of

## 4.2. The Eucharistic Heart

In the pages that follow we enter the heart of the "Gar-nier"spirituality: devotion to the eucharistic Heart. Starting from the centrality of the Eucharist in her christian life, the Mother felt attracted to the adoration and dwelt there, repeating with the psalmist: "Be still before the Lord, and wait in patience" (Ps 36:7). Daughter of the 19th century who preserved and strengthened the devotion to the Sacred Heart of Jesus, Adèle received the divine revelation that impelled her to unite the devotion to the Sacred Heart, with the adoration of the Blessed Sacrament. Thus she fully accepted the invitation of her adorable Master: "Abide in my love" (Jn 15:9). It is precisely in this "abiding" that the charism of Mother Adèle is revealed, and is also the mode of receiving her vocation and the specific identity of her Work: to "Dwell in the Eucharistic Heart of Christ".

It is interesting to note how in the treaties of spirituality

happiness and admiration at the work of God. [ ...] My Father this vision only lasted a few seconds, I think, because I would not have been able to support it without dying. This that happened, this that I have seen, my Father, I am not able to tell you, and although this was much less elevated, than what I felt when I was borne away into the bosom of the Divinity where I was as if in heaven with my God. But here I was very much more moved emotionally in my nature, because it was my own soul that I saw: I was so thrilled at seeing the perfection of its dispositions at that moment, it was the grandeur, the power of the divine operation, just as the Lord said to me: 'Behold this is what I can do in a soul.' [ ...] May God not permit, my Father, that this vision, this marvel that he has shown me, would ever give me one proud thought, since it was the immensity of his power and of his goodness that so thrilled me. [ ...] My Father, disparage me if you so wish; but I feel myself to be in God to such a degree and in his hands that I will be glad of anything that you may say to me even if it is to overwhelm me with reproaches and scorn. ".

the heart of Christ is expressly united to the Eucharist in a relationship of grace and holiness. This is also unmistakably so in the spiritual experience of Mother Adèle: "Grace – recalls Royo-Marin – flows as from its single source for us, from the heart of Christ, in which resides the fullness of grace and of the divinity. Christ communicates to us the grace through the sacraments, mainly through the Eucharist, in which he gives himself to us as food of our souls".[57]

The Eucharist becomes therefore truly a unity with the Heart of Christ, with the Love of God. It is the highest expression, as the same pontiff Benedict XVI teaches, at the beginning of his Apostolic Exhortation, entitled most expressively: *Sacramentum Caritatis*: "The Sacrament of charity, the Holy Eucharist is the gift that Jesus Christ makes of himself, thus revealing to us God's infinite love for every man and woman. This wondrous sacrament makes manifest that "greater love", which impels each one of us to "give his life for his friends" (Jn 15:13). Jesus, in fact, "loved them to the end" (Jn 13:1). With this expression, the Evangelist introduces the gesture of infinite humility of Jesus: before dying on the cross for us, he tied a towel around his waist, he washes the feet of his disciples. In the same way, Jesus in the Sacrament of the eucharist continues to love us "to the end", even to the gift of his body and his blood".[58]

In the following pages it is possible to verify how, in the pierced heart of Jesus, Adèle discovered the greatness of the paschal mystery: Adèle embraces the cross, the sign of the highest gift of Christ immolated for the salvation of the

[57] Antonio Royo-Marin, *op. cit.*, page 540.
[58] Benedetto XVI, *Sacramentum Caritatis*, Libreria Editrice Vaticana, Città del Vaticano, 2007, n. 1.

world. This spiritual attitude is found in modern theology, both with the then theologian Ratzinger, and especially with Durwell, who presents a theology "entirely centred on the paschal mystery, and more precisely on its salvific dimension":[59] "The pierced heart of Jesus – writes the theologian Ratzinger – ... opening itself saves the world. This transformation of the opened heart, reveals the paschal mystery. This heart saves, certainly, but saves by its utter self-giving".[60]

### 4.2.1. *The Centrality of the Eucharist*

"From the age of 20 years or so I have always had a great devotion to the Holy Mass; but it has become like the sun of my life and my joy and my intense happiness for about 40 years. I assisted at the Mass in a large church of a small town. It was during the week, and there were some people. The priest, whom I knew only by sight, was sickly and seemed rather indifferent. At the *Orate Fratres*, I raised my eyes, and I saw Our Lord in place of the priest. He wore the vestments, the white chasuble and had turned toward the people and said very clearly in a loud voice, – and what a voice! – The *Orate Fratres*, but in french, which I still cannot explain. Then, the emotion, the joy that filled my soul made me understand the Mass with an intensity of fervour that I had never had. From that day I cannot express what the Holy Mass is for me and my joy each day assisting at it. And this remembrance so often renewed in my memory and in my heart makes me ever more united to the Holy Sacrifice".[61]

[59] Réal Tremblay, *François-Xavier Durwell, theologian of the Pasqua di Cristo*, Lateran University Press, Città del Vaticano, 2010, p. 8.
[60] Joseph Ratzinger, *Guardare al Crocifisso*, Jaca Book, Milano, 1992, p. 61.
[61] H-15G-003, Dom Columba Marmion.

With these words, written to Dom Columba Marmion, in her letter of 4 November, 1908, the Mother reveals the epitome of her eucharistic spirituality, in which it is possible to highlight two fundamental aspects.

In the first place her own "great devotion" to the Holy Mass, matured from the age of 20 years, and became "like the sun of my life". Also in other circumstances Adèle would express the same concept,[62] such as when addressing her assistant, Monsieur Charles Michel, she confided: "The Mass is for me the sun of my life, the heaven of my soul here on earth".[63] For Adèle the Eucharist not only illumined her life, but unquestionably became the centre of her soul: "Jesus made me understand that his altar would be in the centre of my soul".[64] This message is particularly timely in the light of the apostolic exhortation, in which repeatedly the Holy Father, Benedict XVI stressed: "the holy Eucharist, then, brings to its fullness the christian initiation and represents the centre and end of all sacramental life".[65]

The eucharistic devotion for Adèle expressed itself in an increasing manner, that stimulated and motivated her to participate in daily Mass, so that the Mass became truly the stable focus of her spirituality, a meeting with life. In fact, when, because of her physical weakness, she was not be able to move freely and was accompanied to Lourdes, on the day

[62] Cf. H-15G-038, Dom Columba Marmion: "The Mass always remains the heaven of my life and the source of everything I need".

[63] H-15E-085, Monsieur Charles Michel.

[64] H-15D-078, Abbé Courtois.

[65] Benedict XVI, *op. cit.*, n. 17. See This same centrality of the Mass is also reflected in the following numbers: 2, 12, 27, 64a, 94 and 95. It includes as well the entire exhortation which would definitely bring the Eucharist to the centre of christian life.

of the Assumption in 1877, the grace she asked from our heavenly Mother, was not to be healed, but to be "strong enough to be able to go to Mass and Holy Communion every day".[66]

Mother Adèle participated assiduously at Holy Mass, with a lively fervour, with a preparation and a constant attention, and with the frequent renewal, both at the beginning and during the Mass, of spiritual acts, so that she could be disposed in the best way to live with devotion, the Sacrament of the Eucharist:

> "This morning, at the Mass, before Holy Communion, I renewed repeatedly the acts of abandon which you[67] have told to me to make, then of the acts of humility and above all the acts of love and of union with Jesus".[68]

During the times that she was infirm, especially in some periods because of her rheumatic pains or in the last years of her life, although she was obliged to renounce participating in the Holy Mass, she asked however, to be able to receive always Holy Communion.

This great eucharistic devotion consistently expressed Mother Adèle's profound prayer to God, during which on numerous occasions, she experienced it as being entwined in an upsurge of trinitarian love. She was the humble hand-

---

[66] H-15D-011, Abbé Courtois.

[67] By "you" Adele means her spiritual father l'Abbé Courtois.

[68] H-15D-012, Abbé Courtois. See also in H-15D-017, Abbé Courtois : "This morning [ …] I went to Mass and I was preparing to renew my act of consecration to Jesus in the Eucharist". See also H-15G,005, Dom Columba Marmion: "During the Mass I made my acts of preparation as usual at the beginning of the Mass".

maid who contemplated the gift of the Holy Trinity in the Eucharist:

> "After Communion, I do not know what happened but I thought I had within me, with Jesus, the Holy Spirit all sparkling with light, all afire with love [...]I felt the presence of the Holy Spirit like that of Jesus and through Him I really adored the Father, I adored Jesus and I adored the Spirit himself with an interior fervour that I cannot express! But all this with calm and an ineffable peace [...] Yet I contemplated distinctly the activity within me of each of the Persons of the Holy Trinity".[69]

This same attitude of Trinitarian love was greatly emphasized by the Holy Father, Benedict XVI, which he stresses as: " In the Eucharist is revealed the plan of love that guides the entire history of salvation (cf. Eph 1.10 ; 3.8 - 11). In it the *Deus Trinitas*, who in himself is love (1 Jn 4.7 -8), is fully involved with our human condition. Christ gives himself to us in the paschal Supper under the appearances of bread and wine (cf Lk 22:14-20; 1Cor 11:23-26), and he becomes the whole divine life which reaches us and shares himself with us in the sacramental form. God is perfect communion of love between the Father and the Son and the Holy Spirit".[70]

The second important aspect of the "Garnier" eucharistic spirituality is represented by the *"Orate Fratres"*, decisive call to prayer, which for Mother Adèle is an intense prayer, implicating, that *"my and your sacrifice be pleasing to God"*. This invitation assumes a powerful spiritual significance

---

[69] H-15D-012, Abbé Courtois.
[70] Benedict XVI, *op. cit.* , n. 8.

223

above all if one considers that Adèle perceives it directly from the voice of Christ. It is a sacrifice "my and your", of Christ and of his worshippers. In the commitment to be "pleasing to God" a reciprocity is revealed that allows God to renew the soul of his children, to unite them more deeply and completely with himself. Adèle captures in her own person the abundant fruits of this "intimate union with the immolation of Jesus on the Holy altar which remains always the attraction of my soul, which for the rest rejoices in this union often without looking for it".[71]

Since she was young Adèle stressed that: "during the Mass [...] I received great graces of union with Our Lord".[72] In truth her eucharistic experience enriched her with great graces. It was during the eucharist that she sensed the divine voice, with which God communicated his will to her.[73]

---

[71] H-15D-079, Abbé Courtois.

[72] H-15D-010, Abbé Courtois. Later, eleven years after, in the letter of 19 June, 1887, she writes in H-15D-017, Abbé Courtois: "This morning, [...] I went to Mass and I was preparing to renew my act of consecration to the Eucharistic Jesus; my soul was in the greatest calm, but I could not pray, but I only felt myself powerless and abandoned to his heart. At the Holy Table, a moment before Our Lord came to me (in Communion), I sensed a gentle heat in the surrounding air and when I had received him it was like a fire within me, but in an unspeakable calm [ ...] I offered myself to him without reserve [...]. After a moment Jesus accorded to my soul for the first time in my life a kind of ineffable union that I cannot define".

[73] Cf. H-15D-037, Abbé Courtois: "At the time of the Holy Communion, at the moment of moving forward to the Holy Table, [ ...] I felt so absorbed by the desire to receive Jesus with a pure heart, that I thought I was with our Blessed Lady, and I cannot say why. At the very moment the priest gave me Jesus, I sensed the voice of my Beloved saying to me: "This is our betrothal feast". I no longer knew what to think"; see also in H-

224

Yet again, during the celebration of Holy Mass Adèle experienced spiritual visions, which instilled into her soul "a calm and ineffable peace"[74] and she prayed according to the intentions of the Holy Spirit. The climax of this vision, lived with great humility and gratitude, was a description of

15D-041, Abbé Courtois: "While he was giving me the Sacred Host, I distinctly understood these words interiorly: '*This is the marriage.*' I was troubled by this for a moment and did not dare to swallow the Sacred Host. Finally Jesus came down into me while I was returning to my place, having already forgotten the words I had understood. I bowed down humbly to adore my Saviour, when something altogether extraordinary took place within me. I tremble with happiness every time I think of it.

I found myself stretched out on the cross, crucified with Jesus, and in such a way that my limbs were penetrated by the limbs of Jesus in a manner only to be grasped by experience: it was like a fusion, a transformation of myself in Jesus. My soul was lost in that of his, my whole being melted, poured out into his.

Never having experienced anything like this and not knowing what was happening, I said to the Lord: 'O my God, what is happening? What are you doing?' 'I am taking possession of you, you are mine, you are my bride.'".

[74] H-15D-012, Abbé Courtois. See also other descriptions of visions that occurred during the participation in the Mass and described to her spiritual father, in H-15G-015, Dom Columba Marmion: "My Father, I am somewhat embarrassed to tell you what happened this morning in my soul during Mass. [ ...] Suddenly on high in a shining light I saw my soul unite itself to God, in dispositions so perfect, so conformed to the desire for God that I believed I would die of happiness and admiration at the work of God. [ ...] My Father this vision only lasted a few seconds, I think, because I would not have been able to support it without dying. This that happened, this that I have seen, my Father, I am not able to tell you, and yet this was much less elevated than what I felt when I was borne away into the bosom of the Divinity where I was as if in heaven with my God. But here I was very much more moved emotionally in my nature, because it was my own soul that I saw: I was so thrilled at seeing the perfection of its dispositions at that moment, it was the grandeur, the power of the divine operation".

the Host stained with blood, that Adèle refers in obedience to her spiritual father, Abbe Courtois[75] and shares with her priest-friend, l'Abbé Sauvé:

> "During the consecration and the elevation, the union of my soul with Jesus was great although I was not in an extraordinary state as often happens to me. At the moment in which the priest took a particle of the Holy Host and put it into the chalice I raised my eyes to adore and to contemplate the holy particle. Oh, if you could know what I saw and how I am still moved and impressed by this vision. The fingers of the priest held not a white particle, but a particle of a striking red, the colour of blood and luminous at the same time. [...] The fingers of the priest were red on the right of the particle, as from a blood stain that seemed still wet. [...] I cannot explain to you the wonderful prodigy that came mightily upon me. [...] Then my eyes closed under an impression of profound reverence".[76]

---

[75] For a description of this spiritual experience see also H-15D-076, Abbé Courtois: "throughout the Mass I felt very united to Jesus, especially during the consecration and the elevation, but I did not feel myself to be in a state of extraordinary contemplation. When the priest took a particle of the host that must put into the chalice, I raised my eyes to the side of the altar to adore the holy Particle as I do sometimes. But what a thrill of emotion when I saw this particle completely and entirely red blood! A vivid colour and rich like fresh blood and vermilion. It was at the same time luminous. More, the forefinger on which it dropped was slightly red and damp with blood on the small space [ ...] I found myself as if petrified. Then I lowered my eyes in most profound reverence. [ ...] I do not give much attention to this event and all other spiritual experiences are much more far-reaching for my soul than this event. Now I feel an ardent and continual love and desire to abandon myself more and more to Jesus in the eucharist, to his eucharistic heart".

[76] H-15C-144, Abbé Sauvé.

226

It was around the eucharistic Sacrifice that Adèle gradually developed her vocation. She felt that God had placed within her this deep desire for recollection and divine union with Christ who offers himself to the Father and experienced his call to become a victim, in intimate participation in the Priesthood of Christ. This would be the focus of her vocation and the charism of The Work:

"As I was plunged in the most profound recollection, uniting myself to the Divine Victim for the glory of his Father, I felt myself in the inmost depths of my soul, penetrated by the presence of Jesus within me. He let me hear words (in a language other than ours), which ravished me with love and bliss. He promised me an ever increasing intimate union with his immolation – a continuous participation, if I so wished, in the adorable Sacrifice continually offered.

He made me understand that there is an intimate and universal priesthood, absolutely and necessarily united to his, which should be the portion of all souls, but which is so of only very few. This priesthood is wholly interior, and is only granted to a soul who consents to it, who has desired it, and who to obtain it wills to immolate itself at all times with Jesus; that even so, in reality it is not the soul who immolates itself but Jesus who immolates it with himself. But as the soul wills to be immolated and abandons itself for that purpose, Jesus makes it participate in his state of victim and priesthood at one and the same time. He consecrates [...] and ordains it to an interior priesthood which conforms it to his Eucharistic life more than any other gift it has received. This priesthood communicates to the soul a far more perfect grace of union in view of being immolated to the glory of God, thereby rendering infinite honour to God the Father, since it is no longer separated from the Divine Lamb.

The Lord made me understand that he is calling me to this

227

interior priesthood and that this priesthood is to be the crowning of his blessings, and for this he has been preparing me for a long time. He showed me all the rending asunder and the despoliation he has wrought in me for a considerable time so as to attain this. Now, he wills that I no longer be attached to anything, neither to myself nor to any creature, but to him alone. It is he who breaks my heart with an intensity which appears to me to be a martyrdom wherein his love always wins the victory.

Jesus seemed to say to me that at Christmas he would unite myself to him forever by this remarkable grace whose greatness dazzles me and whose tenderness floods me with ineffable delights. To be, in my soul, the priest of Jesus! How can that be? Is it not folly, extravagance! What am I to think? [...]

Jesus again made me understand that his altar would be in the centre of my soul, that there he would unceasingly immolate me with himself, and that I would immolate myself by abandon. He showed me that for this I had to attain very great purity of heart, soul, mind and body, so that the victim – who would also be priest with Jesus, would not be defiled. Then he told me of the sacrifices necessary for this: 'I will lead you to make them; love, I will give you; difficulties I will smooth out; your wretchedness will be my concern – I take it upon myself".[77]

"My and your sacrifice" thus becomes union with the sacrifice of Christ, the priest who offers himself as a victim of expiation for the salvation of the world, becoming ourselves "living sacrifice". And Adèle felt herself abandoned completely to God, ready to be united to the "holy sacri-

[77] H-15D-078, Abbé Courtois.

fice", "all purified and consumed as a victim".[78] She antici-
pates, in this way, the idea, which was developed during the
Second Vatican Council, which sees the baptized to be
"Holy People, a Chosen Race, a Royal Priesthood": "Mother
Church – reminding us of the document *Sacrosanctum Concilium* – ardently desires that all the faithful should be led to
that full, conscious and active participation in liturgical cele-
brations which is demanded by the very nature of the
Liturgy and to which the christian people as "a chosen race,
a royal priesthood, a holy nation" (1Pt 2.9 ) has the right and
the duty by virtue of Baptism".[79] In this function, recalls the
Council again in *Lumen Gentium*: "the baptized, by regenera-
tion and the union of the Holy Spirit, are consecrated to be a
spiritual house and a holy priesthood, to offer [ ...] spiritual
sacrifices".[80] The "common priesthood" and that of Christ,
the only priest, since "all the faithful form a holy and royal
priesthood, offer spiritual sacrifices to God through Jesus
Christ".[81] The faithful therefore unite themselves to the Sacrifice of Christ, being themselves *"spiritual hosts"*: this same
eucharistic attitude, of uniting themselves to the offering of
Christ on the altar, is rightly emphasized by the mystical
experience of Mother Adèle. In describing the treasures of
grace enclosed in the Eucharist she prayed that it was the
Spirit who was guiding her pen, since, as she wrote, "in
spite of the light in which I saw these things, I feel incapable
of expressing them".[82] The reflection that follows, as

---

[78] H-15C-094, Abbé Courtois.
[79] Second Vatican Ecumenical Council, *Sacrosanctum Concilium*, 14.
[80] Second Vatican Ecumenical Council, *Lumen Gentium*, 10.
[81] Second Vatican Ecumenical Council, *Presbyterorum Ordinis*, 2.
[82] H-15D-053, Abbé Courtois.

recounted in her letter of 20 December, 1887, highlights an aspect of her eucharistic vocation: she feels that Jesus wishes to attract to himself *"host-souls"*:

> The eucharistic soul becomes a host in proportion to her fidelity in receiving these graces and in corresponding to them. In certain souls Jesus acts by himself in such a way that they hardly ever decide anything, or undertake anything, or achieve anything according to their own judgement. In others he hides himself and leaves them more activity, having given them graces and lights for this which appear to be natural; for he expects labours and undertakings from them that call for the cooperation of the powers which man can dispose of himself – these must pay homage to God for them by employing these powers in his service. It is thus at the same time a natural and a supernatural fidelity that Jesus wants from these host-souls....[83]

But above all, "my and your sacrifice" becomes Mother Adèle's experience of union with the Cross of Christ, highlighting how for her the paschal mystery is offered, as a gift, death and resurrection:

> "After having received the Communion [ ...] I bowed down humbly to adore my Saviour, when something altogether extraordinary took place within me. I tremble with happiness every time I think of it. I found myself stretched out on the cross, crucified with Jesus".[84]

---

[83] H-15D-053, Abbé Courtois.
[84] H-15D-041, Abbé Courtois.

Adèle joins the eucharistic experience to the experience of the Cross; the eucharistic memorial re-evaluates the Son's death on the Cross so that it does not remain firm and isolated, but becomes a death which is an eternal memorial, realizing the eschatological dynamic that opens to the resurrection. The theologian François-Xavier Durrwell has elaborated effectively this reflection recalling: "Although the cross was the arrowhead lodged in the earth, it continues, his sacrifice rises above time, "he offered himself through the eternal Spirit" (Heb 9:14). [ ...] Christ in his glorifying death becomes the eschatological sacrifice: he is 'priest for ever in his eternal sacrifice".[85] United with the priesthood of Christ Adèle feels herself to be "Victim", taken from the world, "separated from the world". The 19 May, 1876, anniversary of her First Communion was also the day on which, for the first time, she received Communion in the Basilica of the Sacred Heart of Montmartre and on that occasion she wrote:

> "It was the anniversary of my First Communion and it was also my first Communion at Montmartre. I offered myself to Jesus without reserve, asking him to take me as a victim, either by accepting my life, as I desired, or by giving it back entirely consecrated to his Good Pleasure, without leaving anything for my own personal satisfaction. From that moment, I felt separated from the world.[86]

This state of "victimhood", which is the summit of the Garnier spirituality, reveals not only a spiritual attitude of

[85] François-Xavier Durrwell, *Lo Spirito Santo alla luce del mistero pasquale*, Paoline, Roma, 1985, pp. 58-59.
[86] H-15D-008, Abbé Courtois.

complete offering to God of her own life, but above all expresses that eucharistic attitude of participation in the self-offering of Christ. Jesus is the "everlasting" Victim and Adèle unites herself to God, consecrates herself to him, through Jesus. In this regard, summing up the thought of the theologian Durrwell, Tremblay writes: "Jesus himself is the victim by whom the veil is opened and since he penetrates only once for all through the veil of his immolated flesh (Heb 10:20 f), you can believe that the state of the victim, in virtue of which the sanctuary is opened, lasts eternally. This suggestion of the texts is confirmed by the fact that man can, if he desires holiness, meet Christ in his victim state and be conjoined with him in the very act of his entrance into God. This is what Heb 10:19 f: tells us namely, that the access road to holiness is open, not thanks to the blood of Jesus, but "in his blood". We therefore believe that Jesus is still the victim; we enter into God by means of it, as he has entered into it".[87]

Intensely living the Eucharist Mother Adèle felt the urgent need to plan the spirituality of her new community based on this aspect, as fundamental charism of their fraternal life. In one of the letters addressed to Alice, just before they met definitively at the foot of the Sacred Heart, Montmartre, she says:

> "Every morning, at Holy Mass and Holy Communion we aspire to his love, his grace, we aspire to himself to become with him the true eucharistic hosts, at the same time poor and rich, immolated and living, in which the love, the adoration intimately united to those of the Divine Victim ren-

[87] Réal Tremblay, *op. cit.*, p. 21.

der glory and thanksgiving to God for the Church and begging his Majesty to pour out more and more the treasures of his mercy and his tenderness on the Holy Father and the Clergy".[88]

In this new work the *Orate Fratres* indicates that remaining united, and praying together in the eucharistic *Sacrifice*, not only the sacrifice of the Mother, but also that of the Community of her daughters, would become a continuous and perpetual adoration, a common sacrifice that unites itself to the Sacrifice of the Martyrs, first on the heights of Montmartre and then at Tyburn.

> There is a lot of talk in London of our installation at Tyburn. Here three hundred and sixty years ago the first martyrs shed their blood for Jesus Christ, suffering terrible torture and since then no religious memorial has honoured their memory on earth [...]. And now finally, the Holy Sacrifice will be offered every day on this blessed plot of earth![89]

This is the eucharistic sacrifice united to the sacrifice of the martyrs, and the Eucharist that shines out in the places where the witnesses to the faith knew how to "offer their bodies as a living sacrifice to God" (Rom12:1). Recently the same pontiff, Benedict XVI, in the apostolic exhortation *Sacramentum Caritatis*, has wanted to highlight this close relationship between the eucharist and witness, between Paschal Mystery and martyrdom:

> "There is a witness even to the offering of one's own life, to the point of martyrdom. Throughout the history of the

---

[88] H-15H-019, Alice Andrade.
[89] H-15E-024, Monsieur Charles Michel.

Church, this has always been seen as the culmination of the new spiritual worship: 'Offer your bodies' (Rm12:1). One thinks, for example, of the account of the martyrdom of Saint Polycarp of Smyrna, a disciple of Saint John: the entire drama is described as a liturgy, with the martyr himself becoming Eucharist. We might also recall the Eucharistic imagery with which Saint Ignatius of Antioch describes his own imminent martyrdom: he sees himself as 'God's wheat' and desires to become in martyrdom 'Christ's pure bread.' The Christian who offers his life in martyrdom enters into full communion with the Pasch of Jesus Christ and thus becomes Eucharist with him".[90]

The Garnier sacrifice, born as abandonment to the will of the Father, and lived in conformity to God, develops with the adoration of the eucharist, the living source of inspiration and the foundations of the spirituality of the Work to be accomplished, finally, in an authentic way in Martyrdom. Hers was a martyrdom symbolic of the Community, for which she was called to give a voice in the first person to the witness of the martyrs, who died at Tyburn to defend their faith. Actual Martyrdom for Adèle, was that throughout her whole life she bore in her body, the experience of pain and illness, attaining then, after atrocious suffering, to Christ, her bridegroom. In the last days of her life, Adèle became the "victim" united to the Sacrifice of Christ.

### 4.2.2. *The Adoration of the Eucharist*

"Then Our Lord told me that I was to come before the Blessed Sacrament every day to renew my consecration to

---

[90] Benedict XVI, *op. cit.* , n. 85.

the Divine Will, either in a special visit or before beginning any other prayer [...]. I will see that he will do everything in me [...]. I had to be consecrated to the Church, the Pope and the Clergy".[91]

These reflections were entrusted by Mother Adèle to Abbé Courtois; after God had given her to listen to the inner voice that exhorted her to consecrate herself to his will, manifesting to her even his plan that she renew daily, in front of the Blessed Sacrament, this consecration. The eucharistic prayer, adoration of the Blessed Sacrament are profound attitudes that God had made to mature in the soul of Adèle since her youth, from the time she worked as a teacher at the family De Crochard. As already mentioned, Adèle had visited the Cardinal of Paris to refer to him a divine message which encouraged the cult of the Eucharist in the new Basilica of the Sacred Heart in Montmartre, with perpetual adoration day and night.[92] Recalling this episode Adèle writes:

"…. Montmartre, alone, under the gaze of God alone. I saw myself living near the Tabernacle of the Sacred Heart, spending as much time as possible adoring him, and only living for that, as a victim destined solely for sacrifice. All that I foresaw seemed to me to be strange, impossible, madness. But moreover, in the depths of my soul Jesus assured me that this was his Will and that he would accomplish it".[93]

---

[91] H-15D-060, Abbé Courtois.
[92] Cf. H-12-129, di Père Lémius.
[93] H-15D-005, Abbé Courtois.

235

Adèle grasped immediately in her soul the close link between the Eucharist and Eucharistic Adoration, so much so that her whole existence became involved in this perspective. Her spirituality was showing itself to be, therefore, in full harmony with the teaching of the Church, which recently has been emphasised by the Holy Father, Benedict XVI, in his Apostolic Exhortation *Sacramentum Caritatis*: "As Saint Augustine put it: *'nemo autem illam carnem manducat, nisi prius adoraverit; peccemus non adorando* – No one eats that flesh without first adoring it; we should sin were we not to adore in the Eucharist the Son of God who comes to meet us and desires to become one with us. Eucharistic adoration is simply the natural consequence of the Eucharistic celebration, which is itself the Church's supreme act of adoration. Receiving the Eucharist means adoring him whom we receive. Only in this way do we become one with him, and are given, as it were a foretaste of the beauty of the heavenly liturgy".[94]

Oftentimes during adoration Adèle showed herself to be in ecstasy during which she not only perceived the elevation of her soul toward God, but also that he himself places her soul into a state of ineffable adoration.[95] And even if her days were spent in duties, in commitments and activities,

[94] Benedict XVI, *op. cit.*, n. 66.
[95] Cf. H-15D-035, Abbé Courtois: "I felt as if I were elevated on high the same way as I have already described a few days ago, and it seems to me that a supernatural force raises my Spirit and makes me ascend by degrees. [...] I would like to tell you of the graces of contemplation, of bliss that I have been granted this morning, during two and a half hours, at different times. My God transports my soul in this state of love and ineffable adoration, to where the earth and creatures could not even appear, except in the intervals between this kind of ecstasy". See also H-15D-061, Abbé Courtois.

she always tried to find "one hour in the day to go to adore my God and to lose myself in him".[96]

For Adèle to adore and to love God, reciprocates his great love for us with adoration. For this reason sometimes in speaking of the adoration she shows an attitude of love, as once when she was absorbed in the presence of God, she noted that her soul "feels filled with love and adoration at the feet of Jesus in the eucharist".[97] For Adèle to be with Jesus and live in his presence actualised the pressing invitation of the Master to his disciples: "Abide in my love" (Jn 15:9). This same theme is recalled on several occasions by the Pope also. This was particularly so during the General Audience of 15 June, 2011, when Benedict XVI concluded his speech: "The true worship of God, then, is to give oneself to God and to men, the true adoration is love. And the true adoration of God does not destroy, but renews and transforms. Certainly, the fire of God, the fire of love burns, transforms, purifies, but precisely in this way does not destroy, but creates the truth of our being, and recreates our heart. So then, live truly by the grace of the fire of the Holy Spirit, the love of God, we are adorers in spirit and in truth".[98]

[96] H-15-063, Abbé Courtois.
[97] H-15D-069, Abbé Courtois. See also the already mentioned H-15D-035, Abbé Courtois: "My God transports my soul in this state of love and ineffable adoration ". As well as in H-15D-061, Abbé Courtois: "I remained quite a long time lost, plunged in adoration and love". Or still in H-15D-081, Abbé Courtois: "After communion I live in heaven, in a state of love and adoration". And when she counsels her friend and then sister Alice, she writes in H-15H-008m, Alice:"The Lord Jesus [ …] wants you to remain faithful loving him and adoring him".
[98] Cf. L'Osservatore Romano, Thursday, June 16, 2011, which lists the address of the Holy Father, Pope Benedict XVI, pronounced during the General Audience Wednesday, June 15, 2011.

The vocation of Mother Adèle to adore the Blessed Sacrament affected not only her life, but extended to include a community apostolate, becoming the charism of the Work of the Sisters Adorers of the Sacred Heart of Montmartre. The Sisters not only witnessed to their vocation, but initiated for the first time, on 4 July, 1901, adoration by night for women, who, unable to go to the Basilica of Montmartre, came into their chapel:

> Between Thursday 4 and Friday 5 we have inaugurated the first adoration of Dames at Montmartre. In fact someone had asked to join it at the Basilica but that is not possible. But they gave our address, "Rue de la Barre, 40, chez M. lle Garnier, who can surely help you to realise your desire".[99]

At the moment when her young religious family was likely to be separated for not succumbing to the new laws of the french Government, the Mother urged her daughters to remain united in religious life, "the foundation of our life of adoration"[100] and preferred to leave her country, her beloved France, she, who carried in her soul the fervour of the French National Vow, and went to England, so as not to lose her daughters, the Adorers of the Sacred Heart of Jesus.

From Paris to London, Mother Adèle in her Work always cherished the centrality of the Eucharist and the absolute value of the Adoration of the Blessed Sacrament, so Providence willed that she finally should come to the land of the

---

[99] H-15E-009, Monsieur Charles Michel. See also in H-15F-110, Père Lémius: "I am writing you to tell you that we are beginning the adoration by night for women. It is very moving, [ ...] in our chapel".
[100] H-15F-114, Père Lémius.

Martyrs. His humble, small and poor religious giving herself to God, called and prepared for the court of the Lord, faithful souls to love and adore him:

> At Tyburn the Sacred Heart himself comes to establish his throne of love, his eucharistic adoration on this same land! Yet we are small, poor Religious Men and women, completely new, very imperfect, very ignorant, incapable and very poor whom He has deigned to call to form and prepare his court for him.[101]

In the presence of Jesus in the Eucharist the Sisters Adorers, continue their prayer, always united to the Church, bringing before God their special intentions for the Clergy and for the Holy Father. Their intentions also include the anxieties and fears of all Nations, as well as for Mother Adèle's beloved France and for the new land, England which welcomed them, convinced that the Eucharist in itself contains a social message, in which the peoples learn to share the earthly bread from Christ who is the bread of Life for all humanity. Indeed, Benedict XVI still recalls: "The act of adoration outside Mass prolongs and intensifies all that takes place during the liturgical celebration itself. Indeed, 'only in adoration can a profound and genuine reception mature. And it is precisely this personal encounter with the Lord that then strengthens the social mission contained in the Eucharist, which seeks to break down not only the walls that separate the Lord and ourselves, but also and especially the walls that separate us from one another'".[102]

---

[101] H-15E-058, Monsieur Charles Michel.
[102] Benedict XVI, *op. cit.*, n. 66.

### 4.2.3. *The Devotion to the Sacred Heart*

Devotion to the Sacred Heart, which became widespread in the 17th century by St John Eudes (1601-1680) and, above all, by Saint Margaret Mary Alacoque (1647-1690), had a significant development in the 19th century. Many were the Congregations male and female inspired by the Sacred Heart.[103] There was a proliferation of paintings and prints

[103] Here are some **Congregations of men** which arose in the 19th century: *Brothers of the Sacred Heart,* founded in Lyons in 1821 by father Coindre for the christian education of youth. *Priests of the Sacred Heart of Jesus of Bétharram* (betharramiti), founded in 1832 at Bétharram (in the area of the Atlantic Pyrenees) from St Michel Garicoïts. Congregation of the Sacred Heart of Jesus, clerical Congregation founded by father Joseph Marie Timon David in 1844, for the assistance of youth workers. Missionaries of the Sacred Heart of Jesus, founded in 1854 at Issoudun by father Jean Jules Chevalier. Children of the Sacred Heart of Jesus, the Congregation founded in 1867 by Daniele Comboni, with missionaries active in central Africa. Priests of the Sacred Heart of Jesus, founded in 1878 in Saint-Quentin by father Leon Dehon for missionary purposes. Fraternity of Diocesan Worker Priests of the Sacred Heart of Jesus, secular institute founded in 1883 by Manuel Domingo y Sol.

Here are some **Congregations of women religious**, among which that founded by Adele Garnier, the latest of the end of the 19th century. Betlemite Daughters of the Sacred Heart, founded in Guatemala in 1668 and restored by Encarnacion Rosal in the 19th century. Society of the Sacred Heart of Jesus, founded in 1800 by Saint Madeline Sophie Barat, for the education of youth. Daughters of Charity of the Sacred Heart of Jesus, which arose in 1823 in La Salle-de-Vihiers. Daughters of the Sacred Heart of Jesus founded in Bergamo in 1831 by Teresa Eustochio Verzeri. Teaching Sisters of St Dorothy, daughters of the Sacred Hearts, based in Vicenza in 1836 by Giovanni Antonio Farina. Franciscan Missionary Sisters of the Sacred Heart, founded in Gemona del Friuli in 1861 by Mother Josefa of Jesus. Sisters of Saint Joseph of the Sacred Heart of Jesus, founded in 1866 in Australia by Mary MacKillop. Handmaids of the Sacred Heart, founded in Naples by Caterina Volpicelli the December 27, 1867. Daughters of the Heart of Jesus, cloistered nuns founded in Berchem 1873 by Mary of Jesus Deluil-Martiny. Daughters of Our Lady of

depicting the Sacred flaming heart, almost always placed on the breast of Jesus who was showing it to us men. The pious practice of the first Friday of the month was organised and its members wore a scapular depicting Christ's Heart. The wonderful "Litany of the Sacred Heart" was composed. The month of June was devoted to this cult. In this way the cult of the Sacred Heart of Jesus, which began in the mystical life of souls, spread and penetrated into the social life of peo-

the Sacred Heart, founded at Issoudun in 1874 by Jean Jules Chevalier. Oblate Sisters of the Sacred Heart of Jesus, founded in Montluçon in 1874 by Louise-Thérèse de Montaignac de Chauvance. Small Servants of the Sacred Heart of Jesus for the Sick Poor, founded in Turin in 1874 by Anna Michelotti. Reparation Sisters of the Sacred Heart, founded in Naples in 1875. Handmaids of the Sacred Heart of Jesus, founded in Madrid in 1877 from Rafaela Porras y Ayllón (there is a homonymous Congregation founded in 1865 by Caterina Volpicelli). Sisters of the Sacred Heart, founded in l'Aquila in 1879 by Maria Ferrari. Hospitaller Sisters of the Sacred Heart of Jesus, founded in 1881 in Madrid by father Benedict Menni, alongside the Hospitaller Order of Saint John of God. Missionaries of the Sacred Heart of Jesus, based in Codogno November 14, 1880 by Frances Xavier Cabrini. Handmaids of the Divine Heart, founded in Coria in 1885 by cardinal Marcelo Spinola y Maestre. Servants of the Sacred Heart of Jesus and of the Poor, founded at Leon in 1885 by José María Yermo y Parres. Daughters of the Sacred Heart of Jesus, founded in 1886 in Guadalajara by Atenogenes Silva, devoted to hospital activity. Sisters of the Sacred Heart of Jesus in Ragusa, founded in 1889 by Maria Schinina. Carmelite Sisters of the Divine Heart of Jesus, founded in 1891 by Blessed Maria Teresa of St. Joseph. Agostiniane Sisters of the Sacred Heart of Jesus, kind in Venezuela in 1893 to Maria Alvarado Cardozo. Catechetical Sisters of the Sacred Heart, founded in Casoria by Giulia Salzano February 5, 1894. Apostles of the Sacred Heart of Jesus, founded May 30, 1894 in Viareggio the forlivese Clelia Merloni. Handmaids of the Sacred Heart of Jesus, which was founded in 1894 by Josef Sebastian Pelczar. *Adorers of the Sacred Heart of Jesus of Montmartre*, founded in 1898 by Adele Garnier. Ursuline Sisters Missionaries of the Sacred Heart of Jesus, founded in 1898 in Parma by Mary Lucrezia Zileri dal Verme. In this regard has been consulted on the internet site: *www.wikipedia.org* has been consulted under the heading "Sacred Heart of Jesus".

ples. At the request of Pope Pius IX in 1876 a movement was born and named "Acts of consecration to the Sacred Heart of Jesus". This same Pope instituted the feast of the Sacred Heart throughout the Catholic Church. Chapels, oratories, churches, basilicas and shrines dedicated to the Sacred Heart of Jesus sprang up everywhere.

Notably among the latter is found the Basilica of the "Sacred Heart" of Montmartre in Paris. It was from reading an article of L'Univers newspaper that announced, in 1872, the project for the parisian Basilica that Adèle felt the inner voice that called her to devote herself to prayer at the Sacred Heart, Montmartre Basilica[104] Adèle prepared spiritually to follow this call and four years later, at the age of 38 years, she received permission from her spiritual director, Père Chambellan, to withdraw to Montmartre, "in solitude and prayer in the shadow of the Shrine of the Sacred Heart".[105] But after a very short time, her state of health deteriorated terribly, leaving her – as she recalls – "just the strength to offer my life to the Heart of Jesus, thinking that from the first day He wanted to take his victim".[106] All her projects and her expectations seemed to cease, but her devotion to the Sacred Heart remained solid and constant. It was this that motivated her even more deeply to welcome every situation, joyful or sad, aware that "in the heart of our Master everything is good when he has decided".[107]

Adèle remained throughout this period "nailed to her bed" and in the end, she decided to leave on 13 September, 1876. She serenely left Montmartre with a desire to "live in the Heart of my well-beloved Master", to abide in him:

[104] Cf. H-15D-002, Abbé Courtois.
[105] H-15D-008, Abbé Courtois.
[106] H-15D-009, Abbé Courtois.
[107] H-15C-003, Madame Vosseaux.

"I would have liked so much to die at Montmartre, but for me it is still more sweet to live in the Heart of my well-beloved Master, where I abide by his grace, I hope".[108]

Her return to Dijon, began for Adèle a period of total abandonment to the divine will. Given that she considered that God himself had been calling her to a life of adoration on the Holy Hill, she now lets herself be led wherever God desires. The desire for abandonment grew in her, came to rest in the Sacred Heart, yearning for "a life more intimate with Jesus, most completely dependent on his adorable Heart":[109]

"I felt blest that I lived all entirely and uniquely in Jesus, that his heart enveloped and consumed me and that not only did he accept my self-giving to him, but that he called and awaited my vow to use me as absolutely his possession".[110]

The vow of abandonment which she made on 17 June, 1887 and directly addressed to the Sacred Heart of Jesus, called on her to make "no voluntary obstacle to his action".[111] Hence slowly but surely God had worked in her

---

[108] H-15C-009, Madame Vosseaux.
[109] H-15D-014, Abbé Courtois.
[110] *Ibidem.*
[111] H-15D-016, Abbé Courtois: "O Sacred Heart, I recognize that I am completely incapable of carrying out this vow without your help; but make it because you press me to do so, and because I hope that you would deign to achieve in me what I cannot do by myself. The only thing that I ask you very humbly, O Heart, full of mercy and power, is that you never let me put any obstacle or that I would make the slightest voluntary obstacle to your action or to your operations in me".

soul so as to have neither taste nor choice, to decide on what is more attractive or what is less important, according to her personal inclinations:

> "It seemed to me that Jesus fashioned my soul to have neither taste nor choice, but to take everything that he sent me as the most sure and best way to glorify him, detaching me from my poor personal inclinations [...]. So for the future, Jesus wants to abandon to his Heart my ways of acting: I will take as the most excellent whatever he arranges for me, not following my attractions except only when He would not have put anything else in their place".[112]

Adèle felt her heart in a state of being "torn out", because she now ardently desired to belong wholly to the Heart of Jesus:

> "I did not wish him to take this, my heart, but rather that he would call me whole and entire, there, where he had placed my heart, that is to say: in his bosom".[113] This experience of the "torn heart", is the confirmation of the mystical dimension of a soul that meets God and who, in God, feels totally involved and transformed. In the history of Christian spirituality this same experience, is reported by various mystics in different times and circumstances. Royo-Marin, in paragraph *The renewal or the exchange of hearts* says: "famous among them all is the case of Saint Catherine of Siena. An identical or similar favour was received by St Ludgarde, St. Gertrude, Saint Mary Magdalen de Pazzi, Saint Catherine of' Ricci, Saint John of Val-

---

[112] H-15D-019, Abbé Courtois.
[113] H-15D-028, Abbé Courtois.

ois, Saint Margaret Mary Alacoque and San Michele de Sanctis".[114] The same author traces a valuable explanation of this mystical phenomenon: "Our Lord under the mystic symbol of the change in the hearts, grants, to the person who receives this grace, a double gift: for the creature – provisions and sentiments that reflect the intimate affections of his blessed soul and, for the body of the creature – a heart in harmony with his interior state, like Jesus' Sacred Heart was always in tune with the impulses of his soul. It is a *mystical, not real, exchange of hearts*".[115]

Strengthened by this Mother Adèle experienced the highest mystical graces as unique as the state of ecstasy[116] and the grace of visions.[117] This together with her union with the Heart of Jesus there was nothing more that could discourage or frighten her, nothing disappoint or weaken her, because her soul was completely abandoned to the Heart of Jesus and he himself "confined her as in a fortress that the enemy cannot attack".[118] And if she was tried by the weight of fatigue and weakness, feeling so empty that she was unable to give anything to God, Adèle renewed the strength to gather "without measure from the Heart of Jesus and find

[114] Antonio Royo-Marin, *op. cit.*, p. 1103
[115] *Ibidem*, p. 1104.
[116] Cf. H-15D-037, Abbé Courtois.
[117] Cf. H-15D-061, Abbé Courtois.
[118] H-15D-045, Abbé Courtois: "For Jesus, after he has received in his Heart the abandoned soul, He takes and confines it as in a fortress that the enemy can also attack, but only to be beaten off and rejected far away. The soul that is under the guard of the strong armed one has nothing to fear, except that of being separated from Jesus. He will overcome all obstacles, avoid the dangers and dwell in unassailable peace, love and trust".

myself in charge of infinite riches".[119] Here pulsates the spiritual heart of Mother Adèle, where her only commitment was to dwell in the Heart of God:

> "My task is to plunge ever more deeply into the Heart of my Jesus where I dwell contentedly in the depth of my soul in spite of all the situations in which He makes me move. May the name of the Lord be blessed".[120]

Adèle lived to remain united solely to Him, without fuss about what may be her future, because the future belongs always to his heart, to His good will:

> "I feel his life in me simultaneously as a strength and a sweetness. O dear Father, I remain serene without a reply to this question when my heart poses: What shall I render to the Lord? I do not act any more to find an impossible solution, but I abandon myself always more and more to the Heart of Him who is all love. I cast myself into this furnace to be purified and consumed as pleases him, not me".[121]

Furthermore even when, it was not so much the temptations and distractions of the material world, but that of a certain indifference of the soul that left her in a "miserable and incomprehensible" state, seemed to take the upper hand, Adèle would strengthen that single point and undertake with determination to "abandon myself to the Heart of my beloved: that is the only good thing I must busy myself with to preserve it".[122]

[119] H-15D-058, Abbé Courtois.
[120] H-15D-061, Abbé Courtois.
[121] H-15D-064, Abbé Courtois.
[122] H-15D-071, Abbé Courtois.

It was on 21 June, 1897, that the Sacred Heart would recall Mother Adèle to the Holy Mountain, in the company of her friend Mère Agnes, indicating a new plan of service, love and total offering to God.[123] Other sisters would join them, but in all would reign that sole purpose: to let themselves be guided by the Sacred Heart:

> "The Sacred Heart [ ...] maintains in us all a cordial and joyful charity, through the union he has established among our souls, in order to respond to his appeal, by devotedness to his holy Church, to his Supreme Vicar, our Father, and to all the clergy. This is our vocation which affirms itself more and more each day, and becomes for us an increasingly great happiness".[124]

We belong to the Sacred Heart most truly. It is he who has created our little society; it is he who governs, who supports it, who consoles and rejoices over it. It is he who tests and purifies; and he that strengthens it.[125]

Once she had started the Work, after just one year, the Mother felt weak and that she had now reached the end of her mission, seeing in a younger Sister her natural substitute. As for herself she aspired to remain contentedly and calmly in adoration and prayer, before the Sacred Heart:

> "Moreover, from the point of view of the work, I believe that my mission is finished in what concerns action. It is evident that the Sacred Heart has willed to make use of me to begin, *to open the door*. That is done. I do not feel called to do anything else. I have neither the light nor the grace

---

[123] Cf. H-15F-170, Père Lémius.
[124] H-15C-174, Père Balme.
[125] H-15F-109, Père Lémius.

to do anything. Perhaps it will be necessary for me to remain in appearance the directress or the Superior on account of my age and because I began it. But when our position is regularised, and our Community definitively established I may well be permitted to draw aside, to lead the common life according to the measure of my strength, and to give myself exclusively to prayer and recollection. Our Lord, who knows I beg him daily to accept in his kindness, my life for the Work, will take me when it pleases him. Meanwhile, he will let me live a life of prayer before his Sacred Heart in the Blessed Sacrament.[126]

But it would still be Mother Adèle, the guide who would direct the little community toward the Sacred Heart. She searched to discern God's will and the path to be accomplished, even when the difficulties and anxieties arose strongly and made the road rough and treacherous. The sisters were never lonely because they felt themselves to be at every moment, the Sisters of the Sacred Heart of Jesus, who drew directly from the source, the love that filled their heart and made them strong in the face of every adversity:

> In the Heart of the Divine Master, we will draw without ceasing love from its source. Then with that love we will embrace, cost what it may, the difficulties, the disgusts, the repugnances, the anguish that we will find at every instant on our road.[127]

The new community, united in adoration of the Sacred Heart, made their first vows in the Crypt of the Basilica of

---

[126] H-15D-115, Abbé Courtois.
[127] H-15F-073, Père Lémius.

Montmartre, on 9 June, 1899, on the day of the feast of the Sacred Heart,[128] desiring to walk protected by his merciful love.

In the presence of incapacity or human frailty,[129] the Sacred Heart always remained close to his daughters: "he will work new miracles to encourage, sustain and fortify us".[130] Everything was from the Sacred Heart, everything belonged to Him: their hearts and their assets, both people and things. So also the purchase of the land and buildings in 40 Rue de la Barre, was considered to be the property of the Sacred Heart[131] and in spite of the fact that she had to take out loans with banks, Mother Adèle was not afraid of having to pay the interest within the fixed deadlines: "I do not become anxious unnecessarily – says the Mother – everything was ensured that they had bought for the Sacred Heart, and because He wanted them. The consequences will be what He pleases".[132]

Then, when the French Government decided to confiscate all the assets of Religious Orders and contemplative fraternities, Mother Adèle immediately turned to her devoted friend Monsieur Charles Michel to register him as the holder

[128] Cf. H-15C-159, Abbé Sauvé.
[129] Cf. H-15D-120, Abbé Courtois: "The Sacred Heart takes care of my soul, he takes, he leads, he consoles, he strengthens it and forgives all frailty".
[130] H-15C-189, Père Balme.
[131] Cf. H-15C-194, Père Balme: "The affair of the property is concluded: the Sacred Heart under our name, is the owner".
[132] H-15F-079, Père Lémius. See also in H-15D-119, Abbé Courtois: "Over the temporal affairs I have taken a very long time, [...] I am not anxious for I know that the Sacred Heart deigns to deal with them. We bought a large property near the Basilica. It is the Sacred Heart that we consider as the owner".

of their possessions, stressing that he will be "the man of the affairs of the Sacred Heart", since "when we bought the property of Montmartre we immediately declared that it belonged to the Sacred Heart, so you are the man of business for the Sacred Heart".[133]

The next important step for the Mother was to decide to complete this business, taking into consideration the position adopted by the Government which would disrupt her contemplative community, and to reiterate with absolute firmness that the Sacred Heart not only did not want her daughters separated, but does not intend to separate them.[134]

[133] H-15E-008, Monsieur Charles Michel. See also in H-15E-005, Monsieur Charles Michel: "All the advice that we receive is for urging us to leave the Civil Society, Mère Agnès and I – at least in a fictitious manner – in order not to compromise with our presence the interests of the property, for the fact of our names as associates, would be looked upon as belonging to the Congregation. I would have liked therefore to wait till you had been consulted on this issue, to do as you have had the goodness of proposing to me. But our Superior has now expressly recommended us to carry out as soon as possible, the change of name, so we cannot do otherwise. Therefore, Monsieur, it would be good if you could put your name as Sociétaire and without any movement of funds. I ask this service of you as a great act of charity that you would make for the Sacred Heart. He will not let you nor will you experience any serious annoyance; and I hope that you would willingly accept to be President of the Society [...]. You must, therefore, at least once a year participate in the general assembly, quite often give your signature for the rents or things of that kind, and finally to be in touch with us every so often about the difficulties that may occur. [...] You have worked so generously for the work of the Sacred Heart".

[134] Cf. H-15F-114, Père Lémius: "My good father, [...] I do not believe that the Sacred heart wants us to be separated. That would no longer be religious life. It is absolutely essential that this religious life be the foundation of our life of adoration. You will see! The Sacred Heart will not separate us. On the contrary he will keep us very united for the glory of God and his consolation".

For Mother Adèle the devotion to the Sacred Heart was not a private matter. Nor was it the expression, although commendable, of a personal devotion, but it was the unique offering of her religious family's self-donation to God, the due expression of its specific identity and charism. She felt convinced that the Sacred Heart called them to be together, totally his, by living as "religious".

In particular, the Mother wrote a most earnest and moving letter to Père Lémius, expressing all their suffering in having to leave Montmartre. But she also wrote of the confidence and trust in the Sacred Heart that their departure would become the occasion of a new apostolate in favour of the development of his cult in the new mission in England:

> "*All of us* are attached to the Basilica, right to the depths of our soul. It is our church, it is our cradle, it is always our abode, it is our Cenacle. If it should please the Sacred Heart to banish us from it for a time, nothing would be able to detach us from it. We would return more numerous, more fully developed, emerging from the swaddling bands in which circumstances are forcing us to remain enveloped. We would return in the full light of day, no longer as children who are fearful, but as grown-up daughters who then will take their place in the home.
>
> But Father, to separate in order to live by twos in rooms upon Montmartre, this would be impossible. In three months we would have undone the work of four years, and not one of our Sisters would prefer this situation to exile, even were it to last several years.
>
> For myself, although my heart is torn at the thought of leaving Montmartre, I feel I have the courage for this, and for the responsibility of taking my Sisters abroad. But to have them here, dispersed, I truly do not feel I have the

grace for that. For me, the work thus broken up, would be destroyed. If some of the others could continue it, they would become pious, and perhaps holy, associate Adorers, *but not Religious.* They would have sacrificed the Religious Life for the consolation of not leaving Montmartre. The Sacred Heart would accept them for what they had become, but not for what he had willed in *creating us,* nor for what he wills in exiling *us at this time.*

That which the Sacred Heart wills, my Father, is to strengthen us, to make us increasingly Religious and to mature us. He wills that the house of Montmartre should be transplanted for a brief time into foreign soil, a seed planted for a shoot to spring forth. You will see it, my Father! This is what happens to us, this indeed is our history which the Sacred Heart himself is writing. He wills the creation of the National Vow among the countries of the earth and he is sending us to spread this idea. We shall be there, as we are here, *the daughters of Montmartre praying everywhere for the Pope, the Church, France, and also very specially for the nation which welcomes us.* There, its conversion will be sought through our prayers united to all other prayers made for the same intention.

The cult of the Sacred Heart is not very widespread in England; let us then go and help to spread it. The house of your Fathers in Kilburn bears the name of the Sacred Heart, and that is a comforting thought to us. I think your Fathers will give us a warm welcome. Perhaps with your recommendation they will open their hearts to us straight away.

The good Cardinal in his kindness has very warmly recommended us through M. Thomas and M. Audollent. We are also preparing a leaflet on our work and our aim in England if it will be disposed to welcome us. M. Lefebvre will send this leaflet to these gentlemen for the Cardinal (in London). I am sending you a copy of M. Lefebvre's letter. We discussed Rome as an alternative to England, but he dismissed that idea altogether. We are not sufficiently experienced to go to Rome. Our situation there would be limited and precarious, if indeed we were able to install ourselves there, for M. Lefebvre told us that the Pope does not wish new Congregations to make foundations there, and has said so himself. The Helpers of the Holy Souls, whom Rome had asked for, had difficulties of all kinds before they were allowed to go there. [...]

I know the cost of living in England is very high. We would live a life of poverty, but we would not die of starvation. Oh, Father, the Sacred Heart is there, he will provide for us, and he will not allow us to lack anything. He well knows that it is he himself who is taking us there, and he will watch over us as he does here. He knows that *we are sacrificing everything for the Pope and for our Religious Life.* You will see, yes, you will see this, Father. And you yourself will still be his instrument for us as you have been from the beginning.

My Father, when the apostles left the Cenacle, their sorrow was great! They had to leave those places where they had lived with the Lord, where they had seen him die. They were not rich, they had no assured income. But their good Master had said: 'Seek ye first the Kingdom of God and his justice and all these things will be added to you. Father, I feel this, I know it, I believe it firmly: this trial will redound to the glory of the Sacred Heart, to our sanctification and the *development* of our little Society.

[...] the Sacred Heart is giving us the tremendous consolation of making our perpetual vows before leaving Montmartre. We are hoping to do this in the Crypt when you come back, perhaps on 24 September. ...[135]

---

[135]  H-15F-118, Père Lémius.

Great then was their spiritual emotion when they moved to Tyburn, secure that it was indeed Providence guiding them with a very precise design: "The Lord wants his Sacred Heart to reign here, where these courageous martyrs had their hearts torn out remaining faithful to him".[136] But the permanence in the new headquarters was not without suffering, and everything was accepted as the desire of the divine heart of Jesus. When the dramatic economic problems seem to be solved, the Mother writes to Dom Bede Camm, considered to be one of the founders of Tyburn, and communicates the joy to see that the Sacred Heart still wants them, in the place of the English Martyrs:

> The Sacred Heart has shown us that he now wants us at Tyburn. I say: "He wants us", even if the future, with its plans is still unknown to us, humanly speaking, we can only count on the present. What he is doing at this moment prevents us from leaving here. I do not doubt that he will make us remain permanently.[137]

After a decade of permanence of the Work in England, Mother Adèle was quite happy to see that the cult of the Sacred Heart seemed to develop and bear its first fruits, and as well the Community too, was developing, thanks to the Divine will:

> Tyburn is very much frequented by people; the Sacred Heart attracts souls for eucharistic adoration. Even the cult of the Martyrs was very much in evidence [...].

---

[136] H-15G-058, Dom Bede Camm.
[137] H-15G-105, Dom Bede Camm.

It seems to us that the Sacred Heart has been pleased to bless our religious family that is growing and I think I can say that it is progressing in the spiritual life.[138]

### 4.2.4. *The Eucharistic Heart*

In a vision I saw Jesus saying to my heart by means of a bright light that he willed his Eucharistic Heart to be the special object of adoration at Montmartre and that the Blessed Sacrament should be exposed there day and night.[139]

In these words it is deeply interesting to trace the culmination of the Garnier vocation and charism of Adorers of the Sacred Heart of Montmartre. Adèle was still a young woman of 36 years when she began to perceive that God was calling her to be the Adorer of the eucharistic Heart. Despite initially not finding the immediate encouragement of her ecclesiastical superiors,[140] she already felt her call to the adoration of the Sacred Heart, feeling like a "victim intended uniquely for sacrifice".[141]

---

[138] H-15F-198, Père Lémius.

[139] H-15D-004, Abbé Courtois.

[140] Cf. H-15D-005, Abbé Courtois: "The Cardinal of Paris, Mons. Guibert said to me: "Then, my child, you think that the worship at Montmartre should be especially directed towards the Heart of Jesus in the Blessed Sacrament?" "Yes, Eminence, and this is why Our Lord wishes the Blessed Sacrament to be exposed day and night". He said to me that this did not seem to be possible; as for the devotion to the Eucharistic Heart, it could not be imposed [...] there was the devotion to the Sacred Heart, and then the devotion to the Blessed Sacrament, why look for something else? As a result, it would be precisely Cardinal Guibert to approve, shortly before his death, the Association of the Eucharistic Heart on the heights of Montmartre and to encourage the perpetual exposition of the Blessed Sacrament, first in the provisional chapel and then in the votive church".

[141] *Ibidem.*

Such a vocation represents a notable development in the unfolding spirituality of Mother Adèle. Indeed, first there was her devotion toward the Eucharist and the adoration of the Eucharist; the next step was her deepening of devotion to the Sacred Heart, and this in turn led her to total abandonment to his holy will. Therefore, the call to the eucharistic Heart appears as the synthesis of a spiritual path that combines these "divine attractions" lived deeply, letting herself be guided by the divine will and the "signs" which the Spirit awakens within her, toward a new life: "I would like to unite myself to the Heart of Jesus in the Eucharist, so abandoning myself to Him that I no longer have my own life, but only that life which he would greatly like to form in me".[142]

With the completion of this total abandonment, Adèle discovers her specific, spiritual purpose: her full realisation in God, in his love, in his eucharistic Heart:

> "[...] To live for Jesus, to desire his kingdom, to pray for souls and finally to abandon myself entirely to his Eucharistic Heart, to his love, such is my aim, my sole attraction".[143]

When Adèle discussed with her friend Alice, the future Mère Agnes, the project of her Work, the above citation containing the charism that would unite them and as a result, give witness in the Church finds another expression:

> "We are all totally vowed and consecrated to his Heart living in the Eucharist, focus of love, of devotion, of generosity; nothing must prevent us from pleasing him and

[142] H-15D-026, Abbé Courtois.
[143] H-15D-063, Abbé Courtois.

devoting ourselves to his intentions, which are for us the triumph and extension of Holy Church, the holiness and the freedom of the Sovereign Pontiff and the fidelity and the sanctification of the Clergy".[144]

To adore the eucharistic Heart meant for Adèle to immolate herself as a victim to God, to participate in Christ's own Holy Sacrifice that comprises the supreme act of love that he made for the entire human race. Therefore to adore the Eucharist is to remain ardently united to Jesus, to perpetuate adhering to his sacrificial offering and to contemplate his immense love: "this union with the Heart of Jesus in the Eucharist must be above all, participation in his sacrifice, in the Holy Sacrifice perpetually offered".[145] Adèle would endeavour to ensure that this attitude would be formally specified in the Constitutions that were to be the underpinning of the path of this new Work,[146] to instil full meaning into their religious life.[147] So Mother Adèle wrote to Père Lémius on 29 September, 1901, the first day of their having departed from Montmartre:

[144] H-15H-021, Alice Andrade.

[145] H-15F-073, Père Lémius.

[146] *Ibidem:* "Perhaps it would be more appropriate to specify clearly and formally in the Constitutions that the worship that we give to the Sacred Heart, a cult of love and reparation, must be at the same time always a cult of union with the Heart of Jesus to glorify his Father with Him, through adoration, thanksgiving, atonement, and supplication. Also that this union with the Heart of Jesus in the eucharist must be the participation in his immolation in the Holy Sacrifice perpetually offered. To maintain in us this essential spirit it would be easier if we are bound to it by our Constitutions".

[147] In fact, when faced with the prospect of having to separate, to escape the new laws of the french Government, Adèle wrote in H-15F-114, Père Lémius: "I do not believe that the Sacred Heart wants us to be separated. This would no longer be religious life; and it is absolutely essential that this religious life be the foundation of our life of adoration".

"On our first day of separation, I need to tell you how much our hearts are with you, our dear, good Father. I cannot find words to express the emotions that are brimming over. But the predominant one is this: 'May the most holy Will of God be ever loved, blessed and adored. And may we always fulfil it.' [...]

Father, we have only to lift up our eyes and our hearts to live in the gentle, peaceful submission of love, to abandon ourselves always with all our heart to the Good Pleasure of the Sacred Heart".[148]

In addition, their adoration continued and intimately united them to the supreme Sacrifice that the Martyrs had made to God. Then too, the Mother was to be full of joy that their sisterly love showed, in spite of their incapacity and poverty, this witness through their work of adoration, exactly on the plot of earth where those martyrs gave their lives for God:

"At Tyburn the Sacred Heart is himself to establish his throne of love, his eucharistic adoration on this very same earth! And these are poor little Religious, all new, very imperfect, very ignorant, incapable and very poor, whom he has deigned to call to form and prepare his court".[149]

We have thus run the route of the specific nature of the Garnier spirituality which is fully realized in the adoration

---

[148] H-15F-124, Père Lémius.

[149] H-15E-058, Monsieur Charles Michel. See also in H-15F-198, Père Lémius: "Tyburn and much frequented by the people; the Sacred Heart attracts souls for eucharistic adoration. Even the cult of the Martyrs is very fervent [...]. It seems to me that the Sacred Heart is pleased to bless our religious family that is growing and I think I can say that it makes progress also in the spiritual life. And the two novitiates give us a sweet hope".

of the Eucharistic Heart of Christ. We can note that for Mother Adèle, the Sacred Heart, (unlike the great diffusion of pious practices linked especially with the already mentioned St Margaret Mary Alacoque), is no longer a devotion characterised by practices which, though valid and periodic, such as the first Friday of the month, or a meditative gaze toward an image of the Sacred Heart of Jesus. The image for Mother Adèle is the Eucharist, Christ himself who renews the gift of life: the practice that firmly perdures, is nothing other than an abiding in his love at the foot of the altar. The paschal memorial welcomes the invitation of the Master: "Abide in me, as I abide in you. As the branch cannot bear fruit by itself, unless it abides in the vine, neither can you, unless you abide in me" (Jn 15:4).

Adèle abides in the highest moment of Christ's self-donation – in which God's love unites the offering of his death and resurrection – certain that this manifests the finest fruitfulness for those who "adore God in spirit and in truth" (Jn. 4:23): *the salvation of the world"*.

## 4.3. Mystical Experience

"While (the two disciples) were talking together and discussing, Jesus himself drew near and walked with them. But their eyes were prevented from recognising him. [ …] When he was at table with them, he took bread, said the blessing, broke it and gave it to them. Then their eyes were opened, and they knew him". (Lk. 24:15-31). Like the disciples of Emmaus who testified to their mystical experience, recognising Christ in the breaking of the bread, so too, the disciple Adèle, Adorer of Christ's eucharistic Heart, experienced the presence of God on her spiritual journey, by dwelling in the presence of the Blessed Sacrament. The "images" she received led her to a divine union ever more profound, until finally on the path of Christian perfection, she only felt the call to the holiness of God: "Be holy; for I am holy" (Lv. 11:44), "Be perfect, therefore, as your heavenly Father is perfect" (Mt. 5:48).

### 4.3.1. *The Spiritual Imagery*

Among the approximately 1,500 letters analyzed, sometimes Mother Adèle describes her spiritual experiences using certain images that symbolise what she is going through at that moment. In addition, she does so because she is not always able to describe them with appropriate words for words alone were inadequate at times to convey the meaning of the work of God in her.

In particular she describes her union with God as a fire that burns inside: *"as a fire in me"*,[150] *"like a flame of love"*,[151] *"as a fire of love within me"*,[152] *"as a fire in the heart"*.[153]

---

[150] H-15D-017, Abbé Courtois: "To [ …] the Holy Table, a moment before Jesus came to me (in communion), I felt a gentle heat in the surrounding air and when I had received Communion this was like a fire within me, but in an ineffable calm".

[151] H-15D-012, Abbé Courtois : "I had just recollected myself to adore my God, when I felt surrounded by this flame of love penetrating me on every side, transporting me into God, in heaven [ …] and my soul was increasingly intoxicated with the love of God. I trembled, I was troubled, my body was covered in a cold sweat, I no longer had strength to struggle and finally I let my soul abandon itself to Jesus". See also in H-15D-023, Abbé Courtois: "I want to say that Jesus, having put in my soul the fire of love, I wish to be a thousand and a thousand times more generous than if I had been moved by the thought of rewards promised to faithful souls ".

[152] H-15D-081, Abbé Courtois: "I felt calm, [ …] but like a fire of love within me, like a beneficial dew, [ …] after this night, after midnight

This image of fire clearly expresses how the love of God consumes her, transforms her, reclothes her, resulting in a burning heat in her soul. This was the experience of the two disciples on the road to Emmaus who having lived intimately the eucharistic experience with the Risen Christ reveal: "Were not our hearts burning within us while he talked with us on the road, while he opened to us the Scriptures?" (Lk 24:35 ).

Royo-Marin catalogues these *Fires of Love* among the *Phenomena of affectivity*, stressing that: "It is a fact, fully demonstrated in the life of some of the saints, that the violence of the love of God is manifested at times externally in the form of fire that warms and burns".[154]

After leaving Montmartre in September 1876, Adèle felt a lessening of her spiritual zeal, regarding the vocation to which she felt called to realise, but which on account of her illness she had to desist from pursuing.

---

Mass, after communion I lived in heaven, in a state of love and adoration making me have impossible, strange thoughts of God. He is here, in me, around me, in heaven, on the high altar, everywhere, and keeps me united to Him, in the most ineffable well-being".

[153] H-15G-005, Dom Columba Marmion: "When I went to the Choir for the Office I felt my soul all embraced, so eager to recite the praises of God; and in pronouncing them, I was on fire in my heart and on my lips. During the Mass I made my acts of preparation as usual at the beginning of the Mass. Then, when the acts became more passive, I was swept away into a more intimate union with my Lord Jesus for the sacrifice; and it was as if he would say and do, He himself, everything that he wants, while filling my soul with an immense love, a burning desire to comply with all that he wants to do for me and in me, and what he wants me to do for him. As the Mass progressed my heart burned increasingly and at the time of Communion I felt as if transformed into a single desire: to receive him as he willed to be received, relying solely on Him for this preparation and transformation of my base soul into a pure soul".

[154] Antonio Royo-Marin, *op. cit.*, p. 1089.

261

In these circumstances once turning her gaze to God, she felt like *"his thing, his tiny grain of sand, his small inert stone"*.[155] Adèle felt radically that she became the Lord's possession that she belonged to his greatness; but at the same time this union placed her in a profound attitude of reverence and humility.

Although small, she remained always profoundly aware of belonging to God, of remaining in his Divine immensity. In a similar way Adèle regarded her soul as being immersed in God *"like a drop of water mingling in the ocean"*.[156] She feels such a *"small thing"* that still belongs to God, the one who exalts the humble, and receives the little children who offer all of their love (cf. Lk 18.9 -14).

It is not always the joyful aspects of spiritual intensity and wealth of feelings that Adèle experienced, for sometimes her soul felt *"like a desert"*,[157] in which she continues to yearn for

---

[155] H-15C-010, Madame Vosseaux.

[156] H-15D-017, Abbé Courtois. See also in H-15D-032, Abbé Courtois : "The earth, creatures, ideas, imagination, all disappeared; I was alone with God, and dived down into him as a drop of water in the ocean".

[157] H-15D-083, Abbé Courtois: "I began to see that the Lord is not absent, but only silent and I feel then something like an interior reverence for his presence within me and my union with Him. I suffer less than before in this state, [ ...] I taste also, in this wilderness, a kind of sweetness". See also in H-15G-010, Dom Columba Marmion: "Since Thursday my poor soul has been wretchedly occupied. I could not at any time, apply myself to prayer [ ...] It was like an agony where I was immersed. Assistance at Mass, which has been for many long years, an unspeakable joy to my soul, now leaves me indifferent. Sometimes I think I am in another world, in the midst of a desert, without end, without light, without heat and without any physical relief. It was like an interior martyrdom. I say "like", because I felt crushed, exhausted, what torture [ ...] I do not understand this state, I do not recall having been so tested, despite the fact that I have had many tests in my life. This is less violent and more

God, as the psalmist recalls: "O God, you are my God, for you I long; for you my soul is thirsting. My body pines for you, like a dry, weary land without water" (Ps 62:2).

Moreover, despite the fact that Mother Adèle wishes to perceive the presence of God, her soul experiences the feeling of being *"like a prison"*, closed in a *"heart of marble"*,[158] unable to be moulded according to the plan of God, and to move freely according to the promptings of the spirit, indeed remaining immobile, *"as muzzled"*.[159] But she maintains a firm hope that God will continue to act, to work, to transform her heart of stone, and give her a new heart, a heart of flesh (cf. Ez 36:26).

grievous [...] in spite of this, there is a small light that crosses this immense darkness and that reassures me. It seems to me that this very fine light gives me a strength of will and a peaceable disposition that can only come from God. I understand that this state of death is to show me my total incapacity, powerlessness and abjection. My poor soul, made in the image of God, should be able to ascend to him, to adore , love, praise him. It cannot do anything, because it is all enfolded in its misery [...] I asked God to deign to purify my suffering uniting it to his abandonment on the cross".

[158] H-15D-043, Abbé Courtois: "My soul is enclosed in a prison absolutely black where nothing can penetrate: neither air nor light nor any relief; nothing, nothing, nothing but the oppressive weight of my miserable being. I can do absolutely nothing, I am bound as with enormous chains. I do not feel any taste, any attraction for my God. [...] O my God, I would like to die of love by telling you that I love you. And all I feel in myself is a heart of marble".

[159] H-15D-105, Abbé Courtois: "I am in a situation of soul, that seems to me quite miserable. [ ...] It seems to me that, from a spiritual point of view, I have neither eyes nor ears, nor taste, nor feelings, nor judgment, nor needs. They are as if muzzled: fabrics and bands surround me and I am bound up, so that I am incapable of any movement [ ...] and my soul can neither savour nor feel his divine love, and therefore, has absolutely the idea that to accept all this and to embrace it as the best thing, is to love God for himself alone".

Although her littleness makes her walk spiritually without great certainty, whether or not it is the love of God, or the awareness of being willed and supported by Him, Adèle affirms that she feels the sense of being " *suspended by a thread, but it is the hand of Jesus that holds me*".[160]

Adèle knows that it is God who must transform her, who must form her soul and make it capable of cherishing his joyful presence; by so abandoning herself to the eucharistic Heart she sees herself *"as a vast uncultivated field without a fence'*,[161] *'like a land abandoned"*,[162] who knows however to raise her trusting prayer that, as proclaimed by the prophet Isaiah, God speaks: "I will open rivers on the bare heights, and fountains in the midst of the valleys; I will make the wilderness a pool of water, and the parched ground into springs of water" (Isaiah 41:18).

Always guided by her accompanying spiritual father, l'Abbé Courtois, who, on some occasions encouraged her to accept the divine grace within her, to feel like *"that vase of alabaster filled with a perfume of great value"*.[163] This is an image that Adèle will return to several times in her letters, witnessing to her attitude of complete availability to the divine will: *"I had to be there for him an alabaster vase full of a perfume of great value!"*,[164] the same perfume that anointed the head of the Anointed One of God (cf. Mc 14:3-9).

---

[160] H-15D-013, Abbé Courtois.
[161] H-15D-014, Abbé Courtois
[162] *Ibidem.*
[163] H-15D-023, Abbé Courtois.
[164] H-15D-026, Abbé Courtois: "Even while I am writing you, my spirit is ravished still in all these splendours of grace and of divine love. Jesus made me understand that I was going to be for him an alabaster vase full of perfume of great value! It seemed to me that his love had

264

Another expression that is used by Adèle when it comes to her attitude of complete abandonment to God, is to feel herself *"like molten wax"*,[165] to live and to be moulded with docility.

Adèle feels her soul to be secure, stable, dwelling in God *"like a rock"*,[166] united to her Creator, and like the psalmist who feels stable in his "eternal salvation": "He alone is my rock, my stronghold, my fortress: I stand firm. In God alone be at rest, my soul; for my hope comes from him. He alone is my rock, my stronghold, my fortress: I stand firm. In God is my salvation and glory, the rock of my strength". (Ps 61:3-8)

Sometimes her mystical experience, as described to Abbé Courtois, seems to her to have been an experience of herself *"as a double person"*,[167] a part that remains sensitive, her natu-

---

already purified this vase, so soiled, and had restored in some way its whiteness while leaving its fragility. Then he invited me to open this vase [...]. My soul was opened, and held open to receive the precious perfume of his love, that He alone can give and is intended only for Him, [ ...] God alone". See also in H-15D-039, Abbé Courtois: "This charity, which comes from God, is the perfume of great value that Jesus wishes to put into my heart, slowly drop by drop in this alabaster vase, so fragile".

[165] H-15D-025, Abbé Courtois: "At every moment, I renew this disposition of abandonment or rather I pray to Jesus to renew it, by taking me whole and entire right to the marrow of my bones; right to the most intimate depths of my soul: So that nothing resists him, but that I am without ceasing like molten wax that leaves itself to be penetrated and moulded with the greatest of ease".

[166] H-15D-073, Abbé Courtois.

[167] H-15D-046, Abbé Courtois. See also in H-15D-025, Abbé Courtois: "The superior part of my soul is united to Him in a region of which I simply cannot give you any idea. This does not prevent the rest of my being, i.e. the natural, sensitive part to be always at the bottom, between confusion and misery. It seems to me that I see in me two people in which only one is easy for me to recognise – my miserable me; while the other is like a higher me, also, but that is detached, almost separate, and which remains fixed in God, in his thoughts, in his love".

ral body and the other part refers to her soul, her spiritual part, totally united to God.

Several years later she describes the same feeling to her spiritual father Dom Columba Marmion. Then she speaks of a part of herself which is suffering terribly, discouraged with so much to think about that it is no longer possible to go ahead with the Work, yet also of another part which instead relies continually and calmly on God's Providence, and his immense love.[168]

A few months later she will describe the same similitude, but presenting her state *"as a double life"*,[169] a natural one and a supernatural one (cf. Rom 7).

[168] H-15G-017, Dom Columba Marmion: "It is as if in me there are two persons, one who is suffering terribly, who believes that everything is finished and that it cannot bear for long the torment of its anxieties and responsibility. And then another that is sustained by God, by faith, accepting everything, who abandons herself to all, who, seeing with certainty that she can do nothing except to rely on God and pray to him, dwelling in peace adoring and blessing with all her heart and all her soul with an immense love and intense joy, the Lord her God, the Master infinitely great, powerful and wise, infinitely good, who himself deigns to find some glory in the filial abandonment of his creature, to his Good Pleasure. This person here, dear Father, who dwells united to Jesus in the Garden of Olives and more still on the Cross, crying out to his Father: "my God, my God, why hast thou forsaken me" [...]. Yes, my Father, this cry that seems to say: everything is lost, everything is finished! This cry consoles me and sustains me. In this union with Jesus, I find the explanation for these two persons and I abandon myself more and more to my God although it seems to me at the same time that I am desperate. I am attached to his Cross, I just ask him pity, mercy, compassion, and then I await his help, without being able to do anything or imagine anything".

[169] H-15G-023, Dom Columba Marmion: "It is difficult to give an account of a state so complex, as a double life; one life natural, physical and moral, also sensitive to a certain extent, it is really pitiable, but at the same time a supernatural life, high, living of love, of conformity and of abandonment to the divine Good Pleasure, rejoicing and blessing God in

But the image that is absolutely recurring most is that which Adèle uses in her letters the imagery of light, resplendent and immense: she saw God *"as the sun"*,[170] or he was found gently *"as in the midst of a sweet light"*.[171]

The grace of being united with God is described as a resplendent vista *"as an infinite light... as an ineffable light"*[172] (cf. "In him was life and the life was the light of men" (Jn 1:4).

It was God in her whom she describes *"as the true sun that illuminates the whole of life"*.[173] "I am the light of the

the sufferings he sends her and grateful with a joy full of gratitude that her most cruel tests are those that unite her more to her God.

[170] H-15D-025, Abbé Courtois: "He is in front of me, or in me, I do not know, like the divine sun that, once it has been fixed, no longer allows the eye to distinguish any other thing".

[171] H-15D-034, Abbé Courtois: "Here is more or less what happens to me, at both the morning masses, and in the afternoon before the Blessed Sacrament. I put myself in the presence of God, humbling myself, adoring him, asking him to make his poor daughter what he wants. Then I find myself very gently (I did not notice this at first even though this happened very promptly) as in the midst of a gentle light, but so penetrating that it was as if I was in the midst of it; it crossed over me and I find it equally was within me".

[172] H-15D-049, Abbé Courtois: "I received from my God for the grace of an ineffable union, a ravishing vision like an infinite light in which my spirit was plunged and was lost. [ ...] God alone like an ineffable light enveloped my soul, and penetrated it and he gave me the joy of heaven which no happiness on earth can have any idea".

[173] H-15D-063, Abbé Courtois: "Our Lord deigns to make me practise charity in trivialities, in the most insignificant things, even banal: with the most perfect dispositions that I have never had for the difficult things or very challenging ones. He leads me as if by the hand, here and there, making himself felt as the true sun that illumines all my life, and makes it so, all according to his heart. [...] My soul is lost in him. See also in H-15F-072. It came to my thought to pray to the Sacred Heart, 'of wanting him to give us a guardian Angel for the Work. I hardly had time to express my desire when it had been heard, and I felt wrapped in sweetness and light".

world; he who follows me will not walk in darkness, but will have the light of life" (Jn 8:12). And this light was for Mother Adèle the light of the Eucharist, and in consequence, the Holy Mass is defined as *"the sun that lights up my life"*.[174]

The mystical experience, deep in God, raised the spirit of his elect one, to such heights that Adèle describes her soul: *"how high"*,[175] *"how high to myself"*,[176] and to feel transported *"as in heaven"*,[177] *"as it is in heaven with my God"*.[178]

---

[174] H-15E-085, Monsieur Charles Michel.

[175] H-15D-032, Abbé Courtois: "Saying my rosary, [ ...] and my soul was raised high, not violently but gently and by degrees; I felt thrown increasingly into the divine love, joyful in the eternal goodness, lost in my God, filled with inexpressible happiness". See also in H-15D-034, Abbé Courtois: "I felt like a lifting of my soul on high, by degrees as if it had been taken gently by someone and raised from the ground or rather high from my body. [ ...] I felt a beautiful sweet wellbeing and at the same time I was very frightened of this kind of ascension and because union with God was increasing as this raising up progressed". Also in H-15D-052, Abbé Courtois: "When I am in his presence my soul is raised and held on high without my rejoicing greatly at what is being done in her though I can discern it clearly. But I feel that it is God who draws me and possesses me [...]. So I leave him to do what he wants and do not trouble myself".

[176] H-15D-083, Abbé Courtois: "O my Father, our good Master and adorable Saviour does not stop this torrent of significant favours. Every day or almost every day, at the Mass, my soul is as raised on high from myself and united so intimately, so completely to Jesus immolated, that I live on the altar or better Jesus makes my heart an altar where he immolates me with Himself".

[177] H-15G- 001, Dom Columba Marmion: "And, behold, how I am at Mass, the Office, at Benediction, everything sings in me; I have no more concerns, but I am as if in heaven, loving my God, adoring him and blessing him in everything". See also in H-15G-006, Dom Columba Marmion: "During the day and between my duties, I feel very often that my soul is drawn up on high, with a sweetness or an extreme ardour and therefore mixed with a certain suffering".

[178] H-15G-015, Dom Columba Marmion.

## 4.3.2. *Intimate Divine Union*

"This morning, [ ...] I went to Mass and I was preparing to renew my act of consecration to the Eucharistic Jesus; my soul was in the greatest calm, but I could not pray, but I only felt myself powerless and abandoned to his heart. At the Holy Table, a moment before Our Lord came to me (in Communion), I sensed a gentle heat in the surrounding air and when I had received him it was like a fire within me, but in an unspeakable calm [ ...] I offered myself to him without reserve [ ...]. After a moment Jesus accorded to my soul for the first time in my life a kind of ineffable union that I cannot define. [ ...] its beauty, its splendour, its majesty, his love, his power, his mercy, his wisdom, finally, everything that I am unable to say, captivated me, permeated me from every side. [ ...] This was neither heaven nor the earth; it was an ineffable life between heaven and earth, the life of Jesus communicated to a creature and for a few moments making all obstacles disappear into a perfect union. Oh, how dare I write this word? And therefore I cannot believe or imagine a closer union with my God. It was of such a kind that the soul, I believe, could remain several days without the body suffering, since it was not then using its energies during this time, since it felt nothing [...]. In coming out from this state I felt my soul more than ever unite with Jesus and without any other desire than to abandon myself completely to Him more and more".[179]

In this letter of 19 June, 1887, written to her spiritual father, Abbé Courtois, Adèle describes that *"ineffable union"* or *"intimate union"* or *"divine union"* which characterised her spiritual experience in her soul that had learned to surren-

[179] H-15D-017, Abbé Courtois.

der itself completely to God. Indeed, there is a stronger reciprocity between the act of abandonment and intimate union, two realities which blend and reinforce one another in a single experience of God.[180]

This divine union does impart some moments of ecstasy, in which her soul feels elevated on high toward God:

> "I am experiencing a trial that is like an interior separation. It seems that my soul is low, and my body raised on high – something spiritual, insatiable that is from within me, and makes me suffer and tremble. Then within a short time perhaps two or three seconds, this part so spiritual of my being, becomes in a kind of elevated state – and joyous with an ineffable wellbeing, about which I am not able to say anything, because I do not know what it is. I think: God. And then, that is all. I descend again, and become once more wholly myself".[181]

[180] Cf. H-15D-019, Abbé Courtois : "The end of the instructions became for me a means of a very intimate union with my Beloved. [...] It seemed to me that Jesus was forming my soul in such a way that it would have neither taste nor choice, but would take all that he sent me as *the surest and best means* of glorifying him, by detaching me from my poor personal inclinations. So, in the future Jesus wishes me to abandon to his Heart *my way of doing things*. I am to regard what he arranges for me as being the most excellent, only following my own attraction when he does not put anything else in its place".

[181] H-15D-024, Abbé Courtois. See also in H-15D-034, Abbé Courtois: "I felt like a lifting of my soul on high by degrees as if it had been taken gently by someone and raised from the ground, or rather, high from my body. [...] I felt a beautiful sweet well being and at the same time I was very frightened of this kind of ascension and because the union with God was increasing as this raising up progressed. I was always fearful, and I began to weep and I cried out: 'O my God, where are you taking me and where then am I going? What will happen to me! Then it seemed to me that I was having a different response, that of an impression – a very strong one – of his divine love and that he possessed me. I rested thus for

Mother Adèle embraced this mystical experience with an attitude of great humility, feeling only "a poor creature",[182] unworthy of such divine gifts, but also with the greatest gratitude to God, who worked so magnificently in her soul. Always with the most discrete sensitivity and caution, she desired and allowed her spiritual father to be able to assess these experiences, and to verify their divine consistency and even having fear to use the term "ecstasy" for these so singular spiritual experiences.[183]

Sometimes the state of the union, while causing in her soul an immense joy, became possible only after great suffering and struggles between a sensitive part and a supernatural part,[184] and feeling as if she was "as a double person of

a certain time; as if ravished and then thought no more of what had happened to me but became all lost in him". And yet in H-15G-001, Dom Columba Marmion: "At the low Mass, at the beginning my soul finds itself prostrated in a confusion full of love and yearning. Then it is as if mounting the altar, I find myself in a state of expectation, of attraction and, delightful undoubtedly, but mingled with hunger and thirst. Then it is as if I had within me a choir chanting, praising God with a joy, and love waxing strong. And finally, when the Consecration takes place, the union with Our Lord in the Holy Sacrifice is so intimate, so profound and so powerful that I believe myself to be in heaven yet on the altar".

[182] H-15D-034, Abbé Courtois: "Dear Father, I suffer telling you so many things that the Lord works so magnificently in the soul of the poorest of his creatures: so despicable, being a sinner, the most unworthy, soiled, that to make good her repentance she would need to be rejected, repulsed, buffeted, cast down at the feet of others".

[183] Cf. H-15D-035, Abbé Courtois: "My Father, I am ashamed to have written the word "ecstasy", since this word is not appropriate for a poor creature like me; but it is because there was no other word to describe my state".

[184] Cf. H-15D-025, Abbé Courtois: "At Mass and in prayer, I am in these days, not always, but most of the time, in a state of union that causes me great joy with God in the soul and yet a kind of suffering, con-

which a part remains where my body is, while the other part dwells in God, united indissolubly to him".[185]

"The grace of union" leads Adèle to discover her vocation in an ever more intimate union, to immolate herself, living all the time with Jesus, in the interior priesthood, in ˏwhom this union embraces the whole of time, living in a state of continuous self-offering through the Son, to God, the Father Almighty.[186] This intimate union with the immolation of Jesus on the Holy Altar, remained for Adèle "always the attraction of my soul and the rest rejoices in this union often without looking for it".[187] It was too, the call of God to live "immolated in union with Jesus" which would constitute her apostolate in the Church, the charism that would lead her to unite with other sisters who, dedicated to God, would live as Adorers "for the glory of God and the salvation of souls and, above all, very specially for the sanctification of the clergy":[188]

> "[...] Then Our Lord renewed the announcement of this grace, adding to it practical instructions on this new interior life which will unite me more fully to him and make me enter into a participation of his own priesthood. Not

straining very painfully my nature. This union therefore is absolutely not anything that depends on me, and it seems to me that it is only to be had at the price of this suffering which is like a fight between the sensitive part of myself and the supernatural. It is not easy to explain, but I am afraid that I must tell you, because it is my habitual disposition these days and I believe that it is a work of purification that the Holy Spirit brings about in me".

185 H-15D-046, Abbé Courtois.
186 Cf. H-15D-078, Abbé Courtois.
187 H-15D-079, Abbé Courtois.
188 H-15D-080, Abbé Courtois.

only does he wish me to be immolated in union with him, in the perpetual sacrifice of the altar, as priest and sacrifice of my own self by his divine action, but he vows me too, to an interior apostolate. [...] Then he showed me that this apostolate, like the immolation, should be continual through prayer, suffering and the conformity of abandon. He showed me that each moment of my life, united to him, would be an act of priestly ministry, were I faithful. For that I must attain a purity of which as yet, I have no concept. To the extent that my soul is clothed in a higher degree in this (purity), it will labour more efficaciously for the glory of God, the salvation of souls and most especially for the sanctification of priests.[189]

So Mother Adèle learnt to live in daily life so that her existence became "'union with Our Lord as a life of faith that animates me in spirit close to the eucharistic Jesus".[190] She finds that in this union is "the inner strength that only God can give to me":[191]

"My spiritual state in the midst of these temporal concerns remains one of an habitual union with Jesus. What I feel is an inner strength that God alone can give me, an habitual elevation of my soul to him, a detachment, greater than ever, from all that is not Jesus, a total abandonment in view of glorifying his guidance by filial confidence".[192]

In particular, on being confronted with daily anxieties and the problems of her Congregation, so serious that they

---

[189] *Ibidem.*
[190] H-15G-003, Dom Columba Marmion.
[191] H-15G-027, Dom Columba Marmion.
[192] *Ibidem.*

seemed to devour her soul, she took refuge promptly "in intimate union with Jesus on the cross" which bestows that "grace which comes from the torture of Christ".[193] This union was, for the Mother, the place in which to live, where to stay, and where to dwell. Here is the development and summary of her entire spirituality: in the Cross she welcomes the Heart of Jesus and dwells here:

> "[…] When temporal anxieties lay hold of me in an excessive way, then my recourse is in intimate union with Jesus on the Cross, at the most awful moment of his life, his very Passion, when he uttered this terrible cry: 'My God, my God, why have you forsaken me!' There, my Father, I plunge myself, in the forsaken, heart of my Jesus".[194]

---

[193] H-15G-023, Dom Columba Marmion.

[194] *Ibid.* The whole citation in its context: "When temporal anxieties lay hold of me in an excessive way, then my recourse is in intimate union with Jesus on the Cross, at the most awful moment of his life, his very Passion, when he uttered this terrible cry: 'My God, my God, why have you forsaken me!' There, my Father, I plunge myself, in the forsaken heart of my Jesus [...] and dwell there. It is the pinnacle of his love that he wanted to know, to suffer, to desire the abandonment by his Father! Then this cry that I utter with him; it seems that I have no more faith, yet I know that it is faith alone that makes me utter this cry! It is faith in Jesus, in his love, in his total devotion to his Father. I understand vaguely that this is the culminating point of the suffering of Jesus and at that moment he saved us from despair and made us make with him the most perfect act of love, the act of the most complete abandonment. And I have to tell you, my Father, that these moments are frightening and I do not even dare to think of them [...] and when they have passed, my soul feels calm, serene again, more than ever in God, nailed to the Cross of Jesus and through him completely ready to suffer everything that he wills, and however much he wills. This is the grace that comes from the torture of Jesus".

Mother Adèle always abides in God, both before the Eucharist, in adoration, and also before the cross, in contemplation. Eucharist and Cross are in fact the expression of that single offering, that single victim sacrificed on the altar of God.

Thus she so abides expressing her being with God, at the very hour of the most intense love, when Christ's heart was opened for the salvation of humanity.

### 4.3.3. *The Desire for Holiness*

Revelation reminds us that God desires holiness of every believer: "Be holy; for I the Lord your God am holy" (Lev 19:2). Every Christian must strive after this state of perfection, Christ himself, in fact, teaches his disciples to "be perfect therefore as your heavenly Father is perfect" (Mt 5:48). The apostle Paul also warns the community of Ephesus to raise to God the canticle of praise that emphasizes this call to holiness: "Blessed be God, the Father of our Lord Jesus Christ, who has blessed us with every spiritual blessing in the heavenly places in Christ. Just as he chose us in Christ before the creation of the world to be holy and blameless before him in love, he destined us in love to be his sons through Jesus Christ, according to the plan of love of his will, to the praise of the glory of his grace, which he has freely bestowed on us in the beloved Son" (Eph 1:3 -7).

In the letters written before the foundation of the Work, Mother Adèle's interest was always directed to seek and do the will of God, abandoning herself totally to him. The call to holiness is mentioned in one situation only; in November 1888, when Adèle describes to both Abbé Sauvé and to her spiritual father, l'Abbé Courtois, the vision which she had seen during Mass: the drop of red blood.[195] She sees in this experience not so much any personal satisfaction, full of pride and complacency, but as an opportunity to give glory to God and a reminder of her own sanctification.[196]

Later, her desire for holiness is emphasised, in the outline of the nascent Work, as a reality to be pursued personally and brought forth in the Church:

> But let us not forget that holiness is specially kept in view in the designs of God on our small Work: we must not wish for our sanctification in order only to make us grateful to God, but to have strongly always the desire for holiness, to give him glory according to his intentions. We are all vowed and consecrated to his Heart living in the Holy Eucharist, fire of love, devotion, generosity: nothing must prevent us from pleasing him and devoting ourselves to his intentions which are, for us, the triumph and extension of his holy Church, holiness and freedom of the Supreme Pontiff and the fidelity and sanctification of the Clergy.[197]

When the whole Community was forced to abandon the revered Basilica of the Sacred Heart of Montmartre and the beloved french nation to take refuge in England, the Mother discerned in this experience a trial that "would redound to

---

[195] Cf. H-15D-076, Abbé Courtois.

[196] H-15C-144, Abbé Sauve: "If It is a favour that Our Lord has deigned to grant me that I be permitted to see the Holy Host tinted with blood, I can only try to give the most humble, the most tender gratitude of which I am capable. And I ask him with confidence that he would make me attain that which he wills me to attain for his glory and for my sanctification. [...] I do not wish to go deeper into these things. My only desire is to obtain from all this the fruits that are in the designs of God".

[197] H-15H-021, Alice Andrade.

the glory of the Sacred Heart, our sanctification and the development of our little society".[198]

But it is above all in her later letters we analysed that Mother Adèle stressed this call to holiness, which appears as the culmination of a journey of conversion and abandonment to the Good Pleasure of God:

> "My poor soul has need of your great spirituality, since it is almost always deprived of daily Mass and Communion. It seems to me that I am vegetating and that if the Lord is pleased to let me live yet, I can only take this opportunity once again to sanctify myself. I pray that I may love him more, serve him better and that if my life is useless as to work, it can do some little thing for love and abandonment to the divine Good Pleasure".[199]

Mother Adèle felt that God, after having asked her to give herself to Him, to adore him in his eucharistic Heart, to form the Work that would perpetuate this charism, now a few years before her passover, renews the call to holiness. Adèle asks, for this reason, the support also of her friend priest, Père Lémius. As a hopeful sign for the new year 1920, she invited him to remember her in his fervent prayers that she might respond to her urgent need to be sanctified:

> "My dear Reverend Father, I ask you the charity of some of your fervent prayers, since I have become very elderly (I am already 82 years) and I really need to sanctify myself and to think very deeply about the account that I will have to give to the Supreme Judge! Fortunately He is also the Sacred Heart, and this gives me entire confidence.[200]

[198] H-15F-118, Père Lémius.
[199] H-15G-047, Dom Columba Marmion.
[200] H-15F-211, Père Lémius.

Finally, three years before surrendering her earthly life to God, Mother Adèle, in one of her last letters, humbly and simply asks her friend priest Père Vasseur for prayers to continue to respond to this call to holiness:

> "I still maintain my health; I began my 83rd year with neuralgia that made me feel so well that I am still full of life. But as it pleases God. We are in his hands. Do ask him to sanctify me before I retire from this earth".[201]

The Mother, during her life, was totally abandoned to God, fulfilling his will and realising the Work of the Adorers of the Sacred Heart of Jesus of Montmartre. She found in the Eucharist her support and strength in a long and consoling path that directed her toward holiness. Her intense eucharistic experience purified and conducted her toward the perfection of God because, as our Holy Father, Benedict XVI recalls, the Eucharist is "the origin of every form of holiness": "Dear brothers and sisters, the Eucharist is at the origin of every form of holiness, and each of us is called to the fullness of life in the Holy Spirit. How many saints have lived an authentically real life thanks to their eucharistic piety! From Saint Ignatius of Antioch and sant'Agostino, from sant'Antonio Abate to Saint Benedict, from saint Francis of Assisi to Saint Thomas Aquinas, from Saint Clare of Assisi to Saint Catherine of Siena, from Saint Paschal Baylon to saint Peter Julian Eymard, from sant'Alfonso Maria de' Liguori to blessed Charles de Foucauld, from Saint John Mary Vianney to Saint Therese of Lisieux, from san Pio da Pietrelcina to Blessed Teresa of Calcutta, Blessed Pier Gior-

---

[201] H-15F-063, Père Vasseur.

gio Frassati to Blessed Ivan Merz, to name only a few of the many names, holiness has always found its centre in the Sacrament of the Eucharist".[202]

Holiness, the final stage of a life lived with God and for God, signifies the full fruition of Mother Adèle's mature vocation. This holiness itself, after her death, will be acknowledged in word and gesture, by all who have had the opportunity to share with her part of their own journey. Amen – Alleluia!

\* \* \*

In 1992, through Cardinal Basil Hume, Archbishop of Westminster, London, the application was submitted for the approval of the heroic virtues of Mother Adèle. At the conclusion of this work, I wish to present the following prayer composed by her Congregation for the Canonization of their beloved Mother, sure that her intercession from heaven can still stimulate profound gratitude through her who has been able to witness and live in Corde Jesu here on earth.

---

[202] Benedict XVI, *op. cit.*, n. 94.

# PRAYER FOR THE CANONIZATION OF
## MOTHER MARIE-ADÈLE GARNIER

FATHER, all powerful and ever living God,
we give you glory, praise and thanks
for the life and virtue
of your beloved daughter, Marie-Adèle Garnier.

Filled with the riches of your grace
and preferring nothing to the love
of the Heart of Jesus Christ,
she devoted her whole life
to the adoration, praise and glory
of your Name;
she sacrificed herself by prayer and penance
for the unity and holiness of your Church;
she loved her neighbour with a charity
full of humility and compassion.

Above all, she found the SUN of her life
in the Holy Mass,
and so was consumed with zeal
for liturgical worship
and eucharistic adoration,
and abandoned herself with all her heart
to your most Holy Will in all things.

In your mercy Lord, hearken to our prayer:

"Glorify Your Servant
Mother Marie-Adèle Garnier,
that Your Servant
may glorify YOU".

We ask you this through Our Lord
Jesus Christ, Your Son,
Who lives and reigns with You
in the unity of the Holy Spirit, One God,
world without end. AMEN.

*Imp. David Norris, Vic. Gen. Westminster, 05.27.1976.*

# CONCLUSION

"The Mass has become like the sun of my life".[552] This expression that Mother Mary of Saint Peter loved to repeat frequently, appears, in the light of this study, as the due synthesis of her existence and her work. Adèle Garnier, in fact, spent a long and intense life in a state of radiant abandonment: abandonment to the divine will without reserve, with self-denial, sacrifice, dedication and renunciation completing a much greater picture. Her life project, for which she had to suffer many tribulations, shines today through her choice of life commitment given totally to the Lord and to her daughters: the Adorers of the Sacred Heart of Jesus of Montmartre. The Sun/Christ, understood in the full meaning assigned by christian symbology, becomes the centre – heart – of existence in God, radiating light to all that surrounds it. Adèle, invested with the light of Christ, relying totally and unconditionally upon the Divine Good Pleasure, has achieved in her time a shining work of remarkable spiritual value.

Accompanied by many spiritual fathers, each of whom managed to guide and lead her toward the different – and sometimes painful – stages of her religious journey and allowing herself to be led by the Holy Spirit, Adèle walked a path *that has passed through the acceptance of the cross to the unconditional self-offering to God, in the quest for holiness.*

In this, the basic aspect of her spirituality and of her Congregation, for which the Mother poured out her whole

---

[1] H-15G-003, Dom Columba Marmion.

life, is represented by the adoration of the Sacred Heart of Jesus, by means of which it is possible to reach the highest expression of the merciful love of God toward humanity.

Through contemplation and tireless adoration, Adèle has taught her daughters that there can be drawn from the Eucharistic Heart living food to nourish and increase their love of God and neighbour. The attention given to the Sacred Heart finds in the Garnier spirituality a privileged position since it explicates Christ's love for sinful suffering humanity. Her writings, in fact, show a Christ who calls and directs: Adèle understands from girlhood that the profound motivation of her call and its mission can be found in the merciful love of God.

In addition, the prospect of reparation for her sins and the sins of others indicates that there is an urgent need to collaborate with Christ for the salvation of humanity, giving a contribution of prayer, fatigue and suffering, to repair the damage done by the sins and by the injustices of mankind. In this dynamic of salvation, the Sacred Heart is interpreted as the privileged place which makes explicit the profound dispositions of Christ, all motivated by love.

The devotion to the Sacred Heart acquires in Mother Adèle a significance that goes beyond the devotional practices and votive images, but which develops in the "dwelling with the Eucharistic Jesus" feeling herself a *"host-soul"*: There Adèle finds the heart of the love of Christ. The Eucharist is the Heart of Christ, a sign of love for humanity. The Eucharistic Heart of Jesus, in the spirituality of Adèle Garnier, becomes the climax of her vocation and her mysticism and assumes, therefore, a specific spirituality which is also the great gift that the Mother gives to her Church.

Feeling herself first, victim offered and consumed, with prayer and sacrifice daily, she drew near the hill of the Martyrs of France, Montmartre, and then continued her work in the place of the Martyrs in England, Tyburn, becoming herself "the last martyr of Tyburn". Her testimony remains an example of self-denial and holiness, still present even in our days. The theme of martyrdom, finally, accompanied by a desire for holiness closes ideally the path of life and of the soul.

In this analysis of the figure and spirituality of Mother Mary of St. Peter there are only summaries of the most important lines of the vast and profound Garnier spirituality, whose valid and ample opportunity will certainly be the subject of a forthcoming study. Certainly, it would be appropriate to revisit the contents of the various collections of letters with reference to her biblical spirituality or to include them in the vast context of the devotion to the Sacred Heart, the better to grasp the specific perspective and contribution of Mother Adèle. Again further analysis of some of its content-mystical theology, such as for example the "trinitarian life" or the "Interior Priesthood". The aim of this work, however, was to contribute to making Mother Adèle Garnier known – she is a figure still too little known in the catholic community – and she is the tireless defender of the cult of the Sacred Heart of Jesus and is the custodian guardian of a very important divine revelation:

> He told me that his will was that his Heart, present in the Holy Eucharist, should be the object of adoration on the heights of Montmartre and that the Blessed Sacrament was to be exposed night and day in that place.[2]

---

[2] H-15D-004, Abbé Courtois.

The Church preserves and celebrates the Eucharist and offers thanks to the Lord for all those who, like Mother Mary of Saint Peter have witnessed, worshipped God "in spirit and truth" (Jn. 4:23).

> "The Lord [ …]
>
> Fresh and green are the pastures
> where he gives me repose.
>
> Near restful waters he leads me,
> To revive my drooping spirit.
>
> He guides me along the right path;
> He is true to his name.
>
> You have prepared a banquet for me
> in the sight of my foes.
> My head you have anointed with oil;
> my cup is overflowing.
>
> In the Lord's own house shall I dwell
> for ever and ever.
>
> (Ps. 22:1-6)

These words of the psalmist crystallise the life of Mother Adèle Garnier: Adèle walked with total trust in God, dwelling in front of the eucharistic table, anointed with that common priesthood and remains "host-soul" dwelling in the house of the Lord to adore him; and God has been able to lead, support and strengthen providentially *the path of Mother Adèle.*

# EPILOGUE

## "WELL DONE, GOOD AND FAITHFUL STEWARD"

Rightly is Don Gianmario Piga to be congratulated and thanked on the final, fascinating achievement found in his work –

## THE PATH OF MOTHER ADÈLE GARNIER

This work at the same time comprises his thesis which he defended in order to obtain his doctorate of spiritual theology.

In presenting us with THE PATH OF MOTHER ADÈLE GARNIER he is in fact revealing that this work only became possible on account of the contribution of so many people whose life path converged on, was linked to, associated with or recorded in some way the LIFE-PATH of this great mystic. In the first place it was the family and friends of Adèle Garnier who brought her into this world and formed her and reared her as a young pious girl walking side by side with her into her adulthood.

As devout adult she encountered on her path a succession of spiritual guides providentially arranged to accompany her along her spiritual journey to the summit of sanctity. At each new turning point in her pilgrim path God had, as it were, a new spiritual guide ready to accompany her on the next stage of her spiritual journey. This succession of such guides in fact spanned 63 years of her life.

There were three Jesuits, one Diocesan priest, one Dominican, one Sulpician, two Oblates of Mary Immaculate, and three Benedictines. Each one of these holy men had his own contribution to support, sustain and direct her ever higher towards union with God – and each one with his gifts shared her religious path as God's servant just at the precise moment her spiritual growth needed it. Without this guidance she would surely have faltered on her God-given path.

When her spiritual path led her to greater maturity her spiritual daughters eagerly followed her teaching and discipline, walking with her along the path of her special charism. In addition she travelled along the path of spiritual motherhood through her guidance and encouragement sharing her humble, wise and loving counsel with so many in need.

As Don Gianmario illustrates so clearly, every aspect of Adèle's path is recorded in her letters – and he has studied, pondered and been captivated by what is recorded in these spiritual and mystical treasures. In these letters we can with facility follow almost every step of her path through life. Many of these letters were written at the express request of her spiritual guides who then returned them to our Congregation before they died, or in other cases, after she had died. This is the source and reason why our Congregation archives possess many more than 1500 letters written by Mother Adèle, or written to her (in which case she kept them safely).

If all this were not enough, ever since her passover to the Lord in 1924 – that is eighty-seven years ago – myriads of letters have not ceased to come to us, addressed to Mother Adèle Garnier from persons who seek to follow her path and to receive her spiritual protection. Each year these letters increase in number and confidence in her powerful intercession with God.

In addition, our Congregation archivists have spent long years sifting, classifying, cataloguing all extant letters and writings of our beloved Foundress, Mother Adèle Garnier so that access may be had into the mystical secrets of her path to GOD. Indeed one archivist, Mother Mary John Baptist Brennan spent many years at this meticulous but inspiring labour.

All these persons can claim to have glimpsed and then followed after our Mother along the mystic path she traced for us all as she followed HIM who is the true PATH, the unique TRUTH and the one LIFE.

Such is the hidden treasure placed at the disposal of our dear Don Gianmario Piga – and he has been enraptured, and collated his findings in this unique vision of the PATH of MOTHER ADÈLE GARNIER.

In particular Don Gianmario has captured the essence of our Mother's mysticism centred on the HEART OF JESUS – Trinity, the Eucharist and the Church. He has not only captured this, but has presented it with the greatest precision respecting the unique aspect of "the Garnier" spirituality within the context of liturgical and Eucharistic celebration, with a fineness of balance that attracts and inspires the reader.

What he has so captured is exactly expressed in the Statement of the Charism of Mother Garnier's Benedictine, Monastic Congregation –

*THE HEART of our Saviour*
*is a symbol and compendium*
*of the whole mystery of our Redemption.*
*This HEART of the Son of God*
*is the perennial fount of his inexhaustible love*
*from which arise unceasing supplications to his Father;*
*it is also the source of that love which his Spirit*
*pours forth upon all the members of his Mystical Body.*
*The Church, his Bride, was born from this wounded HEART*
*in the very hour of his redemptive death.*
*Our Congregation too has been born from the HEART of Christ*
*and is called to share intimately*
*in this mystery of his redemptive mediation.*

\* \* \*

*The first and highest expression of our vocation*
*lies in our total consecration to the worship and praise*
*of the adorable Trinity through and in union*
*with the Sacred HEART of Jesus… through participation in*
*– the Eucharistic Sacrifice, divine centre of the liturgy,*
*– the choral celebration of the Liturgy of the Hours,*
*– the Perpetual Adoration of the Holy Eucharist,*
*the supreme gift by which the HEART of Jesus*
*has willed to dwell always in our midst.*

290

*The celebration of the paschal mystery in the Eucharist*
*is the mainstay and renewal of this*
*totally* EUCARISTIC LIFE.

*May God bless you, Don Gianmario Piga.*
*Mary, Mother of the Church, pray for us.*

15 June 2012

MOTHER M. XAVIER OSB
*Feast of the Sacred Heart of Jesus*
*Superior General*

Adorers of the Sacred Heart of Jesus, of Montmartre,
Order of St Benedict,
Tyburn Convent, 8 Hyde Park Place, London, W2 2LJ,
England.

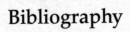

# Bibliography

# UNPUBLISHED DOCUMENTS AND LETTERS

**Letters of Adèle Garnier[1]**

| | | |
|---|---|---|
| – H-15B | Letter 001 | Document Chenille, Chrysalide, Papillon *[1865 – 1868]* |
| – H-15B | Letter 002 | Raphael Document *[1865 – 1875]* |
| – H-15B | Letters 003-058 | To Madame De Crozé, VOL. I *[1869 – March 1876]* |
| – H-15B | Letters 059-127 | To Madame De Crozé, VOL. II *[May 1876 – December 1893)* |
| – H-15B | Letters 128-172 | To Madame De Crozé, VOL. III *[March 1894 – March 1893]* |
| – H-15C | Letters 001-020 | To Madame De Vosseaux *[June 1876 – 1897]* |
| – H-15C | Letters 021-023 | To Père Chambellan *[August 1876]* |
| – H-15C | Letters 138-172 | To Abbé Sauvé *[May 1888 – 1892]* |

[1] This recalls what has already been written in Note 1: *the letters are catalogued and kept in the Archives of the Congregation of the Benedictine Sisters of Tyburn – London, with the following abbreviations: H-15B-001 … H-15C-001 … H-15D-001 … H-15E-001 … H-15F-001 … H-15G-001 … H-15H-001. The initials indicate respectively H: History of the Congregation; 15: the Section relating to the writings of Mother Adele Garnier; A, B, C, D, E, F, G, H: the various volumes corresponding to the Section. Finally, the numerical sequence next, 001-020 …, refers to the sequence number of letters collected in chronological order.*

In addition, I personally wished to integrate each dossier over the years, shown in parentheses, in italics, in which the letters were written.

- H-15G  Letters 233-270  To Various Persons OL. II
  *[December 1910 – December1917]*
- H-15G  Letters 271-323  To Various Persons VOL. III
  *[January 1918 – December 1922]*
- H-15H  Letters 001-025  To Her Sisters
  *[August 1896 – October 1897]*
- H-15H  Letters 026-062  To Members of the Congregation
  *[January 1908 – December 1919]*
- H-15H  Letters 063-149  To Various Sisters, VOL. I
  *[1903 – 1912]*
- H-15H  Letters 150-194  To Various Sisters, VOL. II
  *[1913 – 1923]*
- H-15H  Letters 195-209  To Members of the Congregation
  *[1913 – 1923]*

**Correspondence received from or for Adèle Garnier[2]**

- H-15C  Letters 024-137  From Père Chambellan
  *[May 1876 – July 1892]*
- H-15  Letters 082-138  From Various Persons
  *[1923 – 1930]*

## STUDIES

**Monographs:**

A.A.V.V., *La très Révérende Mère Marie de Saint Pierre, 1838-1924*, Beauchesne Editeur, Paris, 1935.

BOUVY EMILE, S.J., *Mère Marie de Saint-Pierre, Fondatrice et Première Supérieure Générale des Sœurs Adoratrices du Sacré Cœur de Montmartre*, Edition Delwarde, Enghien, 1933.

CAMM BEDE, O.S.B., *The Foundress of Tyburn Convent, Mother Mary of St. Peter, Adèle Garnier, Congregation of the Adorers of the Sacred Heart of Jesus, OSB,* Saint Michael's Abbey Press, Farnborough – Hampshire, 2006.

[2] *Ibidem.*

PLUS RAOUL, S.J., *Adèle Garnier, Mère Marie de Saint-Pierre, Fondatrice des Religieuses Adoratrices du S.C. de Montmartre O.S.B.*, Editons Spes, Paris, 1934.

RIOS ROMANUS, O.S.B., *The Benedictine Congregation of Adorers of the Sacred Heart of Montmartre*, Catholic Records Press, Exeter.

TYBURN CONVENT, *Led by a Star, Mother Marie Adèle Garnier, Biographical and Character Profile*, Volume I (printed by the Congregation).

– *Led by a Star, Mother Marie Adèle Garnier, Response to Divine Vocation, The First Stage: Towards Montmartre*, Volume II (printed by the Congregation).

– *Led by a Star, Mother Marie Adèle Garnier, Response to Divine Vocatio, The Second Stage: Tyburn & Beyond*, Volume III (printed by the Congregation).

**Articles and Essays:**

CAMM BEDE, O.S.B., "Mère Marie de St-Pierre Garnier, Fondatrice des Adoratrices du Sacré-Cœur" in *Revue liturgique et monastique*, X anno, N. 3-4, 1925, pp. 150-54.

DEASE ALICE, "Model Lives in Modern Times. Mother Mary of St. Peter Garnier, 1828-1924, Foundress and First Superioress of the Benedictines of the Sacred Heart at Tyburn" in *Westminster Cathedral Chronicle*, August 1925, pp. 157-158.

## OTHER STUDIES[3]

A.A.V.v., *Welcome the Heritage – the story of Marie Adèle Garnier*, A.C.T.S. Publications, Melbourne, 1975.

[3] The following are Works presented which speak of Mother Adèle Garnier, or of the spirituality of the Sacred Heart with references to the Mother. Others are texts written, studied and disseminated about the Mother herself, such as Abbè Charles Sauvé, Dom Bede Camm, and Dom Columba Marmion.

A.A.V.v., *The One Hundred and Five Martyrs of Tyburn*, Burns & Oates, London, 1917.

A.A.V.v., *Tyburn Hill of Glory – Being the Story of the Benedictines Adorers of the Sacred Heart and their Foundress Mother Mary of Saint Peter (Garnier)*, The Catholic Book Club, London, 1952.

A.A.V.v., *They Died at Tyburn*, Tyburn Convent, London, 1961.

A.A.V.v., *Documents of Mother Foundress on the Congregation, Adorers of the Sacred Heart of Jesus, of Montmartre, Order of St. Benedict*, Tyburn Convent, London, 1996.

A.A.V.v., *Dictionnaire de spiritualité ascétique et mystique, doctrine et histoire*, Beauchense, Paris, 1949, Voce *Abandon*, Vol. I.

A.A.V.v., *La maison sur la colline a Paris*, Mechliniae, 1953.

A.A.V.v., *Montmartre to Sydney, A Journey in the Spirit*, A.C.T.S., Melbourne, 1975.

A.A.V.v., *Gloria Deo per Sacratissimum Cor Iesu*, Tyburn Convent, London, s.d.

A.A.V.v., *La très Révérende Mère Marie de Saint Pierre, Fondatrice et Prémière Supérieure Générale de la Congrégation du Sacré Coeur de Jésus de Montmartre*, Beauchesne, Paris, s.d.

BASTIE JEAN, *Cahier du C.R.E.PÈREI.F., Centre de Recherches et d'Études su Paris et l'Ile de France – La Butte de Montmartre et le Sacré Coeur*, CREPIF, Paris, 1995.

BENEDETTO XVI, *Sacramentum Caritatis*, Libreria Editrice Vaticana, Città del Vaticano, 2007.

BENOIST JACQUES, *Le Sacré Coeur de Montmartre de 1870 à nos jours*, VOL. I, Les Editions Ouvrières, Paris, 1992.

– *Le Sacré Coeur de Montmartre de 1870 à nos jours*, VOL. II, Les Editions Ouvrières, Paris, 1992.

– *Monsegneur Charles et les congrégations féminines au Sacré-Cœur et sur la butte Montmartre (1959 – 1993)*, Les Editions Ouvrières, Paris, 1999.

- *Le Sacré Coeur des Femmes de 1870 à 1960*, VOL. I, Les Editions Ouvrières, Paris, 2000.

- *Le Sacré Coeur, son équipement et la Butte de Montmartre. Contribution à l'histoire du féminisme, de l'urbanisme et du tourisme (1870-1959)*, Les Editions Ouvrières, Paris, 2000.

BRENNAN MOTHER M. JOHN BAPTIST, O.S.B., *Guide to the Crypt of the Martyrs*, Tyburn Convent, London, 1996.

CAMM BEDE, O.S.B., *Tyburn and the English Martyrs*, Art and Book Company, London, 1904.

- *Forgotten Shrines*, Macdonald & Evans, London, 1910.

- *A Birthday of the English Martyrs*, The Neuman Press, Minnesota, 1908.

- *Nine Martyrs Monks*, Burns Oates & Washbourne, London, 1931.

- *Lives of the English Martyrs*, VOL. I, Burns Oates & Washbourne, London, 1904.

- *Lives of the English Martyrs*, VOL. II, Burns Oates & Washbourne, London, 1905.

CLÉMENT MAURICE, *Vie du cardinal Richard, archevêque de Paris*, J. De Gigord, Paris, 1923.

DENIZOT ALAIN, *Le Sacré Coeur et la Grande Guerre*, Nouvelles Editions Latines, Paris, 1994.

DOLLEN CHARLES, *Fire of Love – An anthology of Abbot Marmion's published writings on the Holy Spirit*, Sands & Company, London, 1964.

DURRWELL FRANÇOIS-XAVIER, *Lo Spirito Santo alla luce del mistero pasquale*, Edizioni Paoline, Roma, 1985.

GALOT JEAN, S.J., *The Eucharistic Heart*, Veritas Publications, Dublin, 1990.

LAVALLÉE PAUL, *Le Bienheureux Columba Marmion dans l'intimité de ses lettres*, Editions Sainte-Madeleine, Paris, 2007.

LÉMIUS JEAN BAPTISTE, O.M.I., *Le culte du Coeur Eucharistique de Jésus*, Pierre Tequi Editeur, Paris, 1930.

- *Les miracles eucharistiques et l'Apparition Eucharistique de Bordeaux*, Neau & Cie, Bordeaux, 1923.

- *L'Apparition Eucharistique de Bordeaux et le Saint Sacrifice de la Messe*, Neau & Cie, Bordeaux, 1928.

MARMION DOM COLUMBA, O.S.B., *Le Christ dans ses Mystères*, De Brouwer & Cie, Paris, 1922.

- *Le Christ idéal de Moine*, De Brouwer & Cie, Paris, 1922.

- *Le Christ vie de l'Ame*, Les Editions de Maredsous, 1947.

- *Le Christ idéal du Pretre*, Les Editions de Maredsous, 1952.

- *The English Letters of Abbot Marmion*, Helicon Ltd., Dublin, 1962.

MENDIZABAL RUFO, S.J., *Catalogus defunctorum in renata Societate Jesu, ab a. 1814 ad a. 1970*, apud Curiam P. Gen., Roma, 1972.

MERCIER DÉSIRÉ, *Cardinal Mercier's Own Story*, Gorge H. Doran Company, New York, 1920.

PAGELLE DE FOLLENAY J., *Vie du cardinal Guibert archevêque de Paris* [2 tomes], Poussielgue, Paris, 1896.

PLUS RAOUL, *Sacré-coeur de Montmartre. De 1870 à nos jours*, éditions de l'Atelier, Ivry-sur-Seine, 1992.

OLDMEADOW ERNEST, *Francis, Cardinal Bourne*, Burns, Oates & Washbourne, London, 1940.

RATZINGER JOSEPH, *Guardare al Crocifisso*, Jaca Book, Milano, 1992.

RÉGNAULT EMILE, *Courte Biographie et lettres inédites de la Bienheureuse Marguerite-Marie*, Hébrail, Toulouse, 1890.

ROYO MARIN ANTONIO, *Teologia della perfezione cristiana*, Edizioni San Paolo, Cinisello Balsamo Milano, 2003.

RUMBELOW DONALD, *The Triple Tree – Newgate, Tyburn and Old Bailey*, Harrap Limited, London, 1982.

SAUVÉ CHARLES, S.S., *L'Ange et l'Homme Intimes*, Maison Vic et Amat, Libraire-Editeur, Paris, 1900.

- *Le Chrétien Intime – Le Culte des Mystères et des Paroles de Jésus*, VOL. I, Maison Vic et Amat, Libraire-Editeur, Paris, 1911.

- *Le Chrétien Intime – Le Culte des Mystères et des Paroles de Jésus*, VOL. II, Maison Vic et Amat, Libraire-Editeur, Paris, 1912.
- *Le Chrétien Intime – Le Culte des Mystères et des Paroles de Jésus*, VOL. III, Maison Vic et Amat, Libraire-Editeur, Paris, 1913.
- *Le Chrétien Intime – Le Culte du Coeur de Marie*, VOL. IV, Maison Vic et Amat, Libraire-Editeur, Paris, 1909.
- *Dieu Intime*, Ancienne Librairie, Paris, 1920.
- *L'Eucharistie Intime*, VOL. I, Maison Vic et Amat, Libraire-Editeur, Paris, 1916.
- *L'Eucharistie Intime*, VOL. II, Maison Vic et Amat, Libraire-Editeur, Paris, 1927.
- *L'Incarnation, ou Jésus Intime*, VOL. I, Maison Vic et Amat, Libraire-Editeur, Paris, 1897.
- *L'Incarnation, ou Jésus Intime*, VOL. II, Maison Vic et Amat, Libraire-Editeur, Paris, 1897.
- *L'Incarnation, ou Jésus Intime*, VOL. III, Maison Vic et Amat, Libraire-Editeur, Paris, 1897.
- *Le Chrétien Intime – Les Litanies du Coeur de Jésus*, Maison Vic et Amat, Libraire-Editeur, Paris, 1907.
- *Le Chrétien Intime – Le Culte du Sacré Coeur*, VOL. I, Maison Vic et Amat, Libraire-Editeur, Paris, 1905.
- *Le Chrétien Intime – Le Culte du Sacré Coeur*, VOL. II, Maison Vic et Amat, Libraire-Editeur, Paris, s.d.

SNEAD-COX JOHN GORGE, *The life of Cardinal Vaughan (1832-1903)*, Herbert and Daniel, London, 1910.

THIBAUT RAYMUND, O.S.B., *Dom Columba Marmion – A master of the spiritual life (1858-1923)*, Sands & Company, London, 1942.

TIERNEY MARK, *Dom Columba Marmion*, Columba Press, Dublin, 1995.

TRAMBLAY REAL, *François-Xavier Durwell, teologo della Pasqua di Cristo*, Lateran University Press, Città del Vaticano, 2010.

# APPENDIX

# ANNEX I
## Photos of Mother Adèle

Adèle Garnier at 35 years

Mother Adèle in her Benedictine Habit and Cowl

Mother Adèle Garnier with the new black Benedictine Habit

Mother Mary of St Peter in her first religious habit

In 1585 *GREGORY GUNNE* predicted
that one day a religious house would
be founded at *TYBURN*
His prediction was fulfilled when
*TYBURN CONVENT* was established
in 1903

Commemorative Plaque on the external wall of the Convent

Mother Adèle (centre) with a group of the First Sisters

## Copies of the letters of Mother Adèle

H-15H-153

Tyburn Convent,

6 Hyde Park Place, London, W.

Le 20 Janvier 1919.

Ma très chère Enfant,

Combien vos bonnes lettres nous intéressent et nous
font plaisir ! Que nous sommes heureuses et reconnais-
santes au Sacré Cœur de la protection manifeste dont
il vous a entourées ! Voulez-vous dire à toutes nos
chères enfants merci pour toutes leurs lettres à M. Agnès
et à moi, si bonnes, si filiales, si édifiantes et en même
temps si pleines de bonne humeur et d'une allégresse.
[...] qui nous réjouit. Non mes enfants, vous
n'êtes pas délaissées [...] qu'il vous semble, être comme
[...] vous êtes le petit grain de froment dont parle
N.S. dans le St Évangile et [...] belle et à bon [...]
[...] un jour [...] : Bénissons le Seigneur. Que
vos chères enfants sachent bien que si nous ne répondons
pas [...] à leurs [...] lettres, c'est l'excès
du travail qui en est le cause. M. Agnès est surmenée à
un point que je ne frais Dre, car elle fait son travail de
[...] et toute la besogne
relative à la Congrégation, étant donné [...] (80 ans ¾)
et mon incapacité — Écrire est encore une chose que je
puis faire de temps en temps, mais si peu à la fois ! Si
le bon Dieu [...] bonne à M. Agnès la santé dont
elle a besoin, je serai bien heureuse. Demandez-le dans
vos ferventes prières.
[...] je vous dirai qq. mots sur les choses
extérieures [...] notre [...] Couvent et aussi vos
[...] l'autel. Il faut certainement le payer
et prier en même temps M. Billaux de vous [...]
[...] jusqu'à ce que vous puissiez l'employer.
J'ai [...] les prix convenus avec M. Billaux en
Juillet 1914 et une lettre où il me dit que tous les bois
[...] et qu'il va commencer l'autel. Le prix
indiqué par lui et accepté par nous était 235 fr —
plus 23 fr. pour l'intérieur de la tabernacle. Mais c'est ce
à du être délaissé. Vous verrez aec lui. Je vous
enverrai la note, en cas que nous ne l'ayons pas —
Peut-être serez-vous en mesure de payer l'autel sinon,
vous nous le direz. Les personnes qui avaient [...]
pour l'installation à [...] ont toutes été averties
que la guerre avait obligé [...] à employer
[...] les sommes reçues — Tous les objets en
métal, puisque M. Billaux veut bien les [...]
Ainsi les [...] vous pouvez vous en passer actuellement
cependant prenez aussi les chandeliers 13 fois 52 [150 — Crucifix 9 fr

Tyburn Couvent
Samedi 5 Août
1911

Ma bien chère Enfant,

Je n'ai pas encore pu vous
écrire et je viens presque au dernier
jour pour vous dire que si je ne
vous écris pas, mon cœur maternel
n'est pas silencieux et je parle
souvent de vous à Notre Seigneur.
Je Le remercie de la transformation
qu'Il a opérée en vous jusqu'à
présent et que j'ai pu constater.
Et c'est parce que vous avez voulu
contenter son amour en Lui donnant
votre cœur sans réserve que Lui-
même a rendu votre désir efficace
en vous donnant force et courage
pour vous renoncer vous-même
dans les luttes contre le vieil homme.
Celui-là, il est non seulement
votre ennemi acharné mais il

# Annex III
## Places of Mother Adèle

The Cathedral of Saint Bénigne - Dijon (Wikipedia)

Tyburn Convent - London

Mother Adele's first tomb in Royston

Altar of the Martyrs in the Crypt of Tyburn Convent

Mother Adèle's Tomb at Tyburn

Basilica of the Sacred Heart of Montmartre - Paris

# ANNEX IV
## Personalities Encountered by Mother Adèle

S. Em. Card. Joseph Hippolyte Guibert

Dom Columba Marmion

S. Em. Card. Désiré-Joseph Mercier

S. Em. Card. François-Marie-Benjamin Richard de la Vergne

H. Em. Card. Francis Alphonsus Bourne

H. Em. Card. Herbert Alfred Vaughan

## ANNEX V
# Brief Chronology of the Daughters of Mother Marie Adèle

19 July1930    The Congregation received the papal approbation, July 19, 1930 and was aggregated to the
Benedictine Confederation 24 January, 1964.[1]

22 October 1947[2] *In 1945 the community of Louvigné-du-Désert peti-
tioned the Archbishop of Rennes, Cardinal Clément-
Emile Roques to be separated from the Mother House
now definitively established in England: On 22 October 1947 the Holy See granted autonomy to the french
religious who took the name of Bénédictines du Sacré-
Cœur de Montmartre B.S.C.M.*[3]

1956    Foundation of a Priory in Australia, now at River-
stone.

1961    Closure of the Belgian Priory

23 October 1961 Foundation of the Priory at the Basilica of Montmartre

1962    *The Priory of Louvigné du Désert moved to* Écouen

1963    Tyburn Convent (Priory) restored after World
War II, London

24 January 1964 The "Tyburn Nuns", aggregated to the Benedictine Confederation..

1964    The novitiate at Royston moved to Wadhurst –
England

1970    *Foundation of the Priory at "Notre-Dame de Marien-
thal"-[] Alsace (France)*

---

[1] Guerrino Pelliccia e Giancarlo Rocca (curr.), *Dizionario degli Istituti
di Perfezione* (10 voll.), Edizioni Paoline, *Milano 1974-2003*, Col. 115.

[2] The halt in this new Religious family, which became a Congregation
in 1983, will become evident with writing in progress.

[3] Guerrino Pelliccia e Giancarlo Rocca (curr.), *op. cit.*, col. 1278.

| | |
|---|---|
| 1972 | *Foundation of* Blaru *and then the closure of the* Ecouen Priory *(France)* |
| 1975 | *Foundation of* Dôle *Priory (France)* |
| 1976 | Foundation of Priory of Monasterio Sagrado Corazón in Piura (Peru) |
| 1977 | Closure of the Priory at Montmartre |
| 1978 | Foundation of the Priory at Sanctuary of Notre Dame at Laghet *(France)* |
| 1981 | Transfer of Priory from Piura to Sechura (Perù) |
| 1983 | Approbation of Constitutions by Holy See of the French Congregation |
| 1984 | Foundation of the Priory Sanctuary of La Chapelle-Montligeon – *Normandy* – *(France)* |
| 1984 | Foundation of the Priory at Montmartre, Paris |
| 1992 | Official Petition to open the Diocesan Process for the Beatification of Mother Adèle Garnier. |
| 1992 | Foundation of the Priory – Benedictine Monastery Largs (Scotland) |
| 1992 | Foundation of the Priory in the Cathedral "Notre Dame des Victoires" in Paris |
| 1993 | Construction of the Monastery at Cobh (Ireland), where also the community at Wadhurst transferred. |
| 1994 | Foundation of the Priory at Sanctuary of Curé d'Ars |
| 1995 | Cardinal Jean Marie Lustiger called the Benedictines to the spiritual and material animation of the Montmartre Basilica. |
| 1996 | Construction of the Monastery at Bombay, New Zealand |
| 1998 | *Foundation of Priory at* Sainte-Baume, *Provence* [*(France)*] |
| 2000 | *Foundation of Priory in the Basilica* "San Martin", Tours *(France)* |

| | |
|---|---|
| 2002 | Foundation of Priory, Monastery "Puerta del Cielo" in Loja, Ecuador |
| 2002 | Foundation of Priory, Monastery "Paráclito Divino", Guatapé, Colombia |
| 2005 | Foundation of Priory, Monastery "Madonna dell'Eucaristia", Rome |
| 2008 | *Closure of Sainte Baume and Foundation of Priory at Sanctuary* Notre-Dame di Laus *at Gap (France)* |
| 2009 | Foundation of Priory, Monastery "Cor Iesu Fons Vitae" in Hamilton Diocese, New Zealand |

At the end of this study
I feel the need to thank God
for this "spiritual exercise"
That providentially I was enabled to make.
A heartfelt thanks to Mother Mary Xavier McMonagle,
 Mother General of the "Tyburn Nuns"
 for the trust granted to me,
 by entrusting to me the confidential letters of the Mother Foundress.
 Thanks to Dr. Maria Antoinette Santoro,
collaborator in transcribing the letters
and in translating of the work of Dom Bede Camm on Mother Adèle.
Sincere thanks to Father Dionigi Spanu,
for giving me encouragement and assistance
in drafting these pages.
Thanks to my mother Andreuccia who accompanied me with her suffering
and today in paradise together with my father, Pietro.

*TO YOU*
*who have in your hands this volume,*
*a spiritual path is offered,*
*which sets out to educate your heart*
*and not only your mind and your hands*
*teaching you to dedicate your love*
*in the school of the Eucharistic Jesus.*

*This can become the stimulus*
*for ever- present evangelisation,*
*as in the Heart of Christ*
*the heart of man learns –*

- *to know the true and only meaning of life and his destiny,*
- *to comprehend the value of an authentically Christian life,*
- *to safeguard himself from certain perversions of the heart,*
- *to unite filial love of God with love of his neighbour.*

*For this message, dear to the tradition and magisterium of the Church, I thank dearest Don Gianmario, apostle of the Sacred Heart and lover of the EUCHARIST.*

✠ VINCENZO PELVI
*Archbishop*

VATICAN PRESS